THE THEATRICALITY OF GREEK TRAGEDY

THE THEATRICALITY OF

Greek Tragedy

PLAYING SPACE AND CHORUS

GRAHAM LEY

THE UNIVERSITY OF CHICAGO PRESS

Chicago and London

GRAHAM LEY is professor of drama and theory at the University of
Exeter. He is the author of, among other books, *A Short Introduction to Greek
Tragedy*, also published by the University of Chicago Press.

The University of Chicago Press, Chicago 60637
The University of Chicago Press, Ltd., London
© 2007 by The University of Chicago
All rights reserved. Published 2007
Printed in the United States of America

16 15 14 13 12 11 10 09 08 07   1 2 3 4 5
ISBN-13: 978-0-226-47757-2 (cloth)
ISBN-10: 0-226-47757-6 (cloth)

Library of Congrss Cataloging-in-Publication Data
Ley, Graham.
The theatricality of Greek tragedy : playing space and chorus / Graham Ley.
p. cm.
Includes bibliographical references and index.
ISBN-13: 978-0-226-47757-2 (cloth : alk. paper)
ISBN-10: 0-226-47757-6 (cloth : alk. paper)
1. Greek drama (Tragedy)—History and criticism. 2. Theater—
Greece—History—To 500. 3. Drama—Technique. I. Title.

PA3201 .L48 2007
882'.0109—dc22
2006018877

FOR TERESA AND KIRI,

AND IN MEMORY OF ALICE (1913–2004)

Contents

Preface

SCOPE OF THE BOOK

This book deals with two problems that are central to the appreciation of the performance of ancient Greek tragedy and to our understanding of the art form itself. Through presenting a variety of evidence and conducting a careful review of it in the book, I hope to make the particular nature of these problems accessible to those who may not be specialists or linguists but who do have a strong interest in the ancient Greek theater and in theater in general.

The problem of the playing space is largely empirical because it concerns the disposition of performers, and my approach to it in chapter 1 relies on the practical implications of the surviving scripts and often on those forms of research that have been conducted practically. In order to appreciate the kind of theater that Greek tragedy was, we need to understand the conditions for which the scripts were composed, and, as I observe in chapter 1, to do that we need to work substantially in reverse, from the scripts to the conditions for which they were composed.

The problem of the chorus is of a different kind because it involves questions of music and dancing and our own cultural puzzlement over this kind of performance for which we have no real equivalent. It is, in that sense, an intricate problem, and in chapter 2 I have tried to trace it for the reader, commenting on the various proposals that have been made about different aspects of it. Although I cannot suggest a resolution, I hope that the critique and evaluation of proposals and my own concluding suggestions will lead readers to greater confidence by the close of the chapter.

Both chapters involve considerable detail, of different kinds, but I have kept my attention firmly on the subject of theatricality, despite temptations to digress, for the sound reason that theatricality deserves close attention of this length. References might be extended, but my aim has been to write a satisfactory book rather than an imposing bibliography. I have in general referred to works written or available in English but have included exceptions where I felt that was necessary or appropriate.

It is arguable that the only possible performances of Greek tragedy are those that occur now. Although I have some sympathy with this view, granted my own alignment with modern theater practice, I am not convinced that insights gained from modern productions should be allowed to control our understanding of ancient theatricality. In fact, my hope would be that an increased alertness to ancient theatricality may contribute to producing the challenges that modern productions of tragedy should bring to their audiences. There can be no doubt that Greek tragedy was a kind of performance that is substantially unfamiliar to us, and we stand to gain if its particularities are allowed to affect our own, increasingly diverse sense of theater.[1]

The archaeology of the theater, and the discussion of artifacts and what may be taken to be the visual record, could demand a great deal of the space available, and my decision has been to concentrate on problems other than these. I would refer readers instead to discussions of the theater itself as a construction by Scullion and Wiles, who review the evidence critically and present a sound evaluation of it.[2] I am in general agreement with their findings, in relation to the theater of Dionysus at Athens, to the extent that the evidence from archaeology permits conclusions.

In summary, Scullion and Wiles argue for the existence of a circular terrace on the south slope of the Athenian *akropolis* in the precinct of Dionysus, containing the *orchestra* for performance, with a *theatron* or "watching place" constructed in an extended and elevated arc around it. Further aspects of the construction of the playing space are discussed in the course of my first chapter, and these include the introduction of a *skene,* from which performers may appear and into which they may enter. With these basic ideas in mind, and with the illustrations to accompany the discussion, I hope readers will find no difficulty in following the argument presented.

1. One of the best sources of information on productions of Greek drama (contemporary, modern, and premodern) is the Archive of Performances of Greek and Roman Drama, which has a Web site at www.classics.ox.ac.uk/apgrd.
2. The relevant sections are "The Fifth-Century Theatre of Dionysos," chap. 1, in Scullion (1994), and "The Theatre of Dionysus," chap. 2, in Wiles (1997). I strongly recommend a reading of both. Readers who feel dissatisfied with this apparent consensus should consult Moretti (2000); there will, inevitably, be other contributions to this argument.

RATIONALE FOR THE DIAGRAMS AND DRAWINGS

Since the disposition of performers in the playing space is the principal subject of the first chapter, I have provided a number of diagrams and drawings
as an alternative to presenting photographs of artifacts or theaters, which   xi
are widely available elsewhere and may not be revealing in relation to the
problems I am addressing. The two exceptions I have included are photographs of vase paintings depicting carriages or wagons, vehicles that are relevant to one part of my review of the problem of the playing space in chapter 1. The intention both with diagrams and drawings is to illustrate the
discussions of scenes or sequences from tragedies made in the first chapter.
The moments chosen are specific and cannot reflect the movement or the
minor changes of disposition that were plausibly part even of these "moments" themselves. But I hope that the illustrations will aid visualization of
the theatricality with which I am concerned.

A schematic view of the three significant parts of the Athenian performance space for much of the fifth century BCE is given in figure 1, taken
from *A Short Introduction to the Ancient Greek Theater,* which was drawn for the
first edition by Richard Mazillius, and redrawn for the second edition by
Tony Williams. I reproduce the second version here: it indicates the relative
locations of the *theatron,* the *orchestra,* and the *skene.* But for this book I have
asked Jon Primrose, who has drawn the diagrams, to provide some preliminary plans that examine the configuration of that space hypothetically in relation to two different issues.

Figure 2 explores the dimensions of the playing space without reference
to any surroundings but in relation to the fifty performers of the dithyrambic *choroi* that formed a major part of the festival of Dionysus at Athens
alongside performances of tragedy, satyr-drama, and comedy.[3] These *choroi*
were called "circular" and we have no reason to doubt that description. So I
asked Jon to provide a circular *choros* of fifty with the space it needs in which
to stand, facing outward, and to move or dance in a circular motion. I then
asked him to provide for a circular *choros* that might move or dance outward
to some extent and to indicate the space it would occupy in that position.[4]
This diagram illustrates a circle of performers with a diameter of approximately sixteen meters and one with a diameter of approximately thirty me-

3. I discuss a number of aspects of dithyrambic performance in the second chapter of this
book, on the *choros.*
4. We have no reason to suppose that the dithyrambic *choros* was made into concentric circles. In Jon Primrose's plans, the expanded circle was calculated on the simple expedient
of extended arms, so allowing room for considerable body movement.

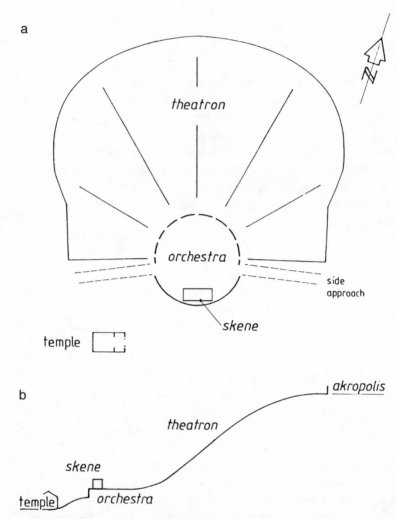

FIGURE 1 *a*, Schematic diagram of the developed fifth-century theater (area 10,000 m² or 107,584 ft²). *b*, side view of theater. (Reproduced from my *Short Introduction to the Ancient Greek Theater,* 2d ed. [Chicago: University of Chicago Press, 2006], fig. 3).

ters. We might assume that the first of these was a minimum for a performance of a circular *choros.*

I follow both Scullion and Wiles in accepting, after Dorpfeld, that the earliest indicative remains of the *theatron* at Athens are of a circular retaining wall that was constructed to allow a level *orchestra* to be created on the hill-

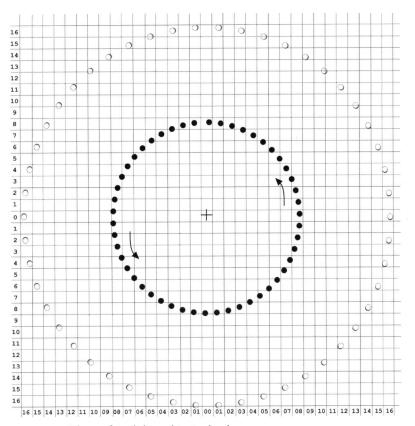

FIGURE 2 Schemes for a dithyrambic circular chorus

side above the temple of Dionysus. This terrace would have contained, as Wiles succinctly describes it, "a circular dancing area half cut into the hillside and half extending from it," with the cutting to the north and the extension, supported by the wall, to the south.[5] A median estimate for the di-

5. Wiles (1997, 45). The shape of the perimeter of the *orchestra* in the fifth-century *theatron* at Athens is the point of contention that prompted the reviews of the evidence and arguments by Scullion and Wiles: some scholars firmly believe that the perimeter was rectilinear rather than circular (Rehm 2002, 39–41 now inclines to this opinion). But the contention may well be more about the defining, lower edge of the banked auditorium than about the shape of the dancing place itself; as it stands, the evidence cited in support of either view is circumstantial, and likely to remain so. The primary importance to the Athenian democracy of the large, circular *choroi* of the dithyramb at the urban Dionysian festivals would seem to leave the construction of a noncircular perimeter to the *orchestra* in

ameter of that circular terrace is twenty-five meters. We could then note that such a space was adequate for the smaller circular *choros* in the first diagram but not suited to the kind of expansion indicated in the wider circle.

In figure 3, I asked Jon to add a *skene* to a circular terrace (or *orchestra*) of twenty-five meters but to show the *skene* in a variety of dimensions. We have no means of knowing where precisely the early *skene* was located, apart from the fact that that it must be to the rear or south of the *theatron* and the playing space, away from and facing the auditorium. It would have been constructed of wood, and its actual dimensions are utterly unknown. At a later period, which is arguably in the later fifth century or in the fourth, stone foundations were provided that must also have been completed by a wooden *skene*. In the absence of secure dating for these foundations and of any indications of the wooden superstructure, our sense of the fifth-century *skene* must remain almost completely hypothetical. Later remains testify that at some point the *skene* was located outside the *orchestra;* but we cannot know whether that was the case in or during the fifth century. We should also allow for the probability that the size and shape of the *skene* changed during the course of the fifth century after its known presence in the *Oresteia* of 458 BCE. Its wooden construction, with the need for renewal and its suitability for adaptation, would make such changes both possible and relatively easy.

For the diagrams in this book, we have adopted the more restrictive option of locating the *skene* within the circular terrace.[6] We have also taken dimensions for the *skene* that allow for an *ekkuklema,* the mobile platform that is

---

need of some explanation: Wilson (2000, 315n33) notes how the dithyramb, in the number of its dancers and its circular form, connects with democratic institutions and building design. Even so, the circular shape of the *orchestra* perimeter shown in the diagrams here should be thought to be provisional, rather than definitive, pending (hopefully) more conclusive evidence or argument. My concern in this book is with the use of the playing space, not with its outline: what happened inside it is of far greater importance to me.

6. Hammond adopts the alternative, of locating the *skene* for the *Oresteia* partly within and partly outside the perimeter of the terrace, presuming that the retaining wall of the terrace was removed in that section to accommodate the construction (1972, 413–14). He provides figures to illustrate this scheme (1972, fig. 3; 1988, fig. 2), which are reproduced by Scullion (1994, figs. 11 and 12). Hammond's argument is criticized briefly but obscurely by Scullion (1994, 49–50), but if the proposal is substantially a "guess," as Scullion states, then in the absence of material evidence it should have the same status as any other. It is worth noting that Hammond's construction is affected in relation to width as well as depth by his belief in a "low stage." Wiles (1997, 52) is inclined to accept a fifth-century *skene* "intersecting the circle" of the terrace on the southern side, for which he cites Hammond's proposal, disregarding Scullion's criticism and the argument that a *skene* would, in the first instance, have been placed on the terrace itself.

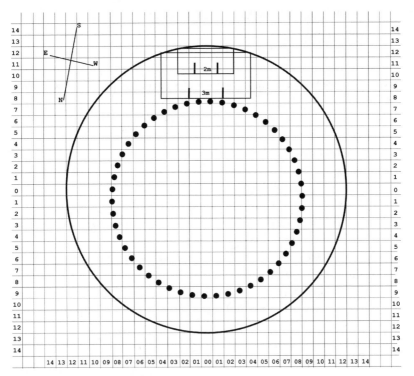

FIGURE 3 Schemes for a *skene* with *ekkuklema*, on terrace

believed to have been projected in a number of scenes from the doors of the *skene*; figure 3 accommodates an *ekkuklema* of, variously, two and three meters frontage. The doors to the *skene* are envisaged as double and folding backward: each of these doors would be one or one and a half meters wide, respectively, and would fold one half or three-quarters of a meter back and to the side in the entrance. The depth of the *skene* would then be calculated pragmatically on the assumption that the *ekkuklema* is a square platform. The sideways extension of the *skene* has been made, proportionally in each case, on the width of the doorway required for the *ekkuklema*, with the frontage being three times that of the doorway.

What stands out from these hypothetical schemes for a *skene* in figure 3 is that the size of the *skene* and its occupation of space vary considerably with what might appear to be only a minor variation in the size of the *ekkuklema*. The creation of an *ekkuklema* larger than three meters square seems to me improbable and unnecessary, and even three meters might be thought to be excessive. I asked Jon to place the smaller of the dithyrambic "circles" on the same diagram, with its center still located on the center of the terrace as a whole, to give some impression of the displacement that would be occasioned by a *skene*. It is possible that the dithyrambic *choroi* performed on the

first day of the festival and that the *skene* was erected in the evening after their performances, which would avoid the problem of any displacement. But unfortunately there is no certainty about the order of performance at the festivals in Athens.[7]

In figure 4, I asked Jon to indicate possible dimensions for a *skene* based on the median between the two measurements for the *ekkuklema* provided in the previous diagram. So the *ekkuklema* in the projections in figure 4 remains at two and a half meters square, while the facades present possibilities from eight and a half meters to twelve and a half meters. These schemes accommodate possibilities for expansion during the course of the fifth century, but the sequence ceases (approximately) at the point where the expansion of the *skene* might become seriously invasive of the playing space on the terrace.[8] The diagram also indicates two circles for the dithyrambic performances, one still centered on the center of the terrace itself, and the other relocated to provide a balanced distance from the *skene* on the south and the audience to the north. With a *skene* even of the largest size indicated here, the dithyrambic *choroi* could perform without restriction; but they certainly could not expect to perform in the absolute center of the terrace, and that qualification probably applies even with the other sizes of *skene* indicated here.

These three preliminary diagrams (i.e., figs. 2–4) form the basis on which the diagrams in chapter 1, illustrating moments from the plays, are drawn. For those remaining diagrams, we adopted the hypothesis of an *ekkuklema* two and a half meters square, with the most extensive of the facades, of twelve and a half meters. We cannot assume an unchanged construction for the *skene* throughout the fifth century, and the addition of a *mechane* (crane) to accomplish the "flying" of gods and other entities (in comedy or tragedy)

7. This arrangement is assumed by Csapo and Slater (1994, 106), and Wiles (1997, 49); but contrast the view of the editors of the revised edition of Pickard-Cambridge (1988, 66).
8. Any proposal for the *skene* that wishes to add doors to the sides of the main (*ekkuklema*) doors would have to envisage either a relatively major occupation of the playing space on the terrace or the construction of a *skene* outside the area established by the original terrace wall, to the south. This is the case with Hammond's construction (n. 6 above), which has a "low stage" in front of three doors for the *Oresteia*. So those who believe that there are indications in some of the comedies of Aristophanes that three doors were available in the *skene* might be well advised to believe correspondingly that a wider *skene* was constructed by that time at least partly outside the playing space established by the terrace.

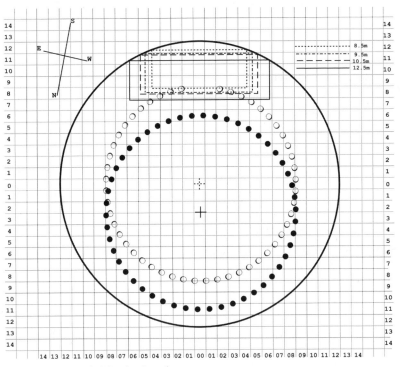

FIGURE 4 Extended facades for a *skene* on terrace

might be thought to demand alterations to its design.[9] Nonetheless, the basic requirements seem to me to vary minimally. Practicable altars, shrines, or tombs involved in the performance of specific tragedies may have been placed at the center of the terrace, or their location may have varied. In the diagrams illustrating "moments" in tragedies in which a substantial property of this kind is involved, I have located it consistently at the median point between the front of the *skene* and the edge of the terrace, some two and a half meters forward of the absolute center, to allow equal space for performers behind it and in front of it.[10]

The key to all the diagrams is simple: circles signify members of the *choros,*

9. The fullest study of this aspect of the *skene* and theatricality is Mastronarde (1990).
10. There is no means of knowing the size of these different objects, and some may have been standard properties, others not. I have asked Jon Primrose to provide a uniform scheme on the plan of an object two meters square as a reasonable estimate of either a standard or a minimum size.

squares signify actors/characters, triangles signify attendants or extras, and the cross signifies the *auletes,* or pipe player who accompanied singing and dancing. Hollow circles, squares, or triangles signify the position from which a performer has moved, and arrows mark the direction of that movement. An altar or tomb that features in a scene is indicated by double, concentric squares situated just below (to the north of) the absolute center of the terrace. The double square signifies either an altar or a tomb with a foundation step.[11]

In three of the diagrams in the first chapter (15–17) we have adopted a simple scheme for a carriage, drawn by two ponies or horses. The carriage is approximately one meter wide, and no more than two meters in length, with an additional one and a half meters for the animals. It is a four-wheeled vehicle, largely for reasons of stability, but also because it may carry a number of people (or properties). Clearly, the vehicles may have varied in construction, but the diagrammatic scheme given is constant and reflects the discussion of this issue in chapter 1. This size of vehicle should be suited to the approach paths of the *eisodoi,* which I have estimated at two meters wide.

For the drawings, Kit Surrey illustrated the same moment as that represented in two of Jon's diagrams (figs. 5, 18). Clearly the value of the drawings is their ability to present depth and angle, rather than an impression of the actualities of costume or gesture supposedly used on the occasion of first production. Their focus is placed on the disposition of performers in the playing space, rather than on the *theatron* itself and the spectators, the landscape background, or the particular construction of the *skene.* The elevation of the *skene* and its form of construction were discussed by Kit and me but are not intended to be authoritative. Similarly, a full complement of spectators has not been shown, and the landscape background is a sketch, although we have included an indication of the older temple of Dionysus below the terrace.

Figures 6 and 7 illustrate the same moment from Euripides' *Suppliants* (fig. 5), and figure 18 illustrates the moment when Astyanax is taken from his mother Andromache in Euripides' *Trojan Women* (fig. 17). All three are drawn as if from different elevations and positions within the *theatron.* Kit's design for the carriage in the scene from *Trojan Women* takes its bearings from the two vase paintings I have included alongside the text in chapter 1. It has wheels that are approximately two-thirds of a meter in diameter. A theatri-

11. Although I have kept the size and the scheme constant, it is unlikely that a complex property such as the shrine of Thetis in Euripides' *Andromache* would be of the same construction as an altar. But for the altars and tombs in the tragedies to which these diagrams refer, the scheme is appropriate enough.

cal vehicle would have to have a secure means for actors to descend from it. So I asked Kit to design a carriage that had a step at the back, with seats (benches) both at the front and the back. Side panels to the superstructure should allow performers to ride securely and give them something to grasp as they stand in the carriage and descend from it.

FURTHER COMMENTS AND ACKNOWLEDGMENTS

I have used the combination "actor/character" repeatedly in this book to establish the physicality of the performer alongside our impression of the character and to emphasize the demands placed on the performer by the script and its realization. On a more trivial level, it may also be worth commenting in advance that, in my references, the abbreviation "no." indicates "number" and "n." indicates "note" (either footnote or endnote) in a source, since this small distinction might lead to an avoidable confusion. Also, a line number followed by the notation "ff." indicates "the line number and the following lines."

I have a number of significant acknowledgments to make, both to institutions and to individuals, for support during the writing of this book. I am grateful to the Leverhulme Trust, for awarding me a fellowship to undertake research for the book, and to the University of Exeter for granting me study leave to match the semester of the fellowship. I was obviously very fortunate to have the graphic skills of Jon Primrose and Kit Surrey, with their patience and their attention to detail, to support the written text. Advice and help from colleagues and friends at Exeter was most important. Conversations with Norman Postlethwaite on proxemics, Larry Shenfield on chariots and carriages, Nic Gayle on music, and Les Read on theaters all contributed greatly. I must add, in fairness and in qualification, that it cannot be assumed that what I have argued or suggested fully represents the opinions of any of the above. In completing the book, I have had the benefit of comments from two anonymous readers for the press, for which I am most grateful.

Some of the material in chapter 2 was published, in a slightly different form, as "Modern Visions of Greek Tragic Dancing," *Theater Journal* 55.3 (2003), 467–80.

Exeter, 2005

other playing spaces —
e.g. theatres, TV studios,
film sets etc.

CHAPTER ONE

The Playing Space

THE SCRIPTS AND THE PLAYING SPACE

The subject of this chapter is the playing space of tragic performance in the fifth century BCE in Athens, and I shall be presenting evidence that the tragic scripts from this period were composed for performance in the open playing space. Despite the abundance of writing on Greek tragedies and on the ancient Greek theater, the practical playing space of tragic performance is the explicit subject of very few studies. Any study of the playing space has to combine what is known of the theater of Dionysus at Athens and its resources with an investigation of the theatricality of the tragedies, matching the scripts and the indications they contain to the space for which they were composed. This is a problematic procedure, made trickier by the absence of any description of performance in progress from a fifth-century observer. So even if we can reach reasonably secure conclusions about the layout and resources of the theater, we have to determine how these were used through a curiously inverted inspection of the scripts themselves. It is "inverted" because we have to work backward from the finished article and try to reconstruct the assumptions that gave rise to it.

With some minimal exceptions, the texts of Greek drama do not contain original stage directions of the kind we have come to expect in modern printed drama.[1] So we are dependent on references in the verbal script to its own implementation or on inferences we can draw from the verbal script about the presence of material objects and about the proximity of performers to each other or to a material object. In this situation there is little point

---

1. Taplin 1977a; Chancellor 1986.

in debating or complaining about the little we have, but it is important to make a cautious appraisal of what we do have.[2] To give a simple example that will appear later in this chapter, if one actor/character says to another "I have brought your bed outside," we should not automatically assume that the other actor/character has been *carried* out on it, without casting our eyes around to see if there are any other indications that may confirm or qualify this assumption.[3]

The verbal script is not a complete performance, or even a secure record of a complete performance. We cannot, ultimately, even be sure of the status of the scripts that have come down to us as texts, and in certain cases scholars have suspected that an original script has been altered or supplemented for performances later than its original production in the fifth century BCE.[4] But the survival of more than thirty mostly complete tragedies from the fifth century and the variety and range of the indications they contain provide a substantial body of material for the investigation of the problem of the playing space. I have not brought fragmentary tragedies into the presentation here, and I have made only a brief reference to *Prometheus Bound* (of unknown date and authorship, but probably from the fifth century) and none to *Rhesos,* which probably belongs to the fourth century, since it seems inadvisable to add greater uncertainties to the problem.[5]

I have stated that there are few satisfactory studies of the open playing space, and Oliver Taplin's influential study *The Stagecraft of Aeschylus* exemplifies the difficulty of studying the open playing space.[6] His consistent focus was placed on what he called "entrances and exits," which he applied to the *choros* as well as to the actors/characters, and his book was constructed in the

2. Any debate about whether there were actions other than those indicated in the verbal script seems a relatively futile one, since it cannot possibly be resolved conclusively, or even satisfactorily. For such a debate, see Taplin (1977b, 28 ff.).
3. I refer here indirectly to Euripides' *Hippolytus,* which I will discuss later in this chapter.
4. Editors of the Greek texts of the plays have the determination of the best version as a prime responsibility. But suspecting the intrusion of additional text, or correcting an apparently corrupt text, are editorial activities that are often hazardous, as editors acknowledge. Page (1934) was relatively confident in advancing suggestions about interpolations in Greek tragedy by actors and later copyists of the texts. But even his doubts should at times be qualified, as I mention in connection with a scene from Euripides' *Iphigenia at Aulis,* which I discuss later in this chapter.
5. *Rhesos* has come down to us ascribed to Euripides, but it is generally believed to belong to a period after his death.
6. Taplin presented a sound (if always debatable) view of the *theatron* at Athens in the fifth century BCE in his app. B and of the *skene* in app. C, although readers should now consult the works I mentioned in the preface: Taplin (1977b), app. B, 434–51, and app. C, 452–59.

form of a sequential commentary on entrances and exits in the tragedies of Aeschylus. In the course of his commentary Taplin also alluded to other, later tragedies by Sophocles and Euripides in an attempt to elucidate not just the "stagecraft of Aeschylus" but also "the dramatic technique of the Greek tragedians."[7] The format of a sequential commentary made the book diffi-   3
cult to read as a study of the playing space, since the continuity of perfor-
mance was obstructed by the focus on entrances and exits and by the relatively limited attention given to what occurs between them, that is, to much
of the substance and action of the play and the performance.

Taplin's terminology had an unfortunate influence on the scholarship of the last generation, stamping the anachronistic concept of "stagecraft" on a form of composition for a singing and dancing *choros* with actors and encouraging the continuing use of "entrance" and "exit" for a playing space for which these terms are inappropriate. Taplin also wrote in passing of "arrivals and departures," and the terminology I advocate is fourfold, taking account of those who "arrive" in the playing space or "leave" it along the side approaches (known diversely as *parodoi* or *eisodoi*), and those who either "appear" from or "enter" the *skene*.[8]

In what follows, I shall refer in the notes to some of Taplin's discussions and to other modern discussions of the tragedies of Aeschylus, Sophocles, and Euripides, although in many cases the full problem of the playing space for tragedy is not truly their subject. The major exceptions in this respect are the theatrical commentaries attached to the translations of Aeschylus and Sophocles edited by Michael Ewans, although the commentaries are not restricted to that single issue.[9] The approach taken by Ewans exemplifies a method that is now becoming far more familiar across a variety of disciplines, including archaeology and classics as well as theater studies, which is that of research through practice. Ewans's method shared by his collaborators was to explore the scripts in workshop or performance and to draw conclusions about their presentation on the basis of a firm interest in the original conditions for which the scripts were composed. Though by no means infallible, practical research tends to offer a different set of observations about the material or problem concerned, and if it is valuable in the case of

---

7. Taplin 1977b, 1.
8. Taplin 1977b, 6. I also use "reappearance," "reentry," and "return." *Eisodos* (plural, *eisodoi*) is a far better term for the side approaches than the alternative *parodos,* which is also used of the "entry song" of the *choros* and so can result in confusion. Taplin argues for *eisodos* wisely (449), and I shall use it here.
9. Ewans 1995, 1996, 1999, 2000.

Caesar's construction of a bridge across the Rhine and other archaeological experiments, it is of obvious and unavoidable relevance to theater studies and the investigation of performance.

4   In this chapter I shall investigate the disposition of actors in the playing space and the disposition of the *choros* and its members in relation to actors/characters. It is that aspect of the *choros* that matters here, and the larger problem of understanding the nature of the *choros* is the subject of the following chapter. Similarly, I have referred merely to "parts" of a song and dance by the *choros* (or an actor/character) without further commentary on choric singing and dancing, since for the purposes of this chapter that is just adequate. I have at times used the neutral term "sequence" for those sections of the scripts I have selected because I am not interested in confronting the reader in this particular enquiry with questions about formal structure and any terminology associated with it. My immediate concern is to offer readers the opportunity to develop a sense of the problem of the playing space through reference to indicative sequences in the surviving tragedies. In relation to the tragedies after Aeschylus, that referencing will be selective; for various reasons, the consideration of the tragedies of Aeschylus has to be more extensive, and I start with this.

THE SURVIVING TRAGEDIES OF AESCHYLUS AND EARLY TRAGIC PERFORMANCE

What evidence there is, from late sources, suggests that Aeschylus began composing early in the fifth century, won his first victory in the dramatic competitions in 484 BCE, and composed about eighty plays, winning thirteen victories. So if the surviving, complete plays of Aeschylus represent a phase in what might loosely be called the "development" of tragedy as a festival performance at Athens, then it is certainly not the earliest phase. On any reasonable calculation, the surviving plays belong to the second part of Aeschylus's life as a composer. There are dates available for *Persians* (472 BCE), *Seven against Thebes* (467), *Suppliants* (late 460s), and the three tragedies of the *Oresteia* (458), *Agamemnon, Libation Bearers,* and *Eumenides,* and while the surviving fragments are interesting, it would be a mistake to attempt to draw firm conclusions from them.[10] It is only reasonable to assume that some of

10. Sommerstein (1996, 13–32) offers a "Life and Times of Aeschylus," with a list of the known titles of plays by Aeschylus.

On *Prometheus Bound,* the case presented by Griffith (1977) has almost universal acceptance, although it has been contested; Sommerstein (1996, 321–27) offers a short summary of the evidence and arguments, with a concluding compromise.

these fragments should date to the period before 472 BCE and *Persians*, his earliest, complete surviving tragedy.[11] Before Aeschylus there is the hidden activity from the time of the introduction of tragedy to festival performance at Athens, which has been traditionally dated to the mid 530s BCE but may be much later than that, toward the close of the sixth century BCE.[12]

To look backward from *Persians* is undoubtedly tempting, but there are very few guidelines indeed if we try to move into the labyrinth of "early" or "original tragedy." Tragedy is a form of performance by a *choros*, but it is next to impossible to determine what that form was like until we see it in the earliest surviving tragedies of Aeschylus. In the *Poetics*, Aristotle states that originally there was only one actor/performer distinguished from the *choros*, and then a second was added, and finally a third.[13] We can be reasonably sure that the composer was the original separate performer and that he remained so until Sophocles decided to withdraw from that role, leaving three actors to perform the differentiated roles in any tragedy, from about or just before the middle of the fifth century BCE.[14]

So we seem to see a requirement for only two actors, doubling roles effectively by means of masks, in the surviving tragedies of Aeschylus before the *Oresteia*, while the *Oresteia* itself requires three actors, with the possibility of four for a brief sequence in *Libation Bearers*, the second tragedy of the trilogy. Most scholars believe that Aeschylus was composing for two actors and the *choros* until the late 460s BCE, close to the end of his life, and only adopted three actors either with or just before the *Oresteia*. The timing of any change from one to two actors is completely hidden from us, although Aristotle states plainly that it was Aeschylus who introduced the second actor. If Aeschylus also adjusted to composing for three only toward the end of his life, then it is an obvious conclusion that the art of composing for two actors and a *choros* was his art par excellence.

Of course, "development" is a tricky concept, which is why I placed it

11. Fragments translated in Weir Smyth and Lloyd-Jones (1957), and a selection in translation in Ewans (1996, 105–24); a discussion in Taplin (1977b), app. A, 416–33, which is unfortunately difficult for those without Greek; accessible discussions of the satyr-play fragments and others incidentally in Sommerstein (1996), esp. in his chap. 3, 53–70, and chaps. 9 and 10, 329–53. I shall not attempt to draw any conclusions from the fragments.
12. Connor (1989) and West (1989) have both shrewdly questioned the traditions associated with Thespis, the legendary founder of tragedy at Athens. Connor would date festival performances of tragedy in the city of Athens to late in the sixth century BCE. He provides sound reasons to doubt the restoration of the phrase "drama in the city," which appears in the translation of the inscription on the Parian Marble in Csapo and Slater (1994), sec. 3, no. 45, 120.
13. Aristotle *Poetics* chap. 4; Csapo and Slater (1994), sec. 2, no. 11, 99.
14. Csapo and Slater (1994), sec. 4, nos. 1–3, 224–25.

above in quotation marks. One of the more obvious traps it sets is the implication that Aeschylus came at the "beginnings" of European drama and theater. It is bound to be tempting to see drama and theater straining in some way to reach the present, to become recognizable to us from an obscure or strange starting point, and the path from ritual origins to secular performance is one that is constantly traced by many commentaries. Aristotle's *Poetics,* the principal theoretical treatise on drama from antiquity, offers a lead here that can be irresistible, since he plainly believes that tragedy did reach its proper form after moving through earlier phases.

The topic of the addition of actors, from one to two to three, is simple enough as an example. The presence of the "actor" at the beginnings of tragedy corresponds with our own modern emphasis on the actor as the elemental component of theater, and the desire for multiplication of this figure is one with which we can easily feel sympathy.[15] In addition, we may well be tempted to believe that we know why the second actor was introduced: the reason must have been an irresistible urge to create spoken dialogue, to move away from a ritualistic, choric form of performance as swiftly as possible to something more manageable.

There are, indeed, exchanges between actors in *Persians, Seven against Thebes,* and *Suppliants,* but we should be unobservant if we classified them as dialogue without qualifying that concept carefully. In most of these scenes, one of the actors/characters present has previously addressed the *choros* alone, and the second actor/character regularly addresses the *choros* first before acknowledging the other actor, responding as much to the concerns embodied in and by the *choros,* and by the present crisis, as to the other character. The presence of the *choros,* rather than the presence of the actor, is a constant factor in the composition of these tragedies, and our sense of "dialogue" needs to be judged accordingly.

Significantly, in *Seven against Thebes,* which introduces two actors/characters before it introduces the *choros,* even the exchange between Eteocles, ruler of Thebes, and the Scout who has been watching the enemy does not take the form of reciprocal dialogue. Eteocles expects a report from the scouts he has sent out, and the Scout arrives and addresses Eteocles, but the king does not respond to him (*Seven against Thebes* 36–77).[16] Reciprocal ac-

15. *The Presence of the Actor* is the title of an influential book by the modern practitioner Joseph Chaikin. In general terms, in reflections on the theater in the later twentieth century, the presence of the actor is seen to be the precondition for the establishment of character, not merely the means to portray character.
16. The debate on the presence of extras for this opening scene is interesting: see, for example, the proposal adopted by Arnott (1989, 21) and Wiles (1997, 115–16), following

knowledgment between these two characters is postponed to the central sequence of the play, but even there it is marginal, subsumed in the public determination of a strategy of defense for the city, which proceeds in front of a tremulous *choros*.

Elsewhere, actors in these early tragedies of Aeschylus regularly address the *choros*, and it can hardly be called speculative to assume that this was the substantial function of the original, separate performer, almost certainly the composer himself. The multiplication of characters, and their effective deployment (appearance or arrival, and reappearance or return) during the length of the drama, is as strong a motive for the addition of the second performer as the potential of exchanges made between them, in which "dialogue" in any modern sense features very little. If we retain the idea of development, it would be more accurate to describe the process as the gradual amplification of a choric form of performance, not a move away from it, even with the addition of a third actor. The extent to which this is evident in the *Oresteia* should emerge from the discussions in this chapter.

But the addition of a third individual performer is not the only resource that distinguishes the *Oresteia* from the preceding tragedies. The script of *Libation Bearers* has a scene of knocking at a door and, indeed, an extended section that involves entrances into and appearances from a structure. Other aspects of the trilogy (e.g., the Watchman apparently on the "roof" at the opening of *Agamemnon*) make it plain to us that Aeschylus is using a solid construction of some sort, for which the conventional name is a *skene* (or *skenai*), literally a "tent." There is no comparable use of a door or of a construction with a presumed interior in the earlier plays, although it is not difficult to imagine or believe (if one chooses) that it was actually present but scarcely used or just not used dramatically at all.[17]

The important consideration is that Aeschylus evidently composes for the *skene* in the *Oresteia* and does not apparently or manifestly do so in the earlier tragedies.[18] The plays by other composers that come after the *Oresteia* adopt this *skene*, and composition continues to take it into account in various realizations that are important to the conception of the dramas, whether tragedy or comedy. So we are faced in Aeschylus's surviving work

---

Calder (1959), in which the audience is addressed by Eteocles as the citizens, in contrast to Taplin (1977b, 129–30), and Ewans (1996, 185).

17. One might speculate on why this construction was called the "tent," and one might also presume that any solid structure (such as that in the *Oresteia*) was preceded by a less solid structure, located somewhere in the *theatron*. There is, however, nothing that can substantiate these speculations.

18. Hamilton (1987) dissents from the prevalent view.

by two modes of composition, which may be closely related: that for a *choros*
and two actors and that for a *choros* and three actors. Accordingly, in relation to the playing space, I shall be concentrating on the continuities and
differences that may be found between Aeschylus's earlier tragedies and
8   the *Oresteia*.

The concept of the playing space sounds very simple, and yet for the ancient Greek theater of the fifth century it is problematic. In the modern theater, we have become accustomed to constant redefinitions of the playing
space, established according to the circumstances of production and the
choices made by directors or ensembles, or even by architects and planners
in the case of predetermined space. For Athens, we need to assume a degree
of regularity not simply in location but in the repeated use of similar conditions for composition and presentation.

The central feature, physically and in conception, is the space in which a
choros sings and dances. The shape of its perimeter may be debated, but its
role in welcoming and accommodating *choroi* for the festival is undoubted,
and that is of far greater importance. Indeed, in the Homeric poems this
kind of space may itself be called "a" or "the" *choros*, in a manner that points
out the cultural consistency of the expectation within a community that
dances will take place and will be watched.[19] So in the space called the theater of Dionysus in Athens, the relationship between the banked *theatron* or
"watching place" and the open space for dancing (usually called the *orchestra*)
is essential. The two elements, as we might be inclined to think of them,
form a unity that is complete in itself. Put in religious terms, the god Dionysus has been honored and satisfied if dances take place that have been
watched, since he himself in the person of his priest and his statue are present in the theater.[20] We might do best to imagine this performative satisfaction in relation to the dithyramb, which deployed no masks or other material properties in the playing space but which united the *orchestra* and *theatron*
on behalf of the Athenian *polis* in honor of Dionysus.[21]

So our own, modern sense of the playing space, in all kinds of ways, may
be at odds with that of the Athenians. We need to remember that the performances of dithyrambs were, in this context of the playing space at Athens,
"theatrical," and in the period of the fifth century and afterward, when there
was a solid *skene*, they may have occurred in front of it but without reference

19. I comment further on this aspect of the word in chap. 2.
20. In fact, we should not be beguiled too much here by etymology. A *choros* is best and
most readily understood by us to be a singing and dancing group, and the *theatron* is as
much a listening place as a watching place.
21. I discuss the dithyramb in chap. 2.

to it.[22] In our reading of plays, in that process of visualization to which we are inevitably drawn, we may easily be distracted by particular aspects of realization and likely production, notably in those cases where we believe we can see the relationship of performer to object. In this respect, the *skene* is bound to exercise a recurrent fascination for commentators, because it offers an elevation and so a possible "frame" for speech and action that accord with many of our modern traditions of "seeing" and of theater.

In such circumstances, we must recall that the singing and dancing of a *choros* were a sufficient satisfaction in themselves and that the *theatron* catered for both seeing and hearing in the elevation of its banked seating. The process of adjusting our perceptions and assumptions needs to be constant, or we shall be continually left with the problem of the playing space: we shall be looking for, and constantly expecting, the wrong kind of theater, in the most fundamental way.

CHOROS, ACTORS/CHARACTERS, AND PLAYING SPACE IN THE EARLIER TRAGEDIES OF AESCHYLUS

Persians

In *Persians,* the costume of the *choros* will have supported the unequivocal definition of the playing space as a "setting" provided by their chant and subsequent song of arrival. The definition is unequivocal not because it is detailed, in local or spatial terms, but because it suggests, for Athenians of that period and for most Greeks until the time of Alexander the Great, the largest geographical and ethnic "other" by which they were impelled to define themselves. The *choros* is of Asia, of Persia, of the cities of Sousa and Agbatana, and if later the audience is offered more insistent references to Sousa (notably at line 761) then these will occasion no perceptual readjustment. The *choros* embodies Persian ambitions and apprehensions and alludes to Persian grandeur, nobility, and wealth, to absent military and imperial might, and to royalty. The *choros* itself is the setting, and the relationship between *orchestra* and *theatron* is settled by its arrival.[23]

22. The alternative is to suppose that the wooden *skene* was erected annually after the day of the dithyrambic performances, in the evening and the following (very) early morning. This is possible but, practically, rather odd and risky, should the dithyrambic performances last until late or should anything go wrong with the construction. Unfortunately, there is nothing that can decide this question for us.

23. Arnott (1989, 135–36) comments on the generality of the setting achieved in *Persians,* as does Ewans (1996, 169).

So it is to the *choros* in this setting, which depends on the relationship between *orchestra* and *theatron*, that the actors/characters of the play come, giving us the needed definition of the playing space for the earliest of our surviving tragedies. My use of the word "definition" here may call for some commentary, since I am apparently employing it in different ways. Aeschylus knew the resources available to him and so knew the playing space, which was also familiar to his audience. His task with each composition was to place a definition on the *choros* and to achieve a definition of the locale or setting insofar as that was required to satisfy understanding and appreciation of the particular tragedy.

Our position is different, since we are working in reverse. We have Aeschylus's definition of the *choroi* in the texts of the tragedies, in the scripts, but we are not familiar as he and his audience were with the playing space for which they were composed. For our part, we need to secure a definition of the playing space, of how it was used, if we are to understand the kind of theater that tragedy was. We might say that the problem of the playing space stands between us and Aeschylus theatrically, much as the texts are usually seen to stand between us and Aeschylus and his original audience, critically or thematically.

To the *choros* come the actors/characters, and the most persistent relationship in the playing space for *Persians* is between the *choros* and the Persian Queen Mother, wife of Darius and mother of Xerxes. It is she whom we first see approaching the *choros,* and she maintains a relationship with the *choros* until the arrival of her son, Xerxes, at the end of the tragedy. What is reported by the Messenger is reported both to her and the *choros,* and the actor/character Darius comes from the underworld to speak to the *choros* and to her. She shares and sharpens the fears of the *choros* by herself reporting her dream, and this simple yet effective paradigm of woman dynast and elders waiting for news of an expeditionary force is one that Aeschylus exploited later in the *Oresteia,* with the dream providing a motif for the second play of the trilogy.

The Queen Mother has come from the palace to the playing space, and in her return (599 ff.) to the playing space after the Messenger's report of disaster she gives to the *choros* a precise description of her progress.

> So I have traced the same path again from the palace,
> but without the carriage and the adornment I had
> before, bringing libations to the father of my son
> to make him well-disposed, offerings that soothe the dead.
> (607–10)

The offerings she lists are milk, honey, spring water, and wine and olives and garlands of fresh flowers (611–18). The lines not only explain what she is intending and doing (i.e., returning to bring propitiatory offerings to Darius) but, in addition, they explain two other matters to the *choros* and to the audience. The second of these is the incidental matter of the contents of the containers that she has brought with her, while the first is the fact that this time she arrives on foot and, in some manner, plainly, without luxury or adornment (the Greek word is *chlídé*).

The passage offers a good example of a necessary technique in the theatrical analysis of scripts, something that we might call retrospective inference. We should not have known that the actor/character of the Queen Mother first arrived in the playing space in a carriage from anything in the script at that point of first arrival. We only come to know this because Aeschylus was keen to create a marked, theatrical effect with the contrasting return of the Queen Mother and to explain it to both *choros* and audience.

The effects of the inference here are important. The Queen Mother "has traced the same path again" from the palace, and so she has arrived in both instances from the same *eísodos,* or side approach into the playing space, and the palace is somewhere other than the playing space. In both instances the actor/character has come to the *choros* in the playing space, which means the *orchestra.* Since it is a level ground signifying a locale, arrival in a carriage is a perfectly consonant resource of this kind of theater. It is, indeed, one that Aeschylus uses again, demonstrably in the first play of the *Oresteia,* but possibly in other instances, and its later use in tragedies by Euripides is of some interest and will be discussed below.[24] We might also note that even when we are quite certain of the existence and deployment of a *skene,* we have no instances of anyone jumping in a carriage from the *skene,* either to visit the *choros* in the adjoining *orchestra* or to rush out to action away from the playing space, like a modern car driver.

The tracing of the "same path" also introduces the possibility that the definition of the locale stretched to definitions of the access to it, with the two *eísodoi* or side approaches signifying distinctive and contrasting directions consistently throughout any given tragedy. Obviously, the alternative to this is that the association was casual and that composers and audience did not care or that some composers sometimes cared and others did not, and there was no standard "convention." Unfortunately, we can do no more

24. Taplin (1977b) introduces these at 75–76, but he attempts to bring all of the examples together at once without adequate discussion, which is unhelpful and unnecessary.

than infer, even if the minimum we are prepared to envisage is that two characters—one leaving and one arriving—should not pass each other in the same *eisodos,* although even this assumption might not be justified.[25] But we do not get references to chance encounters of that sort, either in anticipation or in the event, although characters may be seen and acknowledged as they approach and arrive along an *eisodos.*

Of course, there is much that we do not know, even with the help and employment of a convenient and fortunate retrospective inference such as this. Commentary might consider whether the Queen Mother arrived in black (the black of mourning) on the second occasion, with few or just one attendant(s) or none, in contrast to the adornment of her earlier arrival, which might refer to the number of attendants as well as to costume.[26] On many occasions attendants, either slaves or soldiers, can be inferred, although the numbers are often uncertain. The situation is far easier when a particular attendant is addressed, and retrospective inference then comes into play, determining that this person must have arrived or appeared with a character at an earlier point. Nor can we be sure about the disposition of such figures and "extras" within the playing space, particularly when there would seem to be several or many of them.

But in *Persians* and in this instance, the most important observation by far is that the actor/character of the Queen Mother has come to the *choros* in the playing space and that her scenes with the *choros* proceed on that basis. In that respect, we can also be sure that the actor/character of the Messenger comes to the *choros,* with whom he finds the Queen Mother. His concern is to report the disaster to "the land of Persia and the cities of the whole of Asia" (249–50), a large phrase that revisits the definition of the locale in the broadest sense achieved by the *choros* in its opening chant and song, and he addresses the *choros* first, as they respond with passages of disturbed song and dance (249–89).[27] The Queen Mother is silent and is only addressed by the

25. Both Taplin (1977b, 450–51) and Hourmouziades (1965, 128–36) favor the distinction of the locales signified by the *eisodoi* in tragedy. Wiles (1997) develops this perception by proposing that "these locations are opposites both topographically and symbolically" (134) throughout his chap. 6 (133–60).

26. Taplin (1977b) comments on the presence of attendants first accompanying the Queen Mother as a part of "the wealth and pomp of her position" (79) and on her contrasting return (98–99).

27. Taplin (1977b) seeks an explanation for this "attention to the *choros* at the expense of the actors" (87), as if holding this mode of composition to account for not according with assumptions he draws from later tragedy and from his own pronounced commitment to the actors of tragedy over the *choros.*

Messenger after she speaks (290–301). She then prompts the reports offered by the Messenger, which are addressed to the unity of concern formed by the Queen Mother and *choros* in the playing space.

The things we do not know should be placed carefully against the things we do. One of the obvious questions is if and when the Queen Mother descends from her carriage on her first arrival in the playing space, which also prompts the question of where that carriage might be positioned.[28] Ewans is right to pursue these questions and to ask how the script might best be played over the extent of this scene, and here the merits of a workshop with performers are bound to be outstanding.[29] Unless there are specific indications of disposition in the script, any proposals made from this kind of exploration will be hypothetical. But granted our certainty about the presence of the *choros* and the characters in the playing space, then the limits of the hypothesis will actually be quite tight, which will make the proposals valuable. Most of these issues are unquestionably best "explained" in practice, which alone can explore possibilities and implausibilities with the appropriate freedom and constraints. But there are some matters that it will be useful to isolate for consideration here.

One of these is that of the disposition of the *choros* members when the *choros* is not singing or dancing, or moving to a chant, on its own. This aspect of the *choros* is effectively the only one I shall be considering in this chapter, others being reserved for the second chapter, which will be devoted to the larger problem of the nature of the *choros*. There is really very little indeed that we could claim to "know" about the disposition of the *choros* members at these times.[30] But the arrival of the Messenger offers a good opportunity for some basic comments or queries.

The Messenger addresses the *choros* and then responds to the Queen Mother during the extent of his presence in the playing space. If the *choros* members were placed to the rear of the playing space, away from the audience, after 290 when the Queen Mother first speaks, then any acknowledgment of them would have to be perfunctory were the Messenger also to address the audience in an effective manner. The Messenger must be in a

28. Taplin (1977b) does not consider these practical problems, in the long and, at times, tortuous commentaries on her "entrance" (70 ff.) and her "exit" (92 ff.).
29. Ewans (1996, 175–76) offers an interesting and persuasive vision of the arrival of the Messenger in the playing space and of the subsequent scene. Ewans's assumptions about the playing space are given at xxiii–xxv.
30. Davidson (1986) tentatively proposed that a circular formation might have been appropriate on a number of occasions when the *choros* is not singing or dancing.

position to address both *choros* and Queen Mother and, yet, not be impeded in his repeated delivery of extended and vivid descriptions to the audience. If the *choros* members are grouped around him, then he will be less visible and so will the fact of his exchange with the Queen Mother, which might be hard to distinguish from an exchange with a *choros* member, which is not what Aeschylus can have wanted.

In the finale of the tragedy, the actor/character of Xerxes comes to the *choros* in the playing space, and it is clear that he is in tatters and carrying an empty quiver (1014–25). The audience has been repeatedly prepared for this, in words from Darius (832–36) and from the Queen Mother (845–51). At 1000–1001, the *choros* exclaims that it wondered at not seeing leading warriors following behind his "wheeled tent," a description that clearly refers to a carriage with a superstructure. Since this is a passing reference, unlike the Queen Mother's thorough explanation of her second arrival without a carriage (607–10), modern opinion varies on whether such a vehicle was visible and whether Xerxes made his appearance on it or with it.[31]

It may be that the actor/character of Xerxes has arrived from the opposite *eisodos* to that used by the Queen Mother, as the Messenger may have done, so giving us the earliest example of the two *eisodoi* carrying different significance in the minds of the audience. Those with the pragmatic mentality of the modern stage manager might then care to note that Aeschylus had removed his carriage early in the play, allowing plenty of time for it to be reequipped and brought round to the opposite *eisodos*. Either a carriage with the tattered finery of a superstructure or no carriage at all would contrast with the luxury of that used by the Queen Mother, so short a dramatic time ago, when Persia was thought to be in possession of all its riches. These are issues that cannot be resolved. What matters is that the king comes to the *choros* and chants and sings and dances the final lament with them in the playing space.[32]

There are, in addition, other issues in *Persians* that cannot be resolved, which may distract attention from what we do know. There is nothing explicit in the script itself that helps us with the location or definition of the

31. Taplin (1977b) is inclined to believe that 913 implies that Xerxes "may go literally on his knees" and to dismiss the wheeled tent, or wagon (123), as does Rehm (2002, 249, 388n61). In contrast, Ewans (1996) believes that 1000–1002 "imply that the Elders [the *choros*] can see the carriage but not see the troops who would normally accompany it" (183).

32. Both Taplin (1977b, 127–28) and Ewans (1996, 184) draw attention to the concluding procession that apparently takes both actor/character and *choros* out of the playing space in the final part of the lament.

tomb of Darius, and this accounts for the variety of speculations about it, which can dwarf our general awareness of the playing space.[33] The Queen Mother brings offerings for Darius, and it is the *choros* that tells us it is expecting Darius to "come here, come to the summit of a mound" (657–60), a mound they have earlier (647) identified with the ruler himself in their song and dance of invocation. Darius himself observes that he saw his queen "near the tomb," and received her offerings, and that the *choros* members, whom he addresses, are standing near the tomb (684–88).

Strictly speaking, we cannot know the location of the tomb or whether the actor/character Darius did appear on top of it.[34] We know that Darius refers to the difficulty of leaving the underworld, whose deities take more readily than they let go (688–90), and to his return down below the earth (839). It would be perverse not to allow for the tomb as a material entity, but we cannot be sure that the actor/character of Darius did actually appear above it and disappear into it.[35] The actor/character of Darius first addresses the *choros,* which responds to him in song and dancing, and there is a later exchange between them. He also has an exchange with his queen, whom he addresses apparently to gain a clearer response than the song and dance of the *choros* have provided. The situation is very similar to the scene with the Messenger, and we have no reason to suppose it was not composed for the same playing space as the second arrival of the Queen and the preceding song and dance of the *choros* (598–680), which take place in the *orchestra.*

The remaining issue is of little importance, although it has inevitably provoked a great deal of speculation. At the close of its opening song, the *choros* reverts to the chanting with which it arrived in the playing space and invites itself to sit in or on or beside "this ancient building" in order to reflect (140–43). Very shortly after—some five short lines of the continuing chant—the *choros* sees the Queen Mother arriving (in her carriage) and immediately

33. Ewans practical explorations placed the tomb in a central position at the rear of the playing space (1996, 170), but he concentrates in his commentary on the need for movement in the interpretation of the script (182).
34. Hammond's supposition (1972, 1988) of the existence of a rock to one side of the *orchestra* is perhaps the most radical of all the speculations. Taplin (1977b, 116–17) has a detailed discussion, which refers to the first of Hammond's two essays; Hammond returned to the controversy in the second of his essays (1988, 16–22).
35. Wiles (1997) envisages the tomb at the center of the *orchestra,* and the actor/character of Darius approaching it after "ascending to the *orchestra* from the terrace behind" (79), the method of ascent favored by Ewans. Rehm (2002) would also see the tomb at the center of the *orchestra* but would have the ghost of Darius appearing on top of the *skene* (239), which he is willing to accept was in existence before the *Oresteia* (315n14).

announces that it is falling down before her in reverence. There is no further reference to any building in the script, and the tomb of Darius is never described in that manner. To be quite literal in our interpretation, if the *choros* did "sit" anywhere then they will have had to jump up and bow down almost immediately. Any proposal that the audience is asked to envisage an interior playing space seems vitiated by the Queen Mother driving a carriage into it immediately.[36] We cannot know precisely why Aeschylus included the lines in his script, but we can be sure that they should not prejudice our understanding of his composition for the playing space throughout *Persians*.[37]

Suppliants

Suppliants is a play composed for two actors and a *choros*, an ensemble to which Aeschylus may have added a subsidiary *choros* late in the action. The most likely dating now places the play in the later years of the 460s and, so, after *Seven against Thebes*. But in its use of arrivals by actors/characters, and their return to the playing space, it helps to consolidate the sense of composition for the playing space that we gain from *Persians*, and for that reason I shall consider it first.

The playing space in *Suppliants* is sufficiently defined by the arrival of the *choros*, who have come from Egypt and the Nile and landed in Argos, their actual arrival in the playing space apparently representing the time after the landing. Our initial impressions are confirmed in the opening song, which refers repeatedly to open spaces, the meadows and pastures of Argos rather than the city or human habitation. A closer definition (260–61) is offered by the ruler of the land, Pelasgus, on his arrival in the playing space, but his account does nothing to readjust our sense of locale. The father of the *choros*, Danaus, speaks at 176, and there is no clear indication whether he has been with the *choros* from the beginning or has arrived at this point. But his association with them, in their crisis, on their voyage, and on their landing, is as close as it might be.[38]

---

36. A conceptual "interior" space has also been attractive to some commentators in speculations on the opening of *Eumenides*, the third play in the *Oresteia*: see, for example, Rehm (1988, 290–301; 1992, 100–101; 2002, 89–91).

37. The full range of speculation would include those who believe that either this "building" or the tomb of Darius, or both, point to the existence of a *skene* of some kind. It is easier to determine the existence of a *skene* when entries are made into it or appearances from it and when references are explicit, as they are repeatedly in the *Oresteia*.

38. Taplin (1977b) discusses that issue at 193–94; Ewans (1996, 205–6) disagrees with Taplin, and brings Danaus into the playing space just before the end of the danced song by the *choros*.

The actor/character of Danaus prepares the *choros* for the subsequent arrival of those whom he expects to be the rulers of the land, who will have heard about the landing of the *choros* and are approaching, he presumes, with an armed force of foot soldiers, horses (horsemen), and chariots. Hindsight, or retrospective inference, is helpful here, because the king, Pelasgus, later orders "men" to accompany Danaus to the city (490–503). So, on his arrival, the actor/character of Pelasgus is most likely accompanied by some of the army that was seen from afar by Danaus, and commentators have been tempted to provide Pelasgus with one of the chariots mentioned by Danaus.[39]

This military grouping plainly comes to the *choros* in the playing space, and the actor/character of Pelasgus addresses the *choros* from the beginning. At 319–21 Danaus is introduced by the *choros* to Pelasgus, at the king's request, but Pelasgus holds back his address to the *choros* until he reaches a preliminary decision about he course of action he wishes to pursue. Since this involves the deployment of Danaus as a representative of the *choros* outside the playing space, Pelasgus addresses Danaus directly, and a brief exchange between the two characters finally ensues. Danaus leaves before Pelasgus, but Danaus returns to the *choros* at 600, and perhaps again at 710, if he has left again at 624; there are no explicit indications in the script about his movements at 624 or 710. But Danaus addresses the *choros* closely and directly from 600, until he leaves to seek help at 775.

This is a sequence of arrivals and returns of actors/characters to the *choros* in the playing space, and the *choros* is the addressee of the characters almost constantly, apart from the brief exchange between Danaus and Pelasgus. The arrival of the Herald of the pursuing Egyptians is completely consistent with this form of composition, but when Pelasgus returns the Herald is appropriately addressed by Pelasgus as an individual and replies to him as such in a substantial exchange between them. Whether or not the actor/character of the Herald has others with him cannot be resolved because there are no explicit indications in the script, and indeed there are none in this instance in relation to any military escort for Pelasgus. But it is the *choros* that is the subject of contention in the playing space to which both figures come, and the *choros* is again addressed by Pelasgus, after he dismisses the Herald and before he leaves (954). The text of the last part of the play has been doubted, but as it stands the *choros* asks Pelasgus as he leaves to send their father to them (968–69), and shortly afterward Danaus returns

39. Taplin (1977b, 200–201) argues for attendant soldiers and considers the possibility of a chariot or chariots; Ewans (1996,207, 207n11) counters this with the demands of "the complex movement and choreography needed to realize the rest of this scene in performance."

(980), referring to an apparently visible bodyguard he has been granted by the Argives (985–86).

The sequence of arrivals and returns in this tragedy and the predominance of direct address of actors/characters to the *choros* offer us an impressive sense of certainty about the form of composition for a *choros* in the playing space of the *orchestra,* one that confirms conclusions drawn from the earliest of the surviving tragedies, *Persians.* Actors/characters and *choros* manifestly share the same ground, although the "presence" of the *choros* in this tragedy is what supplies the tension of the play. In this respect, a glance back at *Persians* is helpful. In *Persians* the *choros* belongs to the playing space unequivocally; in *Suppliants,* the opposite is, in one sense, apparently true, since the suppliants are refugees. But this contrast in modes of definition of the playing space is more interesting because it is not absolute. The playing space in *Persians* should exude security, but at the "moment" of the tragic action it does not. In *Suppliants,* the fact of not belonging makes even the first arrival of the *choros* in the playing space insecure. But the belief of the daughters of Danaus in their status as suppliants claiming kinship in a foreign land makes their contested possession of the playing space the subject of the tragedy.

The ground of the *orchestra* in *Suppliants* is at one point described as "this smooth/level precinct" (508) by Pelasgus, who is inducing the *choros* to take up a position in it, since he regards it as being under the protection of the gods. That this is the playing space of the *orchestra* is plain from the fact that the *choros* then sings and dances in it. Earlier in the play, the *choros* was persuaded by Danaus to take refuge on a "this mound/hill of the gods in assembly" (189), and at 430 the *choros* refers to "images" of the gods, expressing a threat in the exchange with Pelasgus just later to hang themselves from these images (455 ff., with their earlier resolve at 160–61). It would seem to be this threat that prompts Pelasgus to send Danaus into the city and to lead the *choros* away from the images, at 506 ff. At a later point, the actor/character of Danaus addresses the *choros* from what he calls "this lookout that receives suppliants" (713), when he sees the ship of the Egyptians. It is difficult, with hindsight, not to associate this reference with his earlier sighting of the Argive army, which was followed immediately by his invitation to the *choros* to take refuge on "this mound." In direct connection with "this mound" Danaus had stated that "an altar is stronger than a fortification" (190), and later in the same scene Danaus encourages the *choros* to show reverence at an "altar shared in common." This picks up what might have been a more general reference from the *choros* at 83–85 to an altar as a protection for refugees.

Several of the Olympian gods are addressed in relation to this mound and altar, as would be expected from the clear indications that the sanctuary is dedicated to the collective gods and that visible attributes such as the eagle of Zeus and the trident of Poseidon are mentioned. The suppliants them- selves have staves of olive decorated with wool, which are symbolic of the plea to Zeus, protector of suppliants, for safety and asylum (e.g., 191–92).

That is a summary of the indications that the script provides, rather than a complete inventory. How far can we make sense of this information, and should it affect our sense of the use of the playing space? There is, it seems, a mound of some sort on which there is an altar dedicated to the Olympian gods, and images of them are visible. The firm implication is that these im- ages are solid rather than pictorial (the threat of hanging), and this might mean freestanding images or, possibly, just high-relief sculpture such as might be found on a frieze. Yet probably more significant for our under- standing of the playing space are the indications of movement to and from this mound. If Danaus invites the *choros* to approach the mound and occupy it as suppliants after the opening song and dance (188–96), then we might assume a distinction of some sort between the open ground of the *orchestra* (in which the dance takes place) and the place of refuge—that is, the mound and altar. This is consonant with Pelasgus's later invitation (508) to the suppliants to leave their place of refuge and come into the "smooth/level precinct," which he regards as also part of the sanctuary and which is (once again) the open ground of the *orchestra*. The *choros* is positioned there for its next dance (524–99), and it is encouraged to remain by the report conveyed by Danaus that the Argives have voted to receive and protect the refugees (600–624), performing the subsequent song and dance there (630–709). These impressions of movement and location would then be confirmed by Danaus addressing the *choros* from the "lookout" or the mound (713) and dis- tinguishing his position from that of the *choros*.

There is no further, explicit indication of movement. But in the exchange between Danaus and the *choros* that follows, Danaus states that he must leave (quickly) to get help; while the *choros* refers to the lack of respect the Egyp- tians have for altars (751–52), anticipating that the Egyptians will not re- frain from seizing them through fear of "this trident" (of Poseidon) and the awesome gods (755–56). We cannot be sure that they have left the open ground of the *orchestra,* and the succeeding dance suggests that they may not have done so. Unfortunately, the text after the arrival of the Herald is in a terrible state, and further conclusions would be unwise. Major uncertainties must also rest over the exchanges between the actor/character of Pelasgus and the *choros* from 348 to 437, which include a sequence in which Pelasgus replies in speech to song from the *choros* (348–417), and a short song from the *choros* (418–37). The *choros* certainly begins and ends this sequence on the mound, by the altar, and it is most plausible to envisage it as Ewans does, with the open ground of the *orchestra* used for the songs and dancing.[40] The alternative is not only inconsistent with the discernible pattern of composition but also requires us to believe that the *choros,* in remaining on the mound, sings but does not dance.

What can be detected in the above reconstruction is a relatively consistent and pragmatic use of the playing space, with the open ground of the *orchestra* used for dancing and distinguished in some manner from another area, which contains the altar and the images of the gods. If this is correct, then it would suggest that Aeschylus has created a playing space within the playing space, composing to allow for the major dances and songs in the open ground of the *orchestra* and integrating that requirement with movement to and from a distinctive but associated locale. Not only is the presence of the *choros* in the defined locale indicative of its insecurity but its movement within the playing space may also presage the desired movement away from sanctuary, in a flux that eventually leads to the release and acceptance that appear to be assured by the close of the play. For the indications that there are in the script to be realized, then an area at the margins of the playing space or a confined area within it seem the necessary, alternative choices for the mound, the altar, and the images of the gods.[41] The rest, unfortunately, we cannot know.

Seven against Thebes

If *Suppliants* was produced in the late 460s BCE, as some fragmentary evidence from papyrus may be taken to reveal, then *Seven against Thebes* may have been, in some respects, a model for it. The comparison is particularly interesting in relation to the issue of the movements of the *choros* within the playing space. If we consider the play from the arrival of the *choros,* then we en-

40. For this reason, Ewans (1996) would place the altar and "statues of the twelve Olympians" in an arc "round the rear perimeter" of the *orchestra* (203). For Hammond (1972), the required mound is accommodated by the rock that he believes stood to one side of the playing space (417–22).

41. Wiles (1997) places the altar in the center of the *orchestra* and believes that the statues "must be close to the altar" (196–97). The *choros* must then dance round "the sacred area of ground" when drawn from it by Pelasgus.

counter once again references to images of the Olympian gods in the initial terror of the *choros*. The *choros* first asks itself to which images of the gods or goddesses it should turn for protection (93–96) and then asks why it does not immediately clasp the images, since this is the time to do so (97–99). These are the gods of the city, and eight Olympians are addressed, with the *choros* later referring to "this assembly of the gods" (219–20), who are bound to the city by sacrifice and public rites (174–80). There is no explicit mention of an altar, which is a repeated reference point in *Suppliants,* but the playing space is defined as "this acro*polís,* a seat [of the gods] that is honoured" (240–41), the acro*polís* (or "high city") traditionally being both an ultimate place of refuge, as a citadel, and a cult center.

At 264–66 the king, Eteocles, asks the *choros* to move "away from/beyond the images" in order to make a better prayer, in contrast to their present terror. He invites them to listen to his prayers and then to raise the propitious, sacred cry and a paean, or song for salvation, "according to the Hellenic custom of the cry accompanying sacrifice, bringing courage to those dear to you, and releasing fear into the enemy" (267–70). His invitation or instruction is then followed by the *choros* dancing and singing (287–368), and with the example of *Suppliants* in mind we should feel confident in concluding that the danced song takes place in the open ground of the *orchestra,* after the *choros* has moved from an area within the playing space that has been dedicated to the images of the gods.

We might then look for further indications of the pattern of movement between the open ground of the *orchestra* and this area within it or on its margins. In its opening song and dance, the *choros* refers directly to its own hesitation in approaching the images and clasping them (95–96), and when Eteocles first addresses the *choros* he refers to "this running-through flight" (191), in a phrase that is recalled later by the *choros* in their evocation of the sack of a city (351). When the *choros* first responds to the actor/character of Eteocles, it does so with song and dance, and there it refers in the past tense to how "I came running up to the images of the gods" and "began prayers to the blessed gods in fear" (214), phrases that are meant to describe its opening song and dance. The past tense recurs at the close of this sung and danced section of the exchange, as the *choros* reasserts that it "came to this acro*polís*" in fear at the shouts and clangor of the enemy (239–41). Immediately after this moment the *choros* hears horses neighing (245), at the opening of a spoken line-by-line exchange with Eteocles, and expresses its fears again and addresses the "gods of the city" and "all-powerful Zeus" in the following lines (251–52). They are said to be clinging to the images during this exchange (258), which ends with Eteocles' instruction to the *choros* to come away from them (264–66).

The most plausible interpretation of these allusions in the text is that the women run to the images at the opening (245) of the spoken line-by-line exchange, as they hear the horses neighing and their fear is renewed.[42] There are, in fact, no indications that they have clung to the images before this point: none in the description of their past movements, none from Eteocles, and none in the opening song, which rather indicates that they do not hold the images. In that case, the dance and song of the *choros* on its arrival would take place in the open ground of the *orchestra,* with reference to the images, and the *choros* would remain there until the renewal of its fear in the spoken line-by-line exchange with Eteocles. His invitation would then draw the *choros* away from the images into the *orchestra,* ready for the danced song that follows (287–368). So we have, in this sequence, an interpretation that corresponds to *Suppliants* in the use of the open ground of the *orchestra* for song and dance and a composition that allows for that as well as for the use of an area within or at the margins of the playing space. Furthermore, the *choros* arrives in the open ground of the playing space, and the actor/character of Eteocles comes to them and addresses them there.[43]

There are no explicit indications in the rest of the script that the images are approached again or involved in the physical action of the playing space. So it is possible, and indeed probable, that they are physically touched and left only once. Nor is there any explicit reference to an altar, or to a mound, nor do actors/characters apparently approach the images. These aspects mark a strong difference from *Suppliants,* which presents a flux of movement from the one area (of the mound) to the open ground of the *orchestra,* and it is possible that the images in *Seven against Thebes* formed a line and that a line rather than an area provided the additional definition of the playing space.

From its arrival, the *choros* has occupied the open ground of the *orchestra,* with one movement away to and back from the images, and after the opening song the actor/character of Eteocles has been involved with it in a long exchange, which includes song and dance from the *choros.* In the later part of

42. Ewans's account of the movements is again impressive and differs in only one detail. He suggests (1996,189, 189n13) that the movement to the images is implied by the final part of the sung exchange with Eteocles at 239–40, which is still in the past tense. I feel that the movement is better motivated by the renewal of fear, just that moment later, at or just before 245, and after the end of the singing from the *choros.*

43. Wiles (1997) constructs a complex argument for placing the "assembly of statues" in an arc at the rear of the playing space (197 ff.), the configuration favored by Ewans.

the play, with the departure of Eteocles to the seventh gate, the *choros* is left to sing and dance on its own in the playing space (720 ff.), and the actor/character of the Scout returns to and addresses it directly (792), engaging in a short exchange, after which he leaves. The text from this point forward has occasioned many doubts, for a variety of reasons, but it would appear that the *choros* sings and dances alone before the two corpses of the brothers are brought to it in the playing space (848–60), initiating a lament from the *choros* over and around the corpses.[44] The final section of the text also includes reference to the arrival in the playing space of Antigone and Ismene (861–62), sisters of Eteocles and Polynices, and contributions from these figures and a Herald form part of the text as we now have it.

23

So the playing space in *Seven against Thebes* is defined, to a considerable extent, by the presence of the *choros* within it, and actors/characters come to the *choros,* and the corpses are brought to it there—if we can rely on this motif, even if not completely on the existing text of the close of the tragedy. This presence is also pronounced in the final section of the allocation of the warriors to the seven gates of the city. The Scout completes his final announcement or description, and Eteocles is engaged by the *choros* in an exchange, in which the *choros* sings and dances (686–711), in a form of composition for the playing space that recalls the earlier exchange between them (203–44).

These observations, taken as a whole, should undoubtedly affect our understanding of the central section of the tragedy, when the *choros* sings and dances after each exchange between the actors/characters of the Scout and Eteocles. At the opening of that sequence, the *choros* has completed singing and dancing in the *orchestra* (287–368), and it announces that the Scout is "bringing some new report of the army to us" (369–70).[45] The *choros* also announces, immediately afterward, the arrival of Eteocles to "learn the report of the messenger" (372–75). Both actors/characters arrive in haste, with the Scout running, as the *choros* describes him. For the rest of the sequence there are no explicit indications about the disposition of the actors and the *choros* in the playing space. But since the *choros* sings and dances at the close of each exchange between the actors, it will do so in the open ground of the *orchestra*.

---

44. The debate is justified and is likely to be endless. Concerned readers would probably do best to refer to an edition such as that by Hutchinson (1985), who provides a clear introduction to the generic nature of the problem (xl ff.), in addition to his notes on 1005 ff. (209–10).

45. This is an action that the Scout repeats later at 792, when he brings the news of the salvation of the city and the death of the brothers.

The experience of the *choros* in the playing space throughout the exchange is emphatically persistent and important.[46]

COMPOSITION FOR THE PLAYING SPACE
IN AESCHYLUS'S *ORESTEIA*

The facts of survival have placed the *Oresteia* in a strange position. Not only is it the only trilogy available to us, but it contains the only complete tragedies by Aeschylus in which the additional resources I have mentioned, those of a *skene* of some kind (with a door) and of the third actor, are manifestly deployed. So we are in the strange situation of observing the effects of these resources on his established mode of composition on only one occasion of production, while at the same time we are conscious that these resources remain substantially unaltered for the period that embraces all the surviving tragedies of his successors. To our limited view, the *Oresteia* occupies a position both at the beginning of something with which we can be relatively well acquainted, with some twenty-five plays by his successors following it, and at the end of something with which we are distinctly less well acquainted, through the three surviving, earlier tragedies by Aeschylus himself. Yet this earlier mode of composition, for the tragic *choros* and two actors, was the mode in which Aeschylus had been exercised for most of his productive life, and one for which he himself may have been responsible.

My approach to the *Oresteia* will attempt to take account of this strange position that it occupies and of the established mode of composition that in the trilogy he was adjusting to new resources. Precisely how new they were, we cannot tell. But they undoubtedly occur at the end of his productive life, and "adjustment" can serve as a salutary, guiding concept in our understanding of the general circumstances.[47] In this respect, it may be helpful initially to list a bare inventory of aspects of the *Oresteia* that are familiar even from

---

46. Ewans (1996) has an excellent discussion of the *choros* in this long scene, commenting that attention in modern critical commentary is concentrated on the speech of the actors/characters, relegating the interventions of the *choros* to "an almost trivial background commentary, musical interludes between serious speech" (192). He concludes, from practical exploration, that "these choral interventions should be performed . . . as sudden repossessions of the *orchestra*" (193). This, of course, would continue the tension between actor/character and *choros* in the playing space established by the composer in the opening of the tragedy.

47. I shall not, in what follows, be attempting to provide a summary critical guide to the *Oresteia* but will be maintaining my attention on selective aspects of composition for the playing space.

our limited awareness of the earlier, established mode of composition for the playing space. In *Agamemnon*, a herald comes to the *choros* with extensive and vivid accounts of military action; in the same tragedy, a royal carriage is drawn into the *orchestra* occupied by the *choros*; again in *Agamemnon*, a *choros* is threatened by force in the playing space; in both *Agamemnon* and *Libation Bearers*, corpses are introduced to the *choros* in the playing space; in *Libation Bearers*, there is a mound representing a grave in the *orchestra*, and a dead king is invoked at this tomb; in *Eumenides*, an image of the goddess Athena is an important reference, and it is used as a place of refuge, from which a suppliant may or may not be drawn; in *Eumenides*, a *choros* is led out finally, by subsidiary figures, to take up residence in a city; and finally, in all three plays the playing space is partly defined by speech from actors before the arrival of the *choros*. This is an aspect that we find in *Seven against Thebes*, nearly a decade before the production of the *Oresteia*, so it is not in itself a product of the new resources. This list is not comprehensive, but it should be strongly indicative of the degree of continuity we should expect and observe in the *Oresteia*. We might also note, in this connection, one very large feature of definition of the playing space, which is the *choros* of elders in *Agamemnon* left behind in the city, and awaiting news of a military expedition, one of a number of features in which the mind of the composer of *Persians* can be seen at work in the first play of the trilogy.

25

But these aspects of continuity, impressive as they are, do not occur as isolated remnants of a former mode of composition in an otherwise changed and adjusted theatricality. Our sense of the probability of continuity is what matters, since it is one means to alert us to what we find in the scripts. The opening of *Libation Bearers* provides a good example, even though the text of the first words of Orestes is unfortunately fragmentary. Orestes is accompanied by Pylades as he arrives, and his words confirm a definition of the playing space fundamentally as the land of Argos and mark a mound and an area within it as the tomb of his father. The composer then places Orestes and Pylades "out of the way" (20), after defining the dramatic moment of the action, which is his return from exile as an (avenging) heir. The *choros* then arrives to dance and to sing in the open ground of the *orchestra*, accompanied by Electra, and by their arrival, carrying libations for the dead, and in the content of their song they confirm the definition of the playing space. The actor/character of Electra addresses the *choros* directly and engages in an exchange with it before approaching the tomb mound of her father. As she traces and steps in the footprints on the ground of the *orchestra* she encounters Orestes and Pylades. Both Orestes and Electra, as the two vocal actors/

characters, join the *choros* in a remarkable, complex, and extended lament for, and invocation of the powers of, Agamemnon, which includes chanting from the *choros* but which is substantially a danced song. The whole scene ends with an extended, spoken exchange between the actor/character of Orestes and the *choros* (510–84).[48]

My description of this scene obviously aims to present it as an unexceptional composition for two actors and a *choros* in the playing space, in terms that are thoroughly familiar from Aeschylus's earlier tragedies, and indeed it does substantially take this form. We might, in addition, note that the vases that the *choros* carries are instrumental in confirming the definition of the playing space—and emblematic of the *choros* and to some extent the play—in a related manner to the suppliant staves in *Suppliants*. But there are features of the composition that diverge from the mode with which we are familiar. The exchanges between the actors/characters of Orestes and Electra are of an intimacy and directness for which there is no precedent in the early tragedies, and it is interesting that the *choros* is induced to interrupt them, or to attempt to do so, on both occasions (264–68, relatively unsuccessfully, and 510–13, successfully). We might justifiably detect here a diminution of the vitality of the "presence of the *choros*" in the playing space in favor of the actors/characters, but one for which there is a subsequent compensation in their total integration in the impressive lament.

We should also note the presence of a potential third performer in Pylades, who may appear to serve the merely functional purpose of a silent extra addressed by Orestes in the opening of the play but who later proves to be decisively vocal (900–902), at a point when three if not four actors/characters are active. We might also observe the lack of symbolic movement by the *choros* between attachment to a distinct area (the tomb mound) and the open ground of the *orchestra*. This was a distinctive feature of both *Suppliants* and *Seven against Thebes*, but Aeschylus has chosen not to use it in *Libation Bearers*. Instead, what we find in *Libation Bearers* is more closely related to the invocation at the tomb of Darius in *Persians*, as we might expect it to be. Indeed, I am always struck by the fact that Agamemnon does not appear at or on his tomb, and this when combined with the presence of Pylades is an interesting aspect of the scene. If the audience was conscious of the fact that three actors were available, as it had some reason to be from the preceding action of *Agamemnon*, then Aeschylus may be teasing the spectators cleverly,

48. I shall comment on the distinctions between speech, chant, and song later in this chapter and in chap. 2.

with the question of whether Pylades will speak or whether he is a silent extra precisely because Agamemnon is going to appear.

Aeschylus has also left a puzzle over the impact of the *skene* in this part of the play. The audience had seen it defined as the palace of Agamemnon throughout the first tragedy of the trilogy, and it is so defined again in the second part of this play. Commentators are divided in their opinions about whether it is an acknowledged element in the definition of the playing space in the first part of *Libation Bearers* or is initially ignored in order to be defined later. The reason that they are divided is the lack of unequivocal indications in the script. We might note two points here. First, if it were "ignored" in the opening of *Libation Bearers,* then Aeschylus would be making a remarkable coup de théâtre, which expects a great deal of his spectators. It becomes quite clear in *Libation Bearers* that the *choros* and Electra have come from the palace, which was the setting of the first play that the audience has just watched. If the *skene* is ignored, then their arrival in the playing space, which is observed over time by Orestes before he withdraws, must be from a side entrance to the *orchestra.* There would, second, be nothing exceptional about an arrival from an *eisodos* if the whole of the first part of the play is viewed in terms of the earlier tragedies and in terms of the mode of composition established in them. Yet it does suggest a remarkable demand on the spectators, both to acknowledge the continuity of the palace from the previous tragedy in the presentation and also to ignore it, or to displace it in their minds, only to replace it later in the play.[49] It is also curious that we cannot detect anything that appears to be conclusive in the script, granted the complexity of the associations involved, which stretch both backward (*Agamemnon*) and forward (the second part of *Libation Bearers*) and are vividly present in the motive that has brought both Electra and the *choros* into the playing space and to the tomb or grave mound of her father.

It is impossible to know how much rumor and theatrical gossip may have played a part in the life of ancient Athens, although once we have the comedies of Aristophanes, from 425 BCE forward, we can gain a sense of how

---

49. The conception that the tomb is in front of the palace, and yet at some distance from it, poses no greater demands on the audience than that of ignoring the *skene.* If the approach of Electra and the *choros* is from an *eisodos,* then Orestes and Pylades might withdraw down the opposing *eisodos.* If the *choros* and then Electra were to appear from the *skene,* all we need to acknowledge is that Orestes and Pylades would be required to "hide" to one side of the tomb mound. Correspondingly, this would allow for a relatively quick revelation of himself by Orestes to Electra, as she traces his footsteps by the tomb. But in neither case is our general sense of composition for the playing space fundamentally affected.

much comedy might choose to play with tragedy and its composers. We cannot tell whether the audience would have come to hear of prospective innovations in advance of the productions and what the level of expectation might be. An innovation like a solid-structure *skene* would surely have occasioned attention in advance, for the obvious reason that it was constructed in a relatively open, public place, and it may well have required public and official approval, since public finance was almost certainly involved. How much the audience may have known in advance about the introduction of a third actor is a question to which the answer is less obvious, because we know virtually nothing about the circumstances of that introduction. A third speaking performer may have been an isolated and brief addition to a tragedy in the first instance and proceeded through various phases to official approval and incorporation, so to speak. What is certain is that *Agamemnon,* the opening play of the *Oresteia,* contains no scenes for three actors/characters speaking together. Aeschylus only reveals his new resource when Cassandra finds her voice, after remaining silent since her arrival with Agamemnon and throughout the reception by Clytemnestra, and only finding it once the actors/characters of Agamemnon and Clytemnestra have entered the *skene.*[50] So she finds her voice only when alone with the *choros,* and it is hindsight rather than the mode of composition that would alert the spectators to the presence of a third actor, since the whole tragedy, including that scene, is composed in the established form that Aeschylus has employed before, with only one or two speaking (or singing) actors and a tragic *choros* involved at any time.

Agamemnon

The Herald in *Agamemnon* comes to the *choros* in a playing space that has been relatively lightly defined so far. The Watchman, whose language seems to imply that he is on the roof of the *skene,* lets the audience know that this (the *skene*) is the hall of the sons of Atreus that is, it seems, in Argos, and both he and the *choros* mention the wife of Agamemnon. But the Watchman gives a far more intense sense of the moment, and the *choros* a far more intense and extended sense of the past at Aulis, than either does of the playing space.

50. I am not here commenting on the division of roles between three actors but on the number of speaking actors/characters in the playing space. The division of roles between three actors for and after the *Oresteia* is generally accepted, with some debate about an additional actor in relation to certain tragedies. A scheme is offered in Pickard-Cambridge (1988, 135 ff.).

What we come to know, unequivocally, is that this is one place to which the climactic result of the Trojan expedition against Troy is tending, a result that is conveyed, first, in a report of the victory and, then, embodied in the arrival of the victorious commander. It is only with the arrival of the Herald that "the soil of the Argive land of our fathers" is immediately and directly greeted (503), with that definition repeated only a few lines later (506) and again immediately (508), and with the greeting extended to the sun that shines on it, to highest Zeus "of [this] land" and to lord Apollo, as savior and healer. The Herald then addresses the "collective gods," an echo of the phrase and term in *Suppliants,* and his own tutelary deity, Hermes.[51] The ground on which the *choros* stands is first in his thoughts, and to be standing on it himself, at last, is as important to the Herald as it will be to Orestes in *Libation Bearers.* It is only after that long greeting that the Herald acknowledges the *skene:* "Hail to the palace of kings, beloved halls, and seats of majesty, and gods who face the sun" (518–19). The Argives must welcome Agamemnon, since the king is coming to them and to "all of these here," a phrase (523) that undoubtedly includes the *choros* within the playing space that is the expectant land of Argos.

It is the *choros* that greets the Herald as an embodiment of that land and that community, and the exchanges that occur are between the *choros* and the Herald, who delivers directly to it his accounts of the siege and of the voyage home. The second of the exchanges (620–35) and the second account from the Herald (636–80) are preceded by a firm invitation from the *choros* to speak of Menelaus, the brother of Agamemnon, and by what appears to be a sharp dismissal of the trust that can be placed in Clytemnestra (615–19). This follows her sole intervention in a scene otherwise composed for the actor/character of the Herald and the *choros* in the playing space, one of the occasions that have prompted unresolved speculations about the timing of her appearances from, and entry and reentries into, the *skene* in the tragedy.[52] The fact is that either Aeschylus has not scripted her appearances from the *skene* with the same clarity and assurance as he has composed for the playing space or he wished to make the actor/character's abrupt use of the *skene* doors a significant quality of this tragedy, obvious and striking in performance but difficult to discern in the text itself. What we plainly have here is the use of a reappearance from and reentry into the *skene* as an interruption of a scene

51. Much of this address seems echoed in Orestes' opening words in *Libation Bearers,* which express related enthusiasm and relief in the return to the homeland after long years of enforced absence.

52. Once again, it is most unlikely that these issues will be resolved, since the indications are insufficient for any certainty.

otherwise proceeding in an established mode, and it differs markedly in that respect from the earlier scene in which Clytemnestra appears from the *skene* to announce the course of the beacon lights from Troy to Argos, which she organized (258–354). Whatever the timing of her appearance, she comes to the *choros* to address it and is engaged from the beginning in a full exchange with the *choros,* in a mode of composition that is unexceptional.

The arrival in the playing space of Agamemnon in a vehicle is also a familiar device of the established mode of composition, as we have seen, to the extent that it may even have been expected by the audience.[53] The *choros* greets his arrival with some twenty-five lines of chanted movement (783–809), addressing him directly, before Agamemnon speaks, and it is clear with hindsight (at 905–7) that he does not immediately descend from the vehicle. It is also clear, from the reference to her by Agamemnon at 950–51, that Cassandra is in the vehicle with him and that she does not descend from it until much later (1070–71). There is nothing to suggest that both actors/characters are not in the same vehicle, and there are no indications of any retinue for the returning and victorious commander.[54] It becomes clear that Clytemnestra is attended, at least in this scene, when she instructs women attendants to lay out the tapestries (908–9), and toward the end of the tragedy Aegisthus has a bodyguard with him that is directed to confront the *choros,* in a display of armed force. Undoubtedly, Aeschylus is keeping the playing space relatively unencumbered in this scene, and this may be as much for reasons of display, in the subsequent unfolding of the tapestries, as for dramatic reasons, since it is imperative that Agamemnon is not guarded if his murder is to be accomplished.

The vehicle brings the actors/characters of Agamemnon and Cassandra into the playing space, and Agamemnon is greeted by the *choros,* which is given ample time by Aeschylus to dispose itself in the playing space in order to accommodate the vehicle after singing and dancing.[55] But Agamemnon, for his part, does not respond immediately to the *choros,* choosing first to greet Argos and its gods in what he terms a "prelude" (*prooimion,* 829) which

30

---

53. I shall consider the nature of the vehicle itself in a subsequent section of this chapter.
54. Taplin (1977b) concludes that there must be attendants but only on the basis of his own rule that "all important figures" are attended in tragedy (304), while Ewans's vision is spare in comparison (1995,143, 143n34). Both reject the more expansive spectacle that speculation and later production may introduce.
55. The welcome of Agamemnon by the *choros* begins in the chant at 783. Taplin (1977b, 302–3) has some worries about exactly when the vehicle is seen, which is a strange concern to have about a gradual approach along an *eisodos* into the playing space.

he sees as his duty. He then addresses the political concerns of the *choros,* expressed to him on his arrival (783–809), and uses the *choros* as the authoritative body to which to make an announcement of public policy. He finally turns his attention to the palace, in which he will again greet and acknowledge the gods (851–54). The progress of the scene to this point accords with and confirms the definition of the playing space and the *choros* and, indeed, of the "moment" that has defined the tragedy. This moment has now been apparently resolved, as the gathering reports of victory and return are confirmed in the united presence of the king with the *choros* in the playing space. The subsequent action of the play and of the trilogy is dependent on an interruption of this sense of completion caused by the reappearance from the *skene* of the actor/character of Clytemnestra.

Once again, there is no indication at all of the timing of this (re)appearance, but there is equally no reason to suppose that Aeschylus introduced the actor/character to the playing space earlier in the scene.[56] It is noticeable that Clytemnestra, on her reappearance, first addresses the *choros* directly in its official capacity (855), coming to it in the playing space in the presence of her husband, and referring to him repeatedly and demonstratively as "this man" (860 and 867), in the context of her supposed past experience of deprivation and anxiety. It is only at the mention of Orestes, their son, whose absence has to be justified to Agamemnon, that she is drawn into using the second-person "your" (878) and "you" (882) of Agamemnon, which she repeats in the elaborate account of her sleeplessness at 890 and 893. She then reverts, from 895 to 896, to describing Agamemnon as "this man" (896) to the *choros,* addressing Agamemnon in terms of endearment in her climactic and crucial invitation to him to descend from the chariot and enter the palace on her terms (905–6). The tapestries are spread to cover the ground between *skene* and the playing space of the *orchestra* (908–9), and only then is there an exchange between Agamemnon and Clytemnestra. The symbolism and significance of this scene have attracted more critical attention than almost any other in Greek tragedy. I shall draw attention here only to the closing words (958–59) of Clytemnestra, in which she asserts the principle that the reunion of Agamemnon with his palace is the true climax of his return, so

---

56. Taplin believes (1977b, 306–7) that the final lines of Agamemnon's speech, when he refers to his intention to "come/go into the palace" at 851–52, were composed to provide the motivation for the actor/character of Clytemnestra to appear to forestall that movement. Ewans (1995) believes that Clytemnestra must appear just before this point, to prevent Agamemnon stepping from the vehicle by being in "his line of vision" before he speaks his final lines (144, 144n37).

asserting contentiously and radically the priority of the *skene* over the playing space of the *orchestra*.

The *skene* also awaits Cassandra, but the power of her vision is expressed fully in the playing space in dance and song, and it contrasts strikingly with Clytemnestra's refusal to remain in the playing space, to which she has briefly come to command or induce the actor/character of Cassandra to step from the vehicle and enter the hall (1035–68). It is the palace and what it contains, the *choros* of Furies that remains inside and never leaves it (1186–87), the phantoms of the dead that sit beside it (1214 ff.), that constitute Cassandra's spoken (and now comprehensible) visions following the danced and sung pain of inspiration (1072–1177). The *skene* broods over the vast scope of her exchange with the *choros* in the playing space, and her resolution to enter it only comes when she envisions the return of an avenger from exile (1280–81), and even then her revulsion from it is almost overpowering (1306–7).

The *skene* terminates the characters of Agamemnon and Cassandra, receiving them from the playing space and from their engagement with the presence of the *choros* in it. The murder of Agamemnon isolates and exposes this presence, as his cries issue to the *choros* from the hall, and the *choros* is left with its inability to affect an action from which it is sundered. In her final reappearance, which is as abrupt as all her other appearances from the *skene,* the actor/character of Clytemnestra not only stands above the corpses (1379) but, after her triumphant announcement and a curt reception (1399–1400) from the *choros,* she also makes an assertion of her separation from them, of her carelessness about whether they choose to praise or blame her action (1401–2). Yet this professed independence from the playing space is illusory, for what immediately follows is an extensive exchange between the actor/character of Clytemnestra and the *choros,* in which Clytemnestra comes to the *choros* in the playing space, speaking to it at first and then chanting, as it dances and sings its experience of horror, disgust, apprehension and lament. The mode of composition is established and familiar, and this applies also to the arrival of a second actor/character in Aegisthus, who is accompanied by a bodyguard and comes to the *choros* in the playing space, willing and prepared to threaten them with physical force (1617 ff., and 1649–53 in particular).

The close of *Agamemnon* almost certainly sees the actors/characters entering the *skene,* with the *choros* left deserted in the *orchestra,* and this separation is emphasized to a high degree in Clytemnestra's closing words, which almost suggest explicitly that the *skene* can dispense with the playing space and the *choros.* Theatrically, the new resource is in debate with an established mode of composition for actors/characters and tragic *choros* in the playing space of the *orchestra*. Its assertions are indeed impressive, but the established mode of composition remains prevalent throughout the tragedy, and the second of the new resources remains fundamentally subservient to it, in the composition of scenes throughout for one or two actors/characters and *choros* in a familiar form. The *skene* has a radical effect on the playing space, but that effect is strictly limited, and it does not displace the *orchestra*. Even the actor/character of Clytemnestra, despite forceful assertions of independence, is brought to the *choros* by the composer, and Aeschylus is more demonstrably interested in playing with the new resource in its effects on the playing space than in substantially changing the theatricality for which he composes. In this respect, the isolation and helplessness of the *choros* at the death of Agamemnon offer a disturbing but only momentary vision of its possible marginalization.[57] Yet if the mode of composition is largely unaltered, the dramatic and threatening potential of the presence of the *skene* is exploited intensely from the beginning through to the end of the tragedy.

Libation Bearers

In *Libation Bearers,* as we have already seen, the *skene* is not allowed to impose on the playing space for the first part of the play, but it is then introduced in what is almost an exaggerated fashion, with fixed attention on its material aspect, as a set of doors. It is as if Orestes returns twice in this play, once to the playing space that is Argos and second to the *skene* that is the palace; as if Aeschylus has chosen to mark what he can still achieve without the *skene,* and what he might do with it. The same may also be true of the other new resource, that of the third actor. In the second part of *Libation Bearers* we are overtly and demonstratively confronted by a multiplicity of actors, as if the composer wishes to bring that multiplicity to our attention in an unprecedented or at least remarkable way. To these ends Aeschylus carefully assigns to the *choros* what is to us, with our limited view of his earlier practice, the distinctive role of playing along with a pretense enacted at the *skene* doors. The *choros* has certainly come to the palace with Orestes, but he has instructed it to "keep silent when necessary and speak according to the circumstances," an instruction (581–82) that might leave us wondering what engagement there may be between actors/characters and the *choros* in the playing space from

57. Taplin (1977b, 331–32; 1978, 34–35) raises the question of whether some lines have been lost at the end of the text, with the result that the *choros* silently leaves the playing space.

now on, and how even the singing and dancing of a tragic *choros* may be accommodated once the plan is put into action. It is as if Aeschylus were preparing to subordinate the playing space and the *choros* completely or temporarily to the actors/characters at the *skene* doors, even to replace one playing space with another.

34

The sequence that follows is indeed extraordinary, but it does not proceed in a uniform manner. Few sequences in Greek tragedy are more attractive to amateur or professional speculation because this sequence involves something that we believe we can all "have a go at blocking," namely, actors/characters appearing and disappearing at and through doors. The sequence begins with Orestes knocking on a door and calling for the slave to answer him. He has said before that he will arrive at the hall carrying his own baggage (560), something to which he draws attention when speaking later to Clytemnestra (675), since it explains why he has no slave(s) with him, but just a companion (the plural "strangers" at 668 indicates firmly the presence of Pylades).[58] The slave answers Orestes tersely (657), and we cannot tell whether he appeared outside or not. Orestes wants to see an authoritative figure in the household, and Clytemnestra finally appears to him, with the exchange passing between them almost certainly at the threshold and not including or even acknowledging the presence of the *choros*. They all enter, after Clytemnestra has instructed her attendant to take Orestes and Pylades to the "men's apartments" in the palace, which importantly suggests a picture to us of internal space. This is the first scene in the surviving tragedies of Aeschylus that is played by the *skene* doors, between actors/characters, and with no reference to the *choros*.

It is, however, immediately followed by a short chant from the *choros*, which refers to their anticipation of becoming involved in the plot ("When shall we show the strength of our voice for Orestes?" 720–21) and to the tomb of Agamemnon, which strongly defined the playing space in the first part of the tragedy. The playing space reasserts its rights, and Aeschylus delivers the actor/character of the old nurse Cilissa to the *choros*, coming to them after she has appeared from the *skene* doors, a sign that the plan of action is in motion. She is addressed by the *choros* and answers it, in a shared status of slavery that ultimately produces complicity. The pragmatic aim is, of course, to deprive Aegisthus of the bodyguard by which he was accompanied at the close of *Agamemnon*. But the integrity of the playing space is also

58. Taplin (1977b, 341–42) has a good commentary on the use of the plural at 713, which in the text as transmitted to us would imply attendants for Orestes and Pylades. This cannot be right, and the text must have been altered.

restored by this exchange and subsequently confirmed by the danced song of the *choros* appealing to the gods for help and by the arrival of Aegisthus, after whom Cilissa had been sent. Aegisthus comes to the *choros* in the playing space and speaks to it, asking for information, but the *choros* sends him into the *skene,* following his entry into it with another chant (855–68), on this oc-

casion anticipating what will happen in the palace, and so preparing us for another scene in which the *skene* may be disjoined from the playing space of the *orchestra.* When the death cry is heard from the palace, the *choros* decides to "stand away" to avoid implication in guilt for the murder (871–72), which gives us a strong sense of Aeschylus preparing for enactment at the *skene* doors and of a temporary suspension of the playing space of the *orchestra.*

The extended sequence between the two chants has been a deft acknowledgment of the continuing involvement of the *choros* at a moment when it might have been marginalized. The spoken exchange (875–934) that follows this sequence is unprecedented, and reconstructions are numerous. For the first time we have three actors/characters speaking in close succession, and the additional problem is that we seem to have four characters: the Slave, Clytemnestra, Orestes, and Pylades. Their voices are all heard within fifteen lines (886–900) of what by any standards is a quick exchange, and all these characters must surely be seen in this same, short section. One of the standard solutions is to suppose that Aeschylus employed a fourth actor for Pylades, who is otherwise an extra, since he only speaks these climactic three lines (900–902), totally unexpectedly.

Technically, the exchanges are simple: Slave and Clytemnestra, Clytemnestra and Orestes, interrupted in a remarkable moment by an interjection from Pylades. The purpose of the scene must be, for the composer, to build up to the confrontation between Orestes and Clytemnestra, who is finally taken inside the palace to be killed. The precise movements cannot be determined from the text, but the Slave seems to go inside the *skene* in response to Clytemnestra's order for an ax to be brought to her (889) because there is no further sign of his presence. The initial exchange between Orestes and Clytemnestra (892–93) is intriguing. Clytemnestra has been told, enigmatically but in a manner that she can interpret, of the death of Aegisthus and, implicitly, the threat to her (885–88); her reaction is to ask for the ax. Orestes then appears:

ORESTES. It's you I'm looking for; this man has had enough.
CLYTEMNESTRA. Ah, my dear, strong Aegisthus! Are you dead?

It may be that the appearance of Orestes, with a gesture, is enough to confirm to Clytemnestra the way the struggle has gone. But "this man" is a strange reference, and one might wonder whether Orestes was carrying some token of Aegisthus with him that we cannot detect (a bloodstained outer garment?). Alternatively, and quite acceptably, we might take it that all know that the fate of Aegisthus is the subject of the minute and that the brief allusion is adequate. There is no indication that the *choros* is involved, and its presence is certainly not acknowledged, but the *choros* closes the scene with comments from the playing space of the *orchestra* (930–31), where it has remained at some distance from the doors of the *skene* (871–72).[59]

36

The song and dance of the *choros* that follows is a celebration, and once again corpses are displayed by an actor/character to a *choros,* as they had been in *Agamemnon.* Also displayed is the netlike device by which Agamemnon was ensnared; Orestes orders it to be spread out, with those doing so standing in a circle (980 ff.), and his speech of justification expands on this theme.[60] So Orestes comes to the *choros* in the playing space, and it is the *choros* that responds to him in the exchange that follows and that ends the play.[61] The onset of terror and of derangement is followed by visions that "spin you round" (1051–52), in the words of the *choros,* and Orestes acknowledges that he has already become a wanderer, his only refuge at the shrine of Apollo in Delphi (1034 ff.), before running off (1061–62).

Eumenides

In the conclusion to the action of *Libation Bearers* Orestes is "driven" (1062) from Argos by the Furies, who are his "mother's enraged hounds" (1054), and the growing numbers of them he sees and the intensity of the vision (*Libation Bearers* 1057) almost suggest an invisible *choros* gradually occupying the

59. I have limited interest in the structure of the *skene* in relation to the inquiry I am pursuing here. But the variety of proposals from commentators includes the belief or the strong assertion that this sequence demonstrates the existence of more than one door in the *skene.* Once again, nothing can really resolve the debate, although it is usually observed that later tragedy seems normally to rely on only one door, while some of the surviving comedies of Aristophanes (from 425 BCE) may be construed as requiring more than one. The sequence as a whole is particularly suitable to the terms of reference established by Taplin for his study, and his detailed account (1977b, 340 ff.) must be a sound starting point.

60. For comments on these two scenes of the display of corpses, see the discussion of *Eumenides* below, and the notes and references there.

61. Wiles (1997) comments that "Orestes must move away from the *skene* into the public space of the *orchestra* when he orders the chorus to stand round him in a circle and display the net" (82–83). In contrast, Ewans (1995) believes that attendants are required (188), following Taplin's brief allusion to the moment (1977b, 357).

playing space, violently displacing the support he has received from the women slaves of the actual *choros*. That virtual presence is made actual in the final scene of the first part of *Eumenides,* when an awakened and frustrated *choros* sings and dances its anger at the escape of its quarry and abuses and accuses Apollo in his own temple precinct (143–77) at Delphi. Once Apollo has come to the *choros* to contest and dispute with it, then the conflict between the definition of the playing space offered by the *skene* (Apollo's temple) and its definition by the *choros* as a place of pursuit can only be resolved by the fact that Orestes has already escaped to Athens. When the Furies arrive in the playing space that is Athens, in the second part of *Eumenides,* they do so in weary pursuit, talking to themselves as they search, following the silent trail, which may mean footprints in the dust as much as the dripping blood they mention (244–53).[62] They do not see Orestes immediately but find him without difficulty. The playing space is defined by their pursuit, and whether at Delphi or at Athens the playing space is the place of their pursuit, as it began to be at the close of *Libation Bearers.*

The principal curiosity of the opening of *Eumenides* is that it depends on the notion that this hyperactive if potentially weary *choros* of righteously vindictive hounds is asleep. Yet the scene with Clytemnestra's ghost is composed very much in the established mode of address by an actor/character to a *choros*. The text unusually contains a notation of sound ("muttering") as the response of the *choros* in an exchange with the actor/character, and whether or not this notation is as original as the script itself, such a response is implied by Clytemnestra's reaction (117–39).[63] Clytemnestra's ghost describes itself as wandering (98), and if this statement is indicative it would conflict with a sudden appearance to a sleeping *choros* from the doors of the *skene*. What is striking is that the ghost addresses the Furies directly from the beginning and even shows its wounds to them (103–4), insisting that the *choros* can see them even though it is sleeping. At the close of the scene, the Furies are visible, dancing and singing in the open ground of the *orchestra* (143–77), where they are confronted by Apollo. All that intervene are three lines, in which individual Furies plainly wake each other up (140–42).

Were we faced by this section of the script on its own or combined with what follows it, we should experience no hesitation in picturing Clytemnes-

---

62. There is, of course, no need to suppose that either the footprints or the blood are literally manifested. Taplin (1978, 36–37) is evocatively insistent on such features as the "relentless coursing" and the "scattered disorder" of the Furies as they arrive in the playing space in pursuit.

63. On these noises, and the "directions" for them, see Taplin (1977a, 122–23).

tra's ghost coming to a sleeping *choros* in the *orchestra,* which then awakes to dance its frustration. It would, in fact, be senseless to construe it in any other way. There is no reason why the exchange between Apollo and Orestes might not take its place as part of this kind of composition, and the demonstrative references by Apollo (67–68) that apparently refer to Furies lying around them both would be highly appropriate to it. In such circumstances, Apollo and Orestes might appear from the *skene* as the temple, with Apollo reassuring Orestes that, now his pursuers were visibly asleep (in the forecourt of the temple), he could leave his place of sanctuary and escape to Athens.

But that easy interpretation is not possible, and it is the opening monologue of the Priestess that firmly sets up different expectations. This figure defines the playing space in great detail, and her reappearance from the *skene* (34) informs us, with hindsight, that the *skene* in this final play is "the house of Apollo," the temple at Delphi that is the seat of the oracle.[64] Her function is to enter the temple in order to sit on the throne of prophecy (27–33), and she reappears from it apparently crawling (36) in horror and shock at what she has just seen inside the *skene.* What she describes is vividly clear: inside the temple, on the *omphalos* or navel stone, is a man with a bloody sword and the olive branch of a suppliant, and near him an amazing group of female beings sleeping and snoring, which she cannot identify but she can describe. This contribution is unequivocal: Orestes and the Furies are inside the temple of Apollo, which is the *skene* that she has entered and from which she has just reappeared.

Inevitably, this confusing and seemingly contradictory set of indications has prompted a variety of practical speculations, which in themselves do little to suggest why Aeschylus should have chosen to compose in this way.[65] The constant factor through the opening sequence is that the *choros* is asleep, and it has to be asleep for Orestes to leave Delphi for Athens, unless the first part of this final play were to have him both reach and then leave Delphi before the *choros* can follow him, something that Aeschylus has not set up at the close of *Libation Bearers.* Yet if Aeschylus has chosen to make the *choros* asleep and also not visible, then it would seem that the most obvious rationale for ·

64. Arnott (1989, 17–18) has an excellent short discussion of the definition of locale and the involvement of the audience in this prologue. As Hammond says (1972, 439n95), "the illusion is at once created that we are there waiting our turn" to consult at the oracle.

65. Hammond (1988, 24–25) solves the problem by having the Furies rush out of the *skene* into the playing space after the Priestess has finished speaking and making Apollo put them to sleep before he speaks to Orestes. This would have the Furies sleeping and waking twice, without any indications that they do so.

the script as it stands must place its emphasis on a visual effect, in the suspense leading to the impact of their ultimate appearance (or arrival) in the playing space.

Those who incline to this view will tend to delay the appearance of the Furies as long as possible, bringing them into sight, from the *skene,* only at the start of their danced song in the *orchestra,* even allowing their awakening to be a scripted event hidden from view in the *skene.*[66] More radical interpretations may play with the idea of a playing space that represents both interior space and exterior space, in order to have a *choros* sleeping in the *orchestra* from the beginning.[67] The compromise is to have the Furies partly visible as soon as possible, which will be after the monologue of the Priestess. The means to do this is the machinery known as the *ekkuklema,* which would seem to have been available to Sophocles, Euripides, and Aristophanes, even in the tragedy that many suspect to be the earliest surviving after the *Oresteia,* namely, Sophocles' *Ajax.*[68]

I find the situation very strange. As I have indicated, so much of the opening of *Eumenides* is conceived and composed in a thoroughly familiar manner for actors/characters and a *choros,* and I am puzzled by the fact that Aeschylus has apparently had the remarkable conception of a sleeping *choros* that awakens but has then apparently made it invisible. There are other puzzling matters. Commentators have been divided in their opinions about whether the *ekkuklema* was used for the introduction of the corpses in the two scenes in *Agamemnon* and *Libation Bearers.*[69] The only apparently explicit indi-

66. Both Taplin (1977b, 369 ff.; 1978, 106–7) and Ewans (1995, 196 ff.) subscribe to this view of the script, with Taplin providing a vivid description of the Furies emerging "one by one or in small disordered groups" from the *skene* (1978, 126–27).

67. Rehm (1988, 290 ff.) argues for this interpretation, combining both internal and external space, with the Furies and Orestes visible (in "internal" space) in the center of the *orchestra* and the Priestess in "external" space behind them and toward the *skene;* and he repeats the scheme in later studies (1992, 100 ff.; 2002, 89 ff.). This allows the ghost of Clytemnestra to come to the Furies in the playing space. Rosenmeyer (1982, 67 ff.) seems to dismiss the notion of interior space while envisaging a similar scenario.

68. In this vision, some of the sleeping Furies would be revealed with Orestes and Apollo, although one commentator has tried to argue for the whole *choros:* so Sommerstein (1989, 93) states the former view, which has been widely held, while Brown (1982, 28) suggests the latter amplification. If only a small number is shown, then these would finally awaken and call out the other members of the *choros.*

69. Those who deny the use of the *ekkuklema* for *Eumenides* may accept its use in *Agamemnon* and *Libation Bearers,* e.g., Ewans (1995, 153, 187, 196n6). Taplin (1977b) offers a summary survey of the *ekkuklema* (442–43), and gives a commentary on *Agamemnon* (325–27), *Libation Bearers* (357–59), and *Eumenides* (369–74), but remains skeptical of the use of the *ekkuklema* even for the first two tragedies.

cation is the one line in *Agamemnon,* when Clytemnestra says, "I stand where I struck" (1379), but even this statement would be valid without making a reference to the *ekkuklema* provided it was taken to refer to her proximity to the dead bodies anywhere in the playing space.[70] The alternative to the use of the *ekkuklema* in these two scenes would be for the bodies to be carried into the playing space, and there is a precedent for that in *Seven against Thebes.* It is noticeable that in both instances, in *Agamemnon* and *Libation Bearers,* the addresses from Clytemnestra and Orestes respectively are made to the *choros* in the playing space, and they are addresses made in public. The scenes are composed as public presentations of the act, and so of the dead bodies, and in this respect they would contrast with the distinctive revelation of an interior scene in *Eumenides,* which is made to the audience rather than to a *choros,* since the *choros* is actually included in the revelation.[71]

I should like to advance a suitably strange hypothesis to account for these phenomena, if only to highlight the degree of continuity that is evident in the modes of composition established and amplified by Aeschylus. My suggestion is that the *ekkuklema* was added to the *skene* as a resource during the period of the composition of the *Oresteia* and that Aeschylus revised his composition of *Eumenides* to incorporate it. The first version of *Eumenides* was composed for a *choros* in the playing space that was asleep or had fallen asleep after arriving at Delphi. In his revision, Aeschylus removed the opening of the play and added the monologue of the Priestess describing an interior scene, which he then revealed in part on the *ekkuklema,* with several sleeping Furies surrounding Orestes at the navel stone. These Furies then remained, once Orestes had been taken from his suppliant position by Apollo, to be addressed by Clytemnestra, and finally the full *choros* appeared from the *skene* and came into the *orchestra* to dance. Aeschylus then decided to present the two earlier scenes, in *Agamemnon* and in *Libation Bearers,* using the same re-

70. Ewans (1995, 154) alludes in passing to the force of this line, without examining this alternative. Taplin (1977b) is alert to the fact that this line is our only signal, and he regards it as "fully integrated" (326), which means that he believes it was not added by a later actor or copyist (who wished to imply the use of the *ekkuklema* by so doing). Wiles (1997) also attaches importance to the line and subscribes to the use of the *ekkuklema* for these scenes and in *Eumenides* (163).

71. The question of agency is surely important: the displays are made intentionally by Clytemnestra and Orestes in addresses to the *choros* and, by implication, to the public of Argos. Wiles's conception of the *ekkuklema* as "in the first instance a device" (1997, 163) is not quite adequate here. Nothing in the scene in *Agamemnon* apart from line 1379 indicates an interior conception, and Orestes invokes the sun in *Libation Bearers* (985–86), as Taplin correctly observes (1977b, 326). The apparatus of murder in both these scenes may be displayed as readily as revealed, even if labor rather than a machine would be involved.

source, but did not (need to) change the script, although he perhaps added line 1379 in *Agamemnon*.[72]

This implementation of a new resource led to a slight discrepancy. In the first two tragedies, what had been a public presentation of the corpses was no longer clearly defined for the audience. There was no explicit suggestion of an interior scene, and the precise situation implied by the use of the *ekkuklema* may have puzzled the audience but without actually disrupting the impact of the address by the actor/character to the *choros*. In *Eumenides* an unequivocally interior grouping was described by the Priestess and then presented on the *ekkuklema,* one from which Apollo and Orestes walked away and which was subsequently addressed from the playing space by the ghost of Clytemnestra. In the first two tragedies, scenes that had been composed in the established mode of an actor/character coming to the *choros* in the playing space were given a slightly changed focus in repeated, referential gestures to the *ekkuklema* in front of the *skene* doors on which the corpses rested. But it was the possibilities for the revelation of an interior scene as elaborated in *Eumenides* that were exploited by the later tragic composers.

As a hypothesis, this proposal might be fairly described as ideal, because it reconciles the diversity of feeling and interpretation expressed by commentators, although doubtless not to their individual satisfaction. It also provokes attention to the question of why the *skene* and the *ekkuklema* might have been conceived, as opposed to when they were introduced, which might not have been at the same time. I find it hard to believe that the *ekkuklema* was not the result of some particular initiative, which may well have been confused in its intentions. The suggestion of the introduction of a *skene,* as the material representation of an aspect of the setting, might more readily be understood as the result of a perception shared between composers. In other words, I can see the creation of a solid *skene,* with doors, as the result of agreement, while I feel that the *ekkuklema* is more likely to be the result of an insistent individual composer who carries others with him. There is no better candidate for that role at that time than Aeschylus. That the idea occurred to him during the composition of the *Oresteia* is no more ridiculous than supposing theater history to be the result of neatness and planning. But the hypothesis might still stand if the *ekkuklema* was an initiative that came from another source, and Aeschylus had to adapt quickly to it. Indeed, it might

---

72. Something more than that may have been involved in altering the script; but the alteration would come to rest substantially in the one line.

even be more attractive to us, since reactions are often easier to envisage than changes of mind.

The second half of *Eumenides* begins with the arrival of Orestes at Athens, and the undoubted presence of an image of the goddess Athena recalls from the earlier tragedies the creation of a distinctive area of the playing space for a suppliant. Since the suppliant is in this case an individual, we do not find those scripted invitations to leave the place of supplication for the open ground of the *orchestra* that Aeschylus provided for the *choros* in *Seven against Thebes* and *Suppliants,* which enabled the *choros* to dance and sing there. Nor can we tell when the suppliant actor/character of Orestes does move away from the image, except to say that he is released from the need to embrace the image by the judgment of the court of Athenian citizens constituted by the goddess Athena. The *choros* of Furies sings and dances twice (321–96, and 490–565) alone with Orestes in the playing space, and for these songs the *choros* must be in the open ground of the *orchestra.* Toward the close of its second danced song, the *choros* pictures the unjust man "in the middle of a whirlpool with which he cannot wrestle" (558–59), and in the chant that leads into its first danced song the *choros* invites itself to "join in a *choros*" (307), calling its song in anticipation a "binding hymn" (306), and then later "a hymn from the Furies that binds the mind" (331–32).

These last two aspects of the script in particular have encouraged commentators to see the first dance as circular, since "join" implies contact or grasp, and this might then be a circular dance round the victim with hands joined, which could be seen readily enough to "bind" him. It is an attractive and by no means implausible vision, but that circle is a supposition, and we cannot be sure where in the playing space the image of Athena was placed.[73]

73. Rehm (1992, 102, 157n12) and Ewans (1995, 210) believe that the image of Athena must be at the center of the *orchestra* to avoid pulling the focus of the second half of the tragedy up toward the *skene.* I suspect that much of this apprehension stems from the belief in a circular, "binding" dance by the *choros* around the actor/character of Orestes. The image and the song were certainly linked together by Taplin: the implication that the *choros* dances round Orestes "is evidence, though of necessity inconclusive, that the statue was somewhere in the *orchestra*" (1977b, 386n1); necessity features again, although to a different purpose, in Taplin's statement that the "near necessity" that the binding spell "should be performed *round* Orestes is strong evidence that the statue was in the *orchestra* itself" (1978, 188n6). Wiles believes that Taplin "argues sensibly" (1997, 83n90) here; but Sommerstein rightly cautions that "nothing in the Binding Song in fact indicates explicitly that Orestes is physically surrounded" and that, were the image near the *skene,* it might "easily fade into the background when no longer relevant to the action" (1989, 123). Podlecki is wary of any conclusion about the location of the image (1989, 13–14), while Heinrichs in his discussion does not mention the location of the image in what he accepts as "a magi-

42

The script informs us that Orestes arrives in the playing space and approaches the temple (literally, "house") and image of Athena, intending to keep his place there and wait for justice (242–43), and the *choros* describes him as "wrapped around the image of the immortal goddess" (259). When the actor/character of Athena arrives in the playing space in answer to his call, she addresses the *choros* and Orestes but engages first with the *choros* (415–35), and only then with Orestes, whom Athena observes "sitting guarding this image near my hearth" (439–40). Her final speech in this scene is initially addressed to Orestes, and refers to the *choros,* but she concludes by addressing the *choros* directly (485–86). Both of these sequences might suggest a separation of Orestes from the *choros,* and the "binding" may be that of the mind. The situation is further complicated by the fact that the suggestion of a temple of Athena and an associated image could hardly fail to evoke the acro*polis* of Athens. But there were no temples on the Areopagus, the rock facing the acro*polis* of Athens, which is the eminently recognizable location for the court that Athena later institutes and describes (681 ff.).[74]

At the close of *Eumenides,* and of the trilogy, the *choros* is conducted from the playing space in a spectacular procession, which has been preceded by an intense and extended exchange between the *choros* and the single actor/character of Athena.[75] In the first part of this exchange Athena speaks and the *choros* sings and dances (778–891), and this culminates in a line-by-line spoken exchange between the actor/character and the *choros,* ending in speech from Athena. Once the *choros* has accepted residence in Athens, it continues to dance and sing in alternation with chanting from the actor/character of Athena (916–1020), and this sequence culminates in final words from Athena (1021–31) as the procession from the playing space begins. The trial scene before that involves the three speaking actors/characters of Orestes,

---

cal circle" for the dance but implies that it should be in the place of the *orchestral* altar (1995, 60–63, 95–96n38). I agree with Sommerstein in doubting whether the position of the image (and of the actor/character of Orestes) is as influential on the use of the playing space as is often assumed, if other aspects of composition are taken into account. Nor do I believe, with Wiles (1997), that the presence of an iconic object (the image) is necessary to indicate Athens to the Athenians, to "denote the public space of Athens" (83).

74. Wiles's (1997) solution to the problem of definition of the playing space in *Eumenides* is to rely on the idea of "schematic space," and his proposal fuses all the potential locations, with some additions to standard perceptions: "Four different Athenian spaces merge into one: the Acro*polis,* the archaic *agora,* the new Agora and the Areopagos" (83–84). Sommerstein (1989) believes of the definition of the location "that one cannot say anything more precise than 'Athens'" (123).

75. For speculations on the theatrical presentation of the procession, see Taplin (1977b, 410 ff.) and Ewans (1995, 221–22), who is even more sparing than Taplin.

Athena, and Apollo with a speaking *choros* and silent jurors in the playing space (566–777), and by its close both Apollo and Orestes have left.[76]

44

The composition for the three actors is interesting. Athena first introduces the court (566–73); the *choros* then addresses Apollo (574–75); Apollo explains his presence and then addresses Athena (576–81); Athena starts the trial but invites the *choros* to speak (582–84); the *choros* then interrogates Orestes, largely in a line-by-line exchange (585–608); Orestes concludes by addressing Apollo, inviting his evidence (609–13). Apollo then first addresses the jurors but is engaged in an interrogative exchange with the *choros* (614–73); there is a brief exchange between Athena and Apollo, before Athena addresses the *choros* (674–78); the *choros* responds by addressing the jurors, and Athena then speaks at length to the jurors as representatives of the Athenians (679–710). The *choros* and Apollo then briefly address the jurors, before exchanging sharp comments with each other (711–33); Athena announces the casting of her vote and instructs the jurors to count the votes (734–43); Orestes appeals to Apollo but is not answered by him (744); the *choros* appeals to their mother, Night (745); Orestes views the alternatives facing him, as does the *choros* (746–47); Apollo addresses the jurors (748–51), and Athena announces the result (752–53). It is greeted with relief by Orestes, who first addresses Athena, then promises Argive loyalty to Athena and the Athenians and leaves with a farewell to Athena and the Athenians (754–77).

This long and intricate sequence has a number of interesting characteristics, of which one of the most striking is the partial displacement of the *choros* by the jurors as addressees of the words of the actors/characters.[77] In terms of composition for the playing space, the *choros* has a rival here, which is a strange effect, unprecedented in our limited vision from the surviving plays and presumably relatively unusual.[78] We might best allow for this by saying that it is

76. Taplin worries at some length over the timing of the departure of the actor/character of Apollo at 403–4 and offers a critical interpretation of it (1978, 38–39). Ewans (1995) comments that Orestes "must now be written out of the drama, to clear the *orchestra* for the final confrontation" (215) between the *choros* and Athena, which demands the full ground of the playing space.

77. Unfortunately, Taplin chooses to comment only on the relative silence of Orestes (1978, 107–8).

78. The brief address to his bodyguard by Aegisthus is plainly not of the same order as this sequence, and the silence of the jurors throughout the scene distinguishes them markedly from such a phenomenon as an additional *choros*. Taplin (1977b) believes that the jurors "were unlikely to have numbered less than ten or more than fifteen" and that "they are to become . . . a supplementary chorus" (393); but that is in relation to his proposal that the jurors sang the escorting hymn for the Furies at the very end of the tragedy (1977b, 411; 1978, 39).

not just the result of the trial of Orestes that supplants the *choros,* potentially canceling its definition and so demanding a change of its status. The presence of the jurors in the playing space, and the address to them by actors/characters, is already a subversion of the status of the *choros,* rather more than an intimation that the *choros* can no longer define—and is already no longer defining—the playing space. There is, as an accompanying feature, very little direct exchange between the actors/characters themselves, despite the many moments in the scene when it might take place. The mode of composition has been altered, but it has not been changed to accomplish a separation of the "dialogue" of actors/characters from the established mode of address to the *choros.* Indeed, that mode is still prominent in the scene, even if Aeschylus has carefully ensured that it is not absolute. The three actors remain a function of composition with the *choros,* or with its rival, in the playing space.[79]

REALIZING THE TRAGIC PLAYING SPACE AFTER AESCHYLUS

The *skene* is a material object, which at the least is a frame for a doorway and a threshold, and a threshold connotes a passage from exterior to interior "space." Once the *skene* has been introduced, it may begin to provide a strong component of the definition of the playing space, as it does noticeably in the *Oresteia.* Characters who appear and reappear from it, who enter it, may also gain strong components of definition from so doing. The *skene* can be, in some instances, the objective of the purpose of an actor/character, and in concealing or containing purposes and actions it may offer a material concomitant to the sequence of the dramatic action. Actors/characters who arrive from the *eisodoi,* or leave down them, may be just as purposeful, but the "exterior" space from which they come or to which they go is less tangible to our practical vision of the theatrical resources.

Above all, a material construction is a potential reference point in a way in which a space is not, and references in the scripts to the *skene* may seem like a certainty that we badly need. It is easy to forget that the way the playing space was defined and exploited until the *Oresteia* was completely acceptable to one if not two generations of composers and spectators. In fact, in many modern commentaries on the tragedies of Sophocles and Euripides, the definition and varied use of the *skene* are far more likely to occasion observations

79. Most critical attention falls on the issue of the relationship of this trial scene to Athenian legal practice: for example, Podlecki (1989, 203–10) offers a critique of Taplin's concerns, and commentaries pursue many aspects of the scene but not that of its composition for three actors and a *choros.*

and discussion than any wider considerations of the playing space as a whole.[80]
So, without necessarily arguing the case, commentators may present us with
two totally different modes of tragic composition and performance: that before the *Oresteia* and that after it.

46   These assumptions need to be questioned, or they will govern our understanding of the use of the playing space after Aeschylus. In order to do so,
we need to acknowledge the variety of indications of activity in the open
ground of the playing space that we find in the surviving scripts by Sophocles and Euripides, evidence that may be related to the presence of a substantial material object apart from the *skene*. The indications that confront
us come in a variety of forms, and the most valuable of them link together a
number of the surviving tragedies, some of which can be dated securely. In
this respect, the most important material object proves to be a tomb or an
altar, which manifestly provides a focus for action in a number of tragedies.
A major study by Rehm has examined the instances of such an object, notably in the tragedies of Euripides, and my own work on Euripides' *Helen* is
of a related kind.[81] The practicalities of performance are of the greatest importance here, insofar as the recognition that performance is practical must
be applied to the later reading of any script that was both composed and produced for given or known conditions. In the discussion that follows, I shall
be referring in my notes to a number of modern commentaries on aspects of
the respective scenes, even if their central concern is not that of the playing
space for tragedy.[82]

ALTARS AND TOMBS IN THE PLAYING
SPACE AFTER AESCHYLUS

The significance of tombs or altars to tragedy is already clear from the early
tragedies and the *Oresteia,* and it remains important, notably under the cultural aspect of Greek society generally termed "supplication," or *hikesía.* This
word includes what we might term "seeking asylum," which is apparent in

---

80. This tendency is pronounced, for example, in both Arnott (esp. 1962) and Hourmouziades (1965).
81. Rehm (1988) and Ley (1991a).
82. In relation to practicable altars as properties I am, like Rehm in his leading study of
the subject, less interested in the dubious evidence for the existence of a *thymele,* or religious altar to Dionysus, in the theater at Athens: see Rehm (1988), Poe (1989), and Ashby
(1991, 1999). Wiles (1997) believes the *thymele* might be a flat stone rather than a raised
altar (71–72).

Aeschylus's *Suppliants,* but it also includes entreaty to an individual for help or support, and it has been studied helpfully by Gould.[83] Part of the mechanism of supplication is the activity of either binding oneself to a place of sanctuary, for direct protection or support from a deity or deities, or "binding" oneself to an individual, in touching knees or chin in an appeal that is understood to take place under the watchful eye of Zeus. The tragedies include many instances of the appeal to an individual, which are marked by references to the accompanying or appropriate actions in the scripts. But they also contain a large number of instances of seeking refuge, for protection or in order to make an appeal, at an altar or a tomb.

47

Some of these instances are of refuge sought by an individual, but others are of refuge sought by a group. In Aeschylus's *Suppliants* this group is the *choros,* and this is also the case in Euripides' *Suppliants,* which does not, however, dramatize the same myth. Euripides' tragedy is deservedly the subject of particular attention from Rehm, whose interpretation seems to me undeniably sound. Rehm is right to insist on practicality, because nothing can be presented in any theater that is not practical when performers, objects, action, and space are involved. But there is one cultural issue that is of considerable importance, and that may not be obvious to all readers, which is that the altars associated with Greek temples were placed outside, most regularly facing the entrance to the temple, and at some distance from it.[84] Our sense of the altar in Christian cultures as belonging to the interior of the church building is inappropriate. Sacrifices and offerings would be made at a Greek altar, and fire might be involved, and in some cults the existence of an altar and a sacred precinct or space might be primary, the construction of a temple for a cult image of the deity being secondary. So the sacred space that contains the altar and any temple is as much an entity in Greek culture as the temple itself, although it would appear that direct contact with an image or with an altar offers the greatest security.

The disposition of performers in the playing space in Euripides' *Suppliants* is revealed by a number of specific indications from the opening of the tragedy, and it becomes clear that what is presented is a temple, represented

---

83. Gould (1973), now republished with a supplement in Gould (2001, 22–77). Kaimio, in one of her categories of close physical contact in tragedy, adopts Gould's distinction between physical and verbal supplication (1988, 49–61). Unfortunately, Kaimio's focus on physicality throughout her interesting study is very narrowly defined and rarely extends to placing the actions she deduces from indications in the scripts into the broad ground of the playing space.

84. Yavis (1949, 56); cited in Ley (1991a, 26n4) and Wiles (1997, 54n119).

by the *skene,* and an altar, and that groups are associated with both, and that one of these groups forms the *choros* of the play. These figures are the "suppliants" of the title, who are defined as the mothers of the seven war leaders who have campaigned against Thebes and died in the battle for the city that was the subject of Aeschylus's *Seven against Thebes.* The women are not named, and the putative number does not match fifteen, which we might expect as the standard number for a tragic *choros;* commentators vary in their reactions to this, some ascribing the attendants who are mentioned in the script to the full complement of the *choros.*[85] These women have symbolically bound the actor/character of Aethra, the mother of Theseus, to the altar, in an attempt to gain her support in their plea to Theseus and Athens to regain the bodies of their sons for burial. The setting is the temple of Demeter at Eleusis, in the territory of Athens. After the opening song from the *choros,* which is addressed in supplication to Aethra, and the arrival of Theseus, Aethra describes the *choros* explicitly as guarding her "in a circle" (103).

The second group is composed of the sons of the dead warriors, and later in the tragedy (794–95) five or six bodies of the warriors are brought into the playing space. After the bodies have been taken away to be cremated, these sons—the grandsons of the women of the *choros*—return with their ashes, forming an additional *choros* that sings and dances in the playing space (1114–64); there are no clear indications there of their number. At the opening of the play the boys are gathered "around" the actor/character of Adrastus (106), whom Theseus on his arrival in the playing space observes at the "doorway" (104), which must be that of the temple. Aethra describes Adrastus as lying down (22), and Theseus describes him as having his head covered by his cloak, in an attitude of grief (110–11). Theseus addresses his own mother first, surrounded as she is by the *choros,* and then Adrastus (fig. 5).

The *orchestra* is, of course, the place for the *choros,* in which it sings and dances. The actor/character of Aethra is with the *choros,* and that its members should be in a circle in order to contain her symbolically at the altar is completely comprehensible. Theseus on his arrival in the playing space first addresses his mother in the middle of this unknown company of women, and these are aspects of composition that are long-established and unexceptional. The presence of an additional, substantial number of other performers with the actor/character of Adrastus at the doors of the *skene* is interesting, since their identity is not revealed by Aethra and only becomes apparent when she answers Theseus after the first danced song from the

85. Collard (1975, 1:18) dismisses all numerical calculations of mothers and attendants in favor of a standard tragic *choros* of fifteen members.

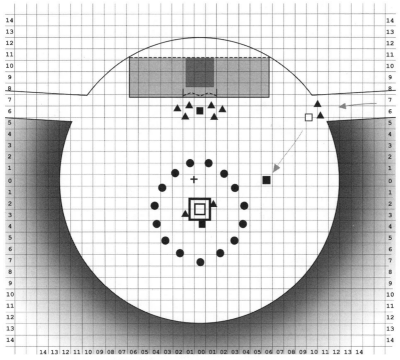

FIGURE 5 Scene from Euripides' *Suppliants* 87 ff.

choros. The spectators may well assume that they will remain mute extras. Their position by the *skene* is probably determined by the presence of the *choros* in the *orchestra* (figs. 6, 7).[86]

Other aspects of the composition are also familiar. Adrastus is invited to the city of Athens by Theseus (354–55), as Danaus was by Pelasgus in Aeschylus's *Suppliants,* and when he returns he remains with the *choros* (589–90) for a scene in which the *choros* is first addressed by the Messenger bringing news of the victorious battle. Only after this exchange with the *choros,* and the Messenger's account of the battle, does Adrastus speak and then engage in an exchange with the Messenger (734 ff.). In fact, the *skene* has a very marginal presence in Euripides' *Suppliants,* a virtual existence as a temple that is clearly defined but that no one enters and from which no one appears, unless it is used (in a manner that is impossible to determine) for the suicidal

86. Rehm's argument and proposal are presented in Rehm (1988, 274–76, 283 ff.). In the same year, Kaimio described the *choros* as "seen around Aethra in the sacred precinct" and placed Adrastus "in a position nearest to the stage building and thus behind the chorus and Aethra" but made no further observation on the playing space (1988, 60–61).

FIGURE 6 Scene from Euripides' *Suppliants* 87 ff.

FIGURE 7 Euripides' *Suppliants* 87 ff. Theseus finds his mother, Aethra, at the altar encircled by the *choros.* In front of the *skene* is Adrastus, surrounded by the sons of the dead war leaders.

leap of Evadne from a "rock" on to the pyre of her husband Capaneus, which is said to be located near the temple.[87]

87. This remarkable coup de théâtre inevitably occasions speculation, but it is impossible to determine how it was achieved from anything in the script. Collard (1975, 1:15–16) offers a brief review. I am, granted my observations on the *skene* at the beginning of this

In Euripides' *Children of Heracles* the *skene* once again represents a temple, but it is used slightly differently. Half of the suppliants are contained within it, and two actors/characters (Heracles' daughter, Macaria, and his mother, Alcmena) successively make their appearances from it. It is also entered eventually by an actor/character (a dependant of Hyllus, the eldest son of Heracles) who has arrived in the playing space and who fetches armor from it. But it remains marginal to the action of the tragedy. As in Euripides' *Suppliants,* there is an altar in the playing space (33), which is distinguished from the interior of the temple as being in full view of the public (44).[88] This is the reason why the daughters of Heracles, with Alcmena, are positioned inside the temple, and the younger sons with Iolaus are placed outside, at the altar.[89] Our full sense of the disposition is completed, in the opening account of it from Iolaus, the aged guardian of the children, by the dispatch before the action of the tragedy has started of the elder sons of Heracles to search out a place to fortify, should they all be expelled from this area near Marathon (45–47). The altar is repeatedly named, with the children and Iolaus seen as suppliants of "Zeus of the *agora*" (70), and the altar as that of Zeus (79, 121, 238–39). So the definition of the playing space depends on the altar, which is dedicated to Zeus but which also implicates the communities of Marathon, situated significantly just inside the boundaries of the larger "land" of Athens (31 ff.).[90]

In Euripides' *Suppliants* the actor/character of the Herald of the Thebans argues with Theseus but does not threaten the suppliants physically (*Suppliants* 399 ff.). In *Children of Heracles* the Herald of Eurystheus arrives with the immediate threat of violence, much as the Egyptian Herald had done in Aeschylus's *Suppliants,* since Eurystheus wants to prevent the children of Heracles from finding a secure base in any foreign country and, if possible, to kill them. Iolaus, threatened once more in a long tale of exile and failed bids for asylum or support, relies jointly on the god of the altar and the people of the land to protect him and the boys from violence, but he is forced to the ground in the struggle with the Herald. At this moment the *choros*

51

---

section, far less concerned in the discussion here with actions in which the *skene* is the obvious reference point.

88. *Children of Heracles* is discussed by Rehm (1988, 303–4) as part of his argument about the location of the practicable altar in fifth-century tragedy and comedy.

89. As Rehm notes (1988, 304), the suppliant sons are addressed or referred to repeatedly during the tragedy, but themselves never speak.

90. The *agora* in Greek communities fulfilled a number of related public functions, as the communal "meeting place" that might contain sanctuaries and law courts and might serve as a market. So it implies, firmly, the *polis* or community in which it is placed. On the implications of "Zeus of the *agora*," see Wilkins (1993, 59–60) regarding line 70.

rushes to him in the playing space, in answer to his shout of appeal to the inhabitants of Athens to protect their city from insult and the gods from dishonor (69–72). The arrival of the *choros* is the counterpart, in relation to the act of supplication in the open at the altar, to the attack of the Herald, since the supplication is an act that anticipates potential assault as much as it hopes to solicit aid.[91]

So the opening song and dance of the *choros* take place first with Iolaus and then with both Iolaus and the Herald speaking (73–108). The dance of the *choros* must protect Iolaus and the boys at or near the altar. The song and dancing conclude with a spoken exchange between the *choros* and the Herald (109–19), and when the Athenian ruler Demophon arrives in the playing space with his brother Acamas he addresses the *choros* first before speaking to the Herald, remarking on the "crowd" that has gathered near the altar of Zeus (120–21). Once the Herald has left the playing space, Iolaus invites the boys to clasp hands (307–8) with Demophon and Acamas in a symbolic linkage of the fates of what are now seen as two kinship groups, presaging a future of alliance. To do this, Demophon and Acamas must now draw near the suppliants (308), if they have not done so before.[92] A circular disposition for the *choros* at the beginning of the sequence (120–35) would be initially protective and would be well suited to the joining of hands and the commitment of alliance to Athens made later by Iolaus as indicated in figure 8. Iolaus is, in turn, invited to leave the altar and go to the house of Demophon, which will be safe even if Demophon is absent, but he declines to cease being a suppliant until the outcome is clear (340–41). The *choros* then dances and sings in the *orchestra,* where the altar must be positioned.

Euripides' *Heracles* offers a different setting, with the *skene* representing the house of Heracles, who is absent from Thebes, but once again Euripides constructs a tragedy around refuge at an altar in the open ground of the playing space.[93] The guardian of the young sons of Heracles is Amphitryon, who has

91. Kaimio considers the act of violence, and mentions "the chorus' entrance," but avoids any consideration of the disposition of actors/characters and *choros* (1988, 73). Mastronarde believes in fundamentally separate spaces for *choros* and actors after the *Oresteia* but advances no arguments for these assumptions (1979, 19n2, 24). Yet in relation to this sequence, he contrastingly assumes that the *choros* does "enter in contact" with Iolaos and is "treating Iolaos first because he is obviously in need of aid" (88).

92. We cannot know if the *choros* was included in this pledge, which is by no means impossible.

93. Rehm (1988, 302–3) discusses *Heracles* and has written extended reviews of the theatrical presentation of the tragedy in later studies (1996, 50–55; 2002, 100–113); Halleran (1985) reviews the "opening tableau" at the altar without considering the location of the altar in the playing space (80–81).

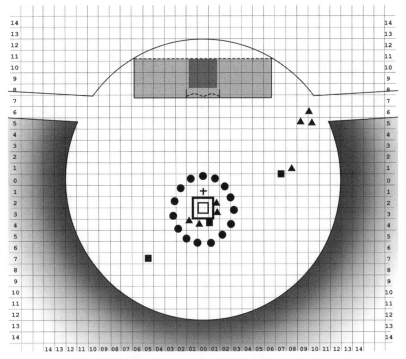

FIGURE 8 Euripides' *Children of Heracles* 120–35. Demophon arrives with his brother Acamas (a silent mask) and addresses the *choros,* which is protecting the young children of Heracles and the aged Iolaus, who are at the altar. The threatening Herald is at some distance.

gathered them at the altar with their mother, Megara. The altar was founded by Heracles himself, after a victory, and dedicated to Zeus the Savior (44–45), whom Amphitryon acknowledges as the father of Heracles. The house itself has been sealed against them, and they are without a change of clothing, food, or drink, sleeping on the bare ground (51–52), while any passage away and over the borders is guarded and blocked against them (82–83).

There is clearly a distinction here between the house from which they are barred and the exposed location of the altar, which stands on bare ground divorced from any domestic resources, with the *eisodoi* to the playing space apparently leading to the equivalent of road blocks (82–83). That the house is physically barred to the family of Heracles is apparent later in the play, when desperation forces Megara to ask the tyrant Lycus to unlock its doors, so that she and her children can find the proper clothing in which to face their impending death (327). From that time forward the *skene* becomes operative in the action of the tragedy, after representing the substance and the inheritance of Heracles' possessions of which the suppliants have been deprived.

The tyrant Lycus's method for displacing and demoralizing the suppliants is to threaten to "heap timbers around the altar on all sides" (240–41) and to set light to them, his language and intention making it absolutely clear that the altar is freestanding.[94] Lycus shows more superficial respect for the sanctuary that the altar offers than had Eurystheus's Herald in *Children of Heracles,* since he does not attempt to drag the suppliants from it. But his threat proves to be decisive in the minds of the suppliant group, forcing them to give up sanctuary.[95] Conversely, the open position of the altar has also allowed for support, provided by the *choros.* Its opening song and dance (107–37) bring the *choros* to the suppliants in the playing space, to a position that the tyrant Lycus then approaches, directly addressing Amphitryon and Megara and referring closely to the suppliant boys (165–66). The *choros* initially says little to Lycus (236–37), but its words are enough, with its supporting presence and his own recent history of oppression, for him to threaten the *choros* for their opposition to his will (247–48). To this the *choros* reacts aggressively, longing to batter and bloody Lycus's skull with their sticks (252 ff.), in a remarkable outburst that, as Megara's thanks and concern (275–76) confirm, belongs to the *choros* rather than to Amphitryon.[96] In figure 9, I have given the *choros* an open formation, allowing for the approach of Lycus and his guards and reflecting both its inclination to resist and its sense of its weakness.

After their progress into the house to dress in clothes appropriate for sacrifice, the suppliants return to the *choros* in the playing space (442–43), and the language of Megara (451–52) and the prayer uttered to Zeus by Amphitryon (497–98) indicate that they are, once again, by the altar, where Amphitryon can address what he believes are his last words to the *choros* (503–4).[97]

94. Rehm (1988, 303) notes the threat but does not comment on the language used by Lycus; Kaimio (1988, 67) does not provide a full translation of the instruction from Lycus in her discussion.

95. Halleran (1985) considers this "solemn moment" of leaving sanctuary to "enter the house" but offers no comment on the movements in the playing space (82).

96. The outburst was attributed to Amphitryon in manuscripts of the tragedy, but Bond rightly endorses an attribution of them to the *choros* (1981, 128–29). Halleran (1985) correctly doubts an act of violence here (81, 82), and he also concludes that the *choros* can "do nothing but verbally condemn Lykos" (82). Kaimio (1988) is interested in the threat but separates the *choros* from Lycus without any consideration of the location of the altar (67).

97. Halleran (1985) has this as a "moving tableau," which he describes as "a slow, stately or solemn entrance" (84).

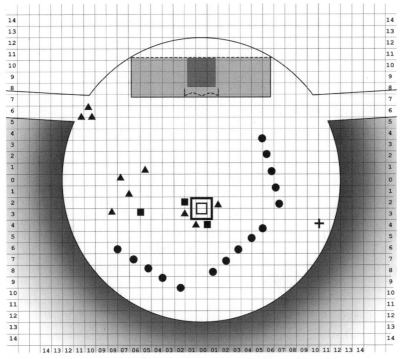

FIGURE 9 Euripides' *Heracles* 255–65. Lycus has just sent away some of his armed guards to fetch wood to burn and smoke the suppliants Amphitryon, Megara, and the young sons of Heracles from the altar. The *choros* is furiously indignant at the threats made by Lycus and abuses and attempts to threaten him in speech.

At this critical point, Heracles appears in an *eisodos* and is seen by both Amphitryon and Megara, who instructs the children to run to him. The actor/character of Heracles plainly greets his house first, on his return, and then his attention turns (525–26) to the children in the open playing space in front of the house and to his wife surrounded by a "crowd" (527), which is the *choros*.[98] He is puzzled, until it is explained to him, why they have so man-

98. This kind of reaction, which is similar to that of Theseus on his first arrival in the playing space in Euripides' *Suppliants,* attracted the attention of Mastronarde and Kaimio, among others. Mastronarde comments that, just as Heracles arrives, "the characters apparently begin to move toward him," but his analysis of the scene is flawed for our purposes by his failure to discuss the location of the altar (1979, 23). Kaimio's description of the scene is more evocative in terms of movement but ultimately suffers from the same vital omission (1988, 41).

ifestly "abandoned my house and hearth" (554). But the eventual progress of all from the *orchestra* into the *skene* proves to be fatal rather than secure.

Euripides' *Andromache* deploys a setting that is related to that in *Heracles,* since the *skene* represents a palace that a woman and child have "abandoned" (37: the word is the same as that in *Heracles* 554), seeking sanctuary at a shrine of Thetis near the palace.[99] Thetis is a sea spirit who is the mother of Achilles, the grandmother of Neoptolemos, and the consort of Peleus, a significant character in the later action of the tragedy, and her actual appearance concludes the play. Andromache, formerly the wife of the Trojan Hector, is a slave and concubine of Neoptolemos, grandson of Peleus and Thetis. Hermione, the wife of Neoptolemos and daughter of Menelaus, has become jealous to the point of threatening Andromache's life; like the title character in *Heracles,* Neoptolemos is absent, and so Andromache is extremely vulnerable, which accounts for her seeking sanctuary at the shrine. The *choros* of women of the locality comes to the actor/character of Andromache in the playing space, and its first danced song in the *orchestra* expresses sympathy with her, while advising her to leave the shrine where she has been so long (117–46). The *choros* hopes to achieve some form of reconciliation, but it also observes that Andromache is a slave in a foreign land and so cannot expect help to come from friends; in this respect, her reliance on sanctuary may be futile.

The actor/character of Hermione appears from the palace and comes to Andromache, insisting that "this house" of Thetis (161), like any altar or even temple, will not protect her: Andromache's best policy, according to Hermione, would be to accept drudgery within the palace itself (164–65). In the argument between the two, Andromache momentarily alludes to the "statue of Thetis" in the shrine, which she claims is looking at Hermione when Hermione threatens her with death (245–46), and Hermione then insists again that Andromache should leave the "sacred precinct of the sea goddess" (253). Andromache will not, unless her life is assured, and so Hermione threatens to "bring fire" to burn her out; there is also, evidently, an altar in the shrine (260). The actor/character of Menelaus also comes to Andromache in the playing space, bringing her son as a hostage, and he, too, refers to the statue of Thetis in the shrine (311). His method is simple, and time

---

99. Rehm (1988, 303) discusses *Andromache.* He concentrates once again, and consistently for his argument, on the presence of an altar but does not mention that the altar is contained within a shrine to Thetis. Wiles (1997) lists the attributes of the shrine and places it at the center of the playing space, summarizing its symbolic significance for the play (200–201).

honored. If she leaves the shrine and dies, then her son will live; if not, her son will die (380–81). And so the crucial decision to leave sanctuary is taken (411): Andromache is seized and held by Menelaus's attendants (425–26) and instructed to "walk toward" the palace (433), from the altar in the open ground of the *orchestra* to the *skene*.

Euripides' *Helen* also marks another separation of sanctuary from palace, with in this case Helen rejecting the palace because of the threat of marriage to the king, Theoclymenus.[100] Her choice of refuge is the tomb of Theoclymenus's father, Proteus, to whom the god Hermes had entrusted her because Proteus could be relied on to keep her safe until she was reunited with her husband, Menelaus (44–48). The background of the play is the version of the myth of the Trojan war in which a phantom of Helen accompanied Paris to Troy, while the "real" Helen was spirited away to Egypt (31–32), and in the opening scenes Helen finds her isolation even more drastically confirmed by depressing reports from Teucrus about her mother and brothers as well as her husband. It is not so much that Theoclymenus is likely to drag her from the tomb of his father by force but that the hope of rescue and of restoration to her past life drastically recedes from her. Nonetheless, Theoclymenus is violent; we hear as the play progresses that he has a homicidal attitude to all Greeks who make a landfall in Egypt, since he expects her husband Menelaus to be among them.[101] So the tomb is symbolic of the hospitality and protection afforded to her by Proteus while he was alive, and its choice by Helen as a place of sanctuary is intended to confront Theoclymenus with the authority of his own father.

The tomb itself is substantial. Menelaus at one point speaks of upright slabs and a base to it (547), and Helen has placed a mattress by it (798); as Theoclymenus says, she has been "living" at it (1228). Menelaus envisages the possibility that Theoclymenus might attempt to starve out both of them if they remained as suppliants at the tomb (981), and he speaks graphically of their possible suicide, with the two corpses lying in blood on the "polished tomb" (981–82), and blood dripping down it. Most significant, in the debate between Menelaus and Helen on the best course of action, the tomb is distinguished plainly as an alternative location to the palace (1083–84). Menelaus asks Helen whether he should go into the house along with her or whether they should both stay seated at the tomb. Helen replies that

100. Rehm (1988, 304–6) discusses *Helen*; I provided notes on the use of the playing space throughout the action of *Helen* in Ley (1991a).
101. This emerges in the scene between Menelaus and the woman Doorkeeper, 437 ff.

Menelaus should stay at the tomb, relying on its protection and on his sword, if need be; but she herself will "go to the palace," to achieve her disguise and her deception of Theoclymenus.

It is the tomb that presents an alternative in the playing space to the will of Theoclymenus, with his lack of respect for guests and foreigners, by opposing to his temperament and inclinations the authority of his father, Proteus. So it is that when Theoclymenus's sister, Theonoe the seer, comes from the *skene* in a procession with torches (865 ff.) Helen's supplication of her relies on the contrast of Theoclymenus with Proteus.[102] Similarly, Menelaus chooses to address Theonoe standing by the tomb (959–61) and, indeed, then addresses the shade of Proteus in that position (962–63). The subsequent resolution of Helen and Menelaus is that Menelaus should stay at the tomb as Helen prepares to deceive Theoclymenus, and it is there that he is found after the actor/character of Theoclymenus has arrived in the playing space (1203). It is plain from the script that Theoclymenus has not seen him there and did not see him when he greeted the tomb on his arrival (1165–66), since what shocked him at that point was Helen's desertion of her place of sanctuary at the tomb (1177–79), and he immediately called for a force to be assembled to chase after her (1180–81). His assumption, once the doors of the palace open, that he sees "those I am chasing still at the house and not escaped" (1184–85) cannot refer to the actor/character of Menelaus directly, who remains as yet unnoticed at the tomb, but it certainly refers to Helen and, perhaps, an attendant.[103]

The reappearance of Helen, like the earlier, solemn appearance of Theonoe from the palace, is an elaborate scene, involving extras as huntsmen with dogs and nets arriving behind Theoclymenus in the playing space, to be ordered by him into the palace as he stands near to the tomb (1170–71) of his father.[104] The actor/character of Menelaus must crouch down on the side of tomb out of sight of Theoclymenus, and the mattress of Helen must be on a side of the tomb that is within his sight. As Theoclymenus shouts for the

102. Kaimio (1988, 59) believes this to be an example of spoken rather than physical supplication and that the actor/character of Helen "remains in the shelter of the tomb." But Kaimio does not discuss the location of the tomb in the playing space.

103. Dale (1967, 143) confidently calls "those" a "ceremonial plural" in her commentary on these lines.

104. What happens next is a matter for speculation, since Theoklymenmos also issues an order later, at 1180–81, for horses and chariots to be brought from the stables. There seems little alternative to the conclusion that the huntsmen and dogs must enter the *skene*, and sufficiently promptly for there to be a short gap in time before Helen makes her reappearance at 1184. Bain (1981, 8–9) discusses the orders given by Theoclymenus.

doors of the palace to be opened and an armed and mounted force to be prepared for the pursuit, with consummate timing the actor/character of Helen appears at the doors of the palace, making a striking impression in a changed mask (face and hair) and changed costume (1186–87). This alteration engages his full attention and curiosity and allows Helen subtly to introduce Menelaus, in his position at the tomb (1203) and in his assumed role in the story she has concocted, to which Menelaus's rags conveniently correspond.

But the most vigorous sequence involving the tomb in *Helen* would appear to be the chase that occurs when Menelaus first tries to speak to Helen, after she has spotted him, and intercepts her as she dashes for safety at the tomb (541–42). The *choros* and Helen have earlier entered the palace to consult with Theonoe, with the *choros* apparently leaving the playing space first (its last lines are at 360–61), perhaps while the actor/character of Helen sings and dances the concluding part of their danced song (362–85). The absence of Helen and the *choros* allows Menelaus to arrive and to remain unknown and to have no way of understanding, in conversation with the woman Doorkeeper and afterward, why it is that there would seem to be two Helens in existence. Menelaus's lonely decision is that he will wait for Theoclymenus. The *choros* then appears from the *skene,* singing its progress into the playing space (515–27), followed by Helen who soliloquizes on the vision of the survival of Menelaus that she has received from Theonoe (528–40). In figure 10a, I have supposed the *choros* to have emerged singing from the *skene* in ranks of three, since this seems most practical, unless we assume extremely wide doors. I have placed the *auletes* (pipe player) away from Menelaus, at the side of the *skene,* from which he can come forward to accompany the *choros.*

Helen announces herself by stating that she is "walking toward refuge at this tomb again" (528), and she is eventually startled by Menelaus (541–42). Her first thoughts are that she will run like a "racing filly or a maenad of the god [Dionysus]" toward the sanctuary of the tomb (543–44). This must suppose that she has not yet reached it, and either her progress from the *skene* doors has been slow or she has wandered about, perhaps moving among the *choros.* The most likely position for the actor/character of Menelaus must be on a side of the tomb facing away from the *skene,* to which he will have withdrawn when he heard the doors opening (at 515). The disposition of the *choros* in that case cannot be certain, but it is unlikely to be around the tomb. Despite what Helen says and fears about pursuit (544–45) and obstruction (550–51), it seems more likely that Menelaus is meant to be astonished (548–49) at the extraordinary resemblance of this person to his wife, and to

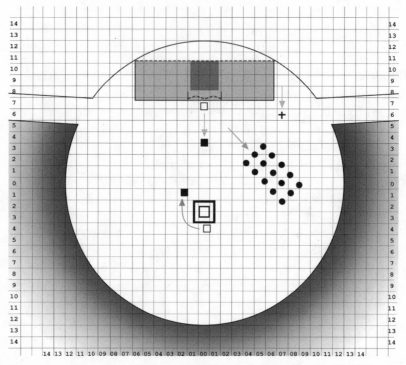

FIGURE 10 *a,* Euripides' *Helen* 528–42. The *choros* has reappeared singing from the *skene,* followed by Helen, who announces that she is returning to her place at the tomb of Proteus. Menelaus has hidden himself behind the tomb.

be keen to address her, rather than that he is purposefully initiating a game of intensive tag. But he too describes her anxious speed of foot ("striving with a fearful stretching out [of the foot]," to give a literal rendition of 546) directed toward the tomb (fig. 10b), and he calls on her to stop running (548 and 555), plainly getting in her way to some extent until at last she reaches her goal (556).

In a later part of the exchanges between Helen and Menelaus, Menelaus expresses surprise that Helen should seek refuge at a tomb by asking her whether there was no altar available or whether this is an Egyptian custom, and Helen in reply compares the security it offered to that provided by a temple (797–98). There is no established location for tombs in relation to associated buildings in Greek society, such as there is for altars in relation to temples, and Aeschylus in *Libation Bearers* offers no clue, as he had offered no indication of the precise position of the tomb of Darius within the playing

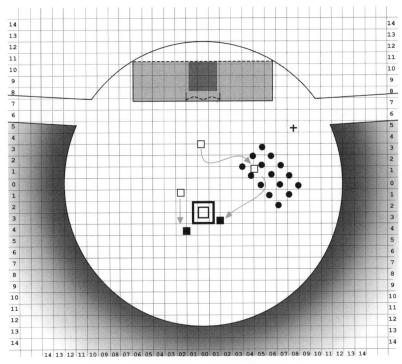

FIGURE 10 *b*, Euripides' *Helen* 543–46. (1) brief display of dodging and blocking by Helen and Menelaus, from (approximately) 543–48; (2) Helen runs to the *choros* (550–51); (3) Helen reaches the tomb of Proteus (556), and Menelaus approaches her there.

space.[105] Menelaus's query might be combined with the later explanation offered by Theoclymenus himself, who on his arrival in the playing space first greets the tomb of his father, implicitly justifying its position by stating that he wished to be able to greet it every time he entered or left his palace ("coming out or going into the house," 1167), which was once his father's. This is a similar pairing to Heracles' description of the movements out of and into his house by his family, to and from the altar in the playing space, and the language used is the same (*Heracles* 622–24).

Euripides in *Helen* may feel the need of justifying this culturally odd collocation of habitation and tomb, and the other example of a tomb or

105. The Greeks in general made use of what we should call cemeteries, set apart from habitation, in the historic period; the Cerameicus in Athens, set just outside the city walls, was one such area. But we have no reason to suppose that the heroic tombs of tragedy were associated with standard burial practices in the minds of the composer or the audience.

"memorial" in the playing space in the surviving, post-Aeschylean tragedies is interesting in this respect. In Euripides' *Bacchae* the "memorial" (*mnema,* a "monument") of Semele is visible by the *skene,* but this is because Semele was destroyed by lightning in the moment of childbirth in the palace itself, whose burnt ruins are supposedly (or apparently) also visible "near" the new palace (*Bacchae* 6–7). There is a suggestion that a flame still flickers from this sacrosanct area, and references are made to that later (596–97, and 622–23), but there are no clear indications of action associated with it, although there are undoubtedly many appropriate opportunities.[106]

The dash to a place of sanctuary within the playing space has an interesting parallel in Euripides' *Ion,* whose unequivocal setting is the temple of Apollo at Delphi and its sacred forecourt, while the place of sanctuary is the altar of the god. The distinction between temple and altar has been made early in the play, by Ion, the temple attendant, in response to questions from the *choros.* In this song and dance shared between them, the *choros* asks Ion if it is lawful to enter the temple, and Ion states that it is not. Those who have made an offering of meal and honey may "go up to the altar," but only those who have sacrificed sheep may proceed into the temple (226–29).

The flight to the altar that occurs later in the play is occasioned by a complicated plot, in which Creusa's attempt to poison Ion is discovered, and the *choros* is told that she is being pursued (1225–26). The actor/character of Creusa runs in, in desperation, to seek help or advice in this emergency from the *choros,* which has also feared for itself as well as for Creusa. Creusa asks the *choros* where she can run for safety, and the response of the *choros* is simple: "Where else other than to the altar?" (1255). The exchange is interesting, since the *choros* is confirming that although Creusa is already condemned to death by law, her position as a suppliant will protect her until her pursuers can actually lay hands on her (1255–57). Her pursuers are then seen arriving, with drawn swords, and the *choros* instructs Creusa to sit at the altar; if they assault her there, they will have a suppliant's blood on their hands (1258–60).[107]

106. Speculation over whether the ruins and the flames were visible is similar to speculation over the nature of the earthquake that shakes the palace, since we have no secure means of knowing what was portrayed. One might possibly compare the references to the thunder of Zeus toward the climax of Sophocles' *Oedipus at Colonus,* 1448–49, but a sound effect is relatively simple contrivance. Truthfully, not much of value can be concluded about the use of the playing space from speculations of this kind.

107. Rehm (1988) chooses not to discuss *Ion,* but this sequence has gained a great deal of attention, little of which has concerned itself with a coherent vision of movement and disposition in a playing space. Wiles argues that there is an absence of what he terms "perspectival realism" in *Ion* and that the audience was presented with "the symbolism of Del-

The actor/character of Ion arrives in a furious rage in the playing space with the other pursuers, and he instructs them to seize Creusa (1266). But it is only later that he calls to them to see the transgressor, crouching at the altar of the god (1279–81). Between these two statements he has apparently addressed Creusa herself, insisting that "neither the altar nor the temple of Apollo shall save you" (1275–76). We might understand any number of things here about Ion's statements, and the implications they might have for the movements of the actor/character of Creusa, but the fact is that Creusa has run to the altar, at the latest by 1279. The situation compels Creusa, with profound ironies, to dedicate her body to Apollo (1285), who had raped her, at his altar and in his precinct, in order to escape death at the hands of their son. Ion's religiosity is offended by the presence of a criminal at an altar, and he states his belief that such wrongdoers should be driven from sanctuary, only to be prevented from so doing by the appearance of the Pythia, priestess and mouthpiece of Apollo's oracle, from the temple. This composition for the playing space by Euripides is very close to the appearance and procession of the actor/character of Theonoe, also a seer, from the palace in *Helen* to Menelaus and Helen at the tomb of Proteus. The tokens that the Pythia brings are destined finally to sunder Ion from the temple, as Apollo sends him away from service (1320 ff.). In the course of the recognition that follows, Creusa is moved by emotion to leave her position at the altar (1401–2), and the culmination is the joyful dance and song in which Creusa and Ion are joined as mother and son (1445–1509), which will take place in the playing space near the altar.

In all these instances that I have discussed, we have a strong sense of composition for the playing space in significant proportions of the tragedies concerned, since the altar, tomb, or shrine contributes strongly to a definition of the space essential to the action in which it is involved. In other tragedies, we may be aware of an altar, but the indications are such that they do not necessarily contribute as firmly to our sense of the playing space. In Euripides' *Electra,* the actor/character of Electra returns to the playing space from the spring and is joined there by the *choros* in dance and song, to be surprised eventually by Orestes and Pylades who have been hiding, occupying what Electra terms a "lair by the hearth" (216–17), to express it literally,

phic space," but he believes that Creusa runs to a symbolic marker at the center of the *orchestra* (1997, 80–81). Other modern contributions to the debate, which has become something of a scholarly puzzle, have included Diggle (1974, 28 ff.), Taplin (1978, 187n9), Mastronarde (1979, 110–12), Bain (1981, 35–36), Halleran (1985, 108), and Kaimio (1988, 65).

which might possibly refer to an altar, but equally might refer merely to a hiding place alongside the house. It is interesting, in this respect, that Electra's reaction is to advise the *choros* to run away down the path (an *eisodos*) while she will escape into the house, but she is immediately prevented from doing so by Orestes and has to kneel in supplication to him (218–21). This would hardly be possible if she were already by the *skene,* and it seems most likely that she is with the *choros* in the playing space and Orestes and Pylades have been hiding nearer to the *skene*.[108] There is no further or expanded reference to an altar in the script, and there would be little point in associating this passage closely with those that we have examined.

There are different kinds of relatively oblique reference in the surviving tragedies of Sophocles. The opening of *Oedipus the King* is impressive, a scene of supplication with extras in the playing space, whose spokesman is a priest of Zeus. Both young and old, the Priest declares to Oedipus, are sitting as suppliants "at your altars" (15–17), and they arise and remove their suppliant branches only at the end of the scene (142–43), once Creon has brought what seem to be reassuring instructions from the oracle of Apollo at Delphi.[109] As a composition for the playing space, the scene can be visualized readily, on analogy with the scenes from the tragedies of Euripides (fig. 11).[110] Yet there is only one other indication in the script that might allow us to envisage how the altar(s) may have been involved in the subsequent action of the play, and that is the reference to Apollo made by Jocasta (918–19). Jocasta has come from the palace, intending to visit the shrines of the gods, such as those outside the playing space that had been mentioned by the Priest of Zeus (19–21). She addresses Apollo first, since he is "nearest" (919), and speaks of coming as a suppliant with prayers, which would suggest a sim-

108. Later, when invited to enter the house by Electra's husband, Orestes addresses his own slaves, telling them to go in (393–94). Later still, the "Messenger" who brings the news of the murder of Aegisthus in the fields is also identified as a slave of Orestes (765–68). So if Orestes and Pylades are, on their first arrival, accompanied by slaves/attendants, as seems likely, then hiding by the house or *skene* is a more persuasive option for a group of at least four or five in total.

109. As Rehm points out, the suggestion that the spectators are taken as the suppliants is made awkward by these instructions, given to some of the suppliants by Oedipus at 142–43, to remove their suppliant branches and get up from their position at the altars. The instructions are confirmed by the Priest (147–48): Rehm (1992, 110n2, 157–58), with the references given there; see also Seale (1982, 215n3, 255n4).

110. In his full theatrical commentary on the script, based on a workshop, McCart (in Ewans 1999, 268–69, 268–69n8) draws on Ashby to suggest that a position for the altars both centrally and to the front margins of the *orchestra* may be most practicable. It might be tempting to see some kind of relationship between the composition here and that of the opening of Aeschylus's *Seven against Thebes,* but the uncertainties make speculation particularly fragile.

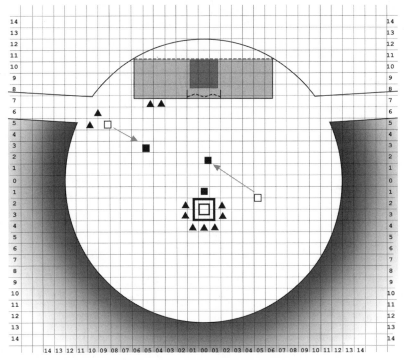

65

FIGURE 11 Sophocles' *Oedipus the King* 91–92. The Priest has seen attendants signal (78–79) that Creon is returning from Delphi (along an *eisodos*), and Oedipus addresses Creon firstly at a distance. The suppliants are gathered at the altar.

ilar intention to that of the suppliants in the opening scene. An altar identified as that of Apollo in the playing space would be totally appropriate, but there are no further references to amplify the vision.[111]

In Sophocles' *Electra*, there are slighter indications than these. At one point late in the tragedy Electra prays to Apollo, kneeling and referring to the offerings she has made (1376–83). This might well suggest the presence of an altar, and offerings have indeed been made to Apollo earlier in the tragedy by Clytemnestra, with Electra close to her and in the presence of the *choros* (630–31).[112] But the indications for the playing space in the text

111. See McCart's commentary (in Ewans 1999, 289–90), with the notes there. As in his discussion of the opening scene, Seale does not reveal where he believes the altar to be in the playing space (1982, 237).
112. Seale (1982) avoids the problem of the playing space by stating equivocally, in relation to Clytemnestra's offerings, that the altar of Apollo "stands in front of the palace" (63); for Electra's prayer, he adds a "statue of Apollo" (73). Like McCart on *Oedipus the King*, Ewans

are slight, perhaps the most interesting being that the Tutor arrives immediately after Clytemnestra's prayer and addresses the *choros* first, asking for
identification of the palace and guessing that the person they see may be the
wife of Aegisthus (660–61) and, then, immediately addressing Clytemnes-
66   tra. This might establish the presence of Clytemnestra, Electra, the Tutor,
and the *choros* in the playing space close to an altar of Apollo, but neither
Sophocles' *Electra* nor his *Oedipus the King* offer us the kind of detail that we
find in Euripides.

Probably the most interesting of Sophocles' surviving tragedies in this respect is *Oedipus at Colonus,* but it calls for very careful analysis. There is, of
course, no reason why a script should declare its use of the playing space to
us expressly, particularly if its composer plays a major role in its implementation in production, or expects to do so. Sophocles had died before *Oedipus
at Colonus* was produced, but the script reveals no determined attempt to render its realization explicit.[113] The opening presents the problem of the playing space for the tragedy.

Oedipus is old, weary, and blind, an outcast from Thebes and a wanderer,
supported by his daughter Antigone and led into the playing space, which is
unknown to them, at a distance from the city of Athens (14–15, and 24), and
apparently sacred, with "laurel and olive trees and vines" mentioned (14–17)
by Antigone. As wanderers, they will almost certainly arrive in the playing
space from an *eisodos.* The stone Oedipus sits on is unpolished by human hand
(19), and to him and his daughter comes the actor/character of a Man of the
locality. This Man declares the place where Oedipus is sitting to be ground
sacred to the Eumenides (36–37) and, apparently, points to a statue of the
horseman Colonus (58–59). Although Oedipus is initially urged to move
away from the sacred ground, when he hears to whom it is sacred he myste-
riously declares himself a suppliant and states that he will never leave this
"seat" of supplication (44–5), something that the Man accepts until he has
further authority (47–48, and 75–80). Oedipus then prays to the Eumenides,
calling the place where he is a "grove" (98) and referring to the "rough seat"
on which Antigone has placed him (101). Curiously, after this solemn statement of intention and significance, and once the arrival of the old men who
will form the *choros* is announced by Antigone, Oedipus actually asks to be

_____

(2000) has an altar just forward of the center of the *orchestra;* his conclusions about
Clytemnestra's and Electra's prayers should be read in the context of his dispositions for
those scenes (195 ff. and 209 ff., respectively).

113. This makes the whole problem even more intriguing: would the production itself have
presented precisely what Sophocles had in mind?

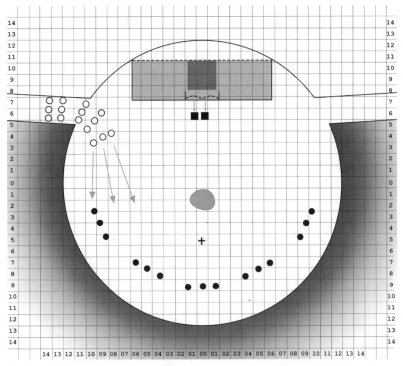

FIGURE 12 Sophocles' *Oedipus at Colonus* 138–49. The *choros* has arrived searching for the intruder, Oedipus, who appears from the *skene* with Antigone at 138, and will be led to the rock. The *choros* keeps its distance both from the sacred precinct of the grove and from Oedipus himself.

moved out of the path and into the grove, so that he can judge the feelings of the old men (113–16).

The *choros* arrives to sing and dance a search for Oedipus and sings of the "grove" and of the "sanctuary" or "precinct" of the goddesses whom it shudders to name, but Oedipus cannot be seen (118–37). The actor/character of Oedipus then reveals himself to the *choros,* from his hiding place in the grove, joining the *choros* in a chanted exchange (138–49), perhaps accompanying his movement (fig. 12). In the second part of the danced song, the *choros* warns Oedipus that he might stray into the "glade" and must keep silence until he has moved away from it (150–69). At the end of a short chant Oedipus then agrees to remove himself (175), and in the second part of the danced song in which he joins with Antigone and the *choros* he moves "forward," farther and farther, toward "these seats" from which no one will drive him, according to the *choros* (176–77). He is finally guided to what the *choros* describes as "this slab of living rock" (192), and he hopes to be seated there (195–96), although after this is mentioned he is still moving forward, leaning on his daughter. Unfortunately, when he declares his identity the *choros* ignores its own pledge and orders him away (226), off the rock on which they had placed him and out of the country (233–34), although Antigone protests. The whole sequence continues and ends in dance and song.

In some respects this setting recalls and continues the long-established use of the playing space to represent an act of supplication. But instead of the altar or tomb that Euripides places away from the *skene,* we would appear to have a "slab" of rock that is outside the sacred ground and, quite plainly, on the same secular ground as that on which the *choros* is dancing and will later stand.[114] Correspondingly, the sacred place of initial supplication is removed from the *choros* and also permits concealment. We know that the *choros* must be in the *orchestra* and that would be the place for the slab of rock and for the extended sequence of dance and song that includes both Antigone and Oedipus in conjunction with the *choros.*[115] This would then, of course, place Oedipus in the *orchestra* for the whole of the rest of the tragedy, until its conclusion, and draw the action of the play toward him. We might conclude that the *skene* represents the opening (through its doors) to the sacred grove of the Eumenides, in which Oedipus conceals himself and his daughter and from which he appears to the *choros,* after the *choros* has searched the *orchestra* and been unable to find him. The alternative is to suppose that the *skene* was not used at all in this tragedy and that the grove is located somewhere else, toward the margin of the *orchestra.*

But the ending of the tragedy, in which Oedipus walks into the grove, will make that construction awkward, unless we assume that he leaves down an *eisodos* to the grove. It would have to be an *eisodos,* because he is followed by his

114. Seale (1982) emphasizes the importance of the "formal compartmentalisation of the acting space" (113) but does not make any allowance for the involvement of the actors/ characters with the *choros* and the position of the *choros* as an instructor (114, 119 ff.); contrast the analysis by McCart (in Ewans 2000, 257 ff.). Kaimio (1988, 15) is concerned with the physical conduct of Oedipus by Antigone in this opening scene but, apart from stating that Antigone "leads him towards the chorus," includes no consideration of the playing space.

115. Wiles (1997, 188) bizarrely sees a "rock" at the center of the *orchestra* as suitable for both locations, since Oedipus has disappeared into the grove in the interim; Wiles apparently relies for this perception on a modern production (188n6)., which was inevitably conceived for very different resources.

two daughters, by Theseus, and by at least one other man, and all of these characters return to the playing space after Oedipus has vanished while in the grove.[116] But it is extremely difficult to understand what possible advantages Sophocles would have gained from not using the *skene* to represent the grove. So it seems most likely that Oedipus entered the *skene* toward the end   69 of the tragedy, followed by the other actors/characters and that they then reappeared from it successively.[117] We have no firm indications at all of where the statue of the horseman, Colonus, might be placed in the playing space if, as seems plausible, that statue was in view, and no action apparently depends on its presence.[118] What is clear is that in the last of his tragedies Sophocles was composing for performance in the open ground of the playing space and relying on close interaction between actors/characters and *choros* within it.

PERFORMERS AND VEHICLES IN THE PLAYING SPACE

By comparison with the careful location of a significant altar or tomb in the playing space, which is used by Euripides to a greater or lesser extent to compose a number of tragedies, the second material presence in the playing space that his scripts plainly reveal seems far more incidental. But the location of vehicles in the *orchestra* in these tragedies, clearly occasioning action, also incidentally provides us with a second body of evidence about the use of the playing space after Aeschylus. Their introduction to the playing space is a discernible instance of what we might assume to be a continuing standard practice, affected only to a limited if impressive degree, as it is in the *Oresteia,* by the presence of the *skene*. In the early tragedies and the *Oresteia,* the introduction of a vehicle to the playing space is only one component in the established mode of composition, part of the essential pattern of the arrival and

---

116. The rock on which Oedipus is initially placed by Antigone would then have to be at the mouth of the *eisodos;* and this *eisodos* would have to remain unused throughout the tragedy until its conclusion. We should then have to assume that all the actors/characters arrive and leave down the same *eisodos,* including the actor/character of Ismene, who must leave down an *eisodos* at 509 to reach the "far side of this grove" (505).

117. Wiles (1997) offers a set of propositions about conceptual space and large properties (trees, the statue of Colonus) but does not explore this playing space in relation to the opening scenes (146–51). Nonetheless, his conclusion is that Oedipus enters the *skene* toward the close of the tragedy (165–66). Seale (1982) also believes this to be the case (136–38). It is difficult to relate the sketch in Jebb's (1928) commentary from his influential series to the actualities of the playing space (xxxviii); but he directs Oedipus out along an *eisodos* toward the close of the tragedy (237–39).

118. Both Wiles (1997, 148) and Jebb (1928, xxxviii) make diagrammatic suggestions for its location in relation to their conception of the grove.

disposition of actors/characters with *choros* in the *orchestra*. It might be assumed to have that status in the tragedies of Euripides; or it might, alternatively, be assumed to constitute a more exceptional allusion to an older practice that has now substantially changed. In this respect, the instances that we find, and what they show us, must be placed alongside the other kinds of indication and evidence that I outline in this chapter.

70

The vehicles in the tragedies of Aeschylus are tangible entities, on which actors/characters stand or are seated, and we have no reason to believe that they were drawn by ancient equivalents of pantomime horses. The standard term for chariot is *harma,* and it is a word that is used by all three tragedians but, noticeably, not in relation to these theatrical vehicles. Yet in relation to the arrival of Agamemnon and Cassandra many commentators prefer to propose a chariot to us, although the sole descriptive reference to the vehicle terms it an *apene* (*Agamemnon* 906), which would be more obviously translated as a carriage or wagon.[119] The symbolic associations of a chariot for a returning war leader, particularly in relation to the Homeric epic *Iliad* in which they feature as an accoutrement, are obvious. But chariots were not used for warfare at this time in Greece, and the only available model would be that of a racing chariot, driven at the Hellenic games (including the Olympic games) by specialist charioteers.

Larry Shenfield, who has written a thesis on the chariot in Greece, points out to me that chariots may carry two people at the most, standing up, of whom one has to drive the horses, which would number either two or four.[120] These chariots were small, light, and potentially unstable, with the driver standing backward of the axle to take the weight of the yoke pole off the backs of the horses, in order to increase speed and mobility. My feeling is that their practicality for theatrical performance must surely be questioned, in association with the issue of theatrical terminology. If we propose a chariot for *Agamemnon,* against the indications of the term used to describe the vehicle, we are either assuming that the actor of Agamemnon can drive a chariot with another actor (Cassandra) standing beside him, or we are assuming that the chariot was walked in by an attendant. The balance of a chariot on the axle depended considerably on the position of the occupant(s); when Agamemnon steps down in the script, there would be a reasonable chance of either him or Cassandra losing their balance.

119. And some editors and commentators pass by it in silence. It might be worth noting that an outstanding editor of *Agamemnon,* Fraenkel, in his note on the arrival of Agamemnon unobtrusively assumes that the vehicle is a wagon (1950, 2:370–71).
120. Shenfield 2001.

The alternative is to accept that an *apene* or wagon was indeed used, as it might generally be for travel over roads. In *Persians,* the more general term *ochema*(*ta*) is used (*Persians* 607) by the Queen Mother to describe the vehicle in which she arrived in the first instance in the playing space. We have no particular reason to assume that she arrived in a chariot, and if she was at-   71
tended by women traveling with her, a carriage would be both practical and appropriate. The carriage in the painting by the Amasis painter (fig. 13) is a two-wheeled vehicle, but there were also four-wheeled versions, as the second of the vase paintings shows (fig. 14), which might carry more people or material goods.[121] Passengers traveled sitting down in these vehicles, and the driver might be separated from the passengers. Tragic actors may have been more suitably positioned for descent from the theatrical vehicles in such an arrangement, and I have to say (most unheroically) that I have always wondered how the actor/character of Agamemnon had his boots pulled off, while still standing in a chariot, without losing his balance. Carriages were associated with weddings, and it is a standard observation that they were "heroized" into chariots in celebratory paintings on vases.[122] So either the chariot or the carriage might readily carry connotations of the wedding, something that would be highly appropriate to a critical interpretation of most of the tragic scenes. In all of the scenes in the surviving tragedies of Euripides the word *apene* is used, alongside more general terms for a vehicle (such as *ochema*[*ta*], *ochos,* or *ochoi*).

In figures 15–17, I have adopted a simple scheme for the carriage, drawn by two ponies. The carriage is approximately one meter wide, and no more than two meters in length, with an additional one and a half meters for the animals. It is a four-wheeled vehicle, and its size would be suited to the approach paths (*eisodoi*), which I have estimated at two meters wide. In the third drawing (fig. 18), which illustrates the same moment from Euripides' *Trojan Women* as figure 17, the wheels are approximately two-thirds of a meter in diameter, and the carriage has a practicable step at the rear, with seats (benches) both at the front and the rear. It does not seem to me at all likely that costumed actors would descend from the front of the carriage. Side

121. It is, of course, impossible to say whether vehicles were adopted, adapted, or made for performances. But I can see little point in the added labor of making the essential structure, although a superstructure might be adapted or added according to requirements. The festival cart of Dionysus pictured on vases might be an example of such an added or altered superstructure, if what is pictured is not purely imaginary (Pickard-Cambridge 1988, fig. 13).
122. For example, Rehm 1994, 14.

FIGURE 13 Wedding procession, with a two-wheeled carriage. Attic vase, from the middle of the sixth century BCE. The Metropolitan Museum of Art, Purchase, Walter C. Baker Gift, 1956. (56.11.1)

FIGURE 14 Wedding procession, with a four-wheeled carriage. Attic vase, from the middle of the fourth century BCE. National Archaeological Museum, Athens. (1630)

panels to the superstructure would allow performers to ride securely and give them something to grasp as they stand in the carriage and descend from it. The moment illustrated in figure 15 is that just before Agamemnon has his boots pulled off by a female slave, in order to step down onto the tapestries. The household women slaves who have spread the tapestries wait by the doors to the *skene;* an attendant stands at the heads of the ponies, in addition to a driver.

Euripides' *Iphigenia at Aulis* is one of the last of the surviving tragedies, which was produced posthumously by Euripides' son along with *Bacchae* and another lost tragedy. The play is set in the Greek camp at Aulis, as the expedition waits to sail against Troy, and the *skene* represents the tent of Agamemnon. The *choros,* of young women who have sailed from Chalcis across the straits to marvel at the Greek armament and its heroes, is not initially acknowledged by any of the actors/characters. When the Messenger comes to announce the arrival of Clytemnestra and Iphigenia, he reports that mother and daughter are resting briefly, after their long journey, with the horses let loose to graze (420–21), and that Clytemnestra has brought the child Orestes with her (418–19). The *choros* is abruptly warned by Agamemnon not to reveal anything of the shameful deception in which Agamemnon and

74

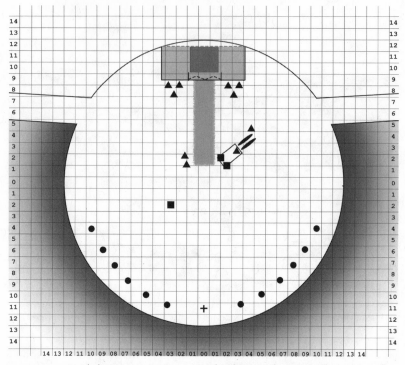

FIGURE 15 Aeschylus's *Agamemnon* 940–41. This diagram shows a smaller version of the early *skene*. Agamemnon is about to have his boots pulled off before stepping onto the tapestries. Cassandra remains seated, and silent, in the carriage. Clytemnestra is at a distance from Agamemnon and the tapestries.

Menelaus have caught themselves (542), and its danced song leads to the arrival of the mother and children.

Clytemnestra responds favorably to the words of welcome from the *choros,* taking them as a good omen, and then instructs some men, presumably her attendants, to remove the dowry gifts from the carriage and carry them into the tent (610–12). The details of the scene accumulate as she continues. Iphigenia is asked to leave a carriage drawn by young horses (613), which is, incidentally, the same kind of vehicle as that in which Laius was traveling when he met and was killed by his son Oedipus in Sophocles' *Oedipus the King,* and the description marks for us what we might term a domestic carriage for travel in contrast to a war chariot.[123] The women of the *choros* are then asked

123. In *Oedipus the King* the carriage carrying Laius appears only descriptively, in a dialogue between Oedipus and Jocasta. There it is introduced as an *apene* (753) by Jocasta, and

to help Iphigenia down from the carriage by offering their arms to her (615–16), and Clytemnestra also asks for "the support of a hand" in stepping down gracefully herself (617–18). Others of the *choros* are asked by Clytemnestra to stand at the fillies'/colts' heads, since unless they are spoken to they may be jumpy (619–20); and, finally, she tells others to take Orestes, whom she introduces as the son of Agamemnon, still an infant (621–22). This last pair of lines confirms that it is the *choros* to whom she is speaking, rather than attendants she might have brought with her, since these would not need to be introduced to Orestes.

Clytemnestra then speaks to her baby, and we cannot tell whether she has taken him back again from a member of the *choros* or handed him to an attendant woman of her own, although none has been indicated. The baby receives no further mention throughout the scene that follows but must, at some point, be taken inside the *skene,* since he is carried out from the *skene* much later in the tragedy by Iphigenia, called to do so by Clytemnestra (1117–19). Iphigenia has been standing apart from her mother, because Clytemnestra calls her to stand by her side, so that the unknown women of the *choros* may call Clytemnestra happy seeing the two of them together (627–29). The final instruction to Iphigenia is to speak to Agamemnon, who has appeared from the *skene.* In what follows, Iphigenia effectively asks permission to run to her father before her mother moves, to embrace him, but Clytemnestra addresses him formally (631–34). There is no further mention of the carriage.[124]

Oedipus alarmingly reports that he encountered such an *apene,* drawn by young horses (802–3), just as Jocasta describes it. Laius was traveling from Thebes to Delphi, accompanied by an escort but in a carriage, and this suggests that carriages could be considered appropriate for men as well as women on journeys. One might debate the number of animals, but in sympathy for the effort involved I give the plural.

124. The authenticity of much of this sequence has been doubted, notably by Page (1934), in a detailed commentary on the shortcomings of the Greek text (158 ff.), and he believed that supplements to a script unfinished at Euripides' death began with the first production (207 ff., "Epilogue"). There is certainly a problem with the preceding announcements by the *choros* (590–606), but the scene is analogous to the other arrivals by vehicle in Aeschylus and Euripides. Only in Euripides' *Ion* is a woman character who has arrived in comfort from a distance introduced without a vehicle; but Creusa may be considered to have arrived first at the sanctuary as a whole, before arriving in front of the temple of Apollo itself in the playing space. In Sophocles' *Oedipus at Colonus,* we are told (311 ff.) of the arrival of Ismene on a pony, although it is not clear whether the animal is seen or not. If this sequence were an interpolation into the script of *Iphigenia at Aulis* by actors, then it would, interestingly, indicate continuity in assumptions about the use of the playing space. Taplin (1977b) is inclined to doubt the authenticity of the scene (77, 77n1) while Halleran (1985) apparently does not (11, 11nn29, 28). Although neither argues a case, Halleran has a particular interest in what he calls "entrance announcements," something that informs his view.

The *choros* is here for the first time closely involved with actors/characters in the playing space, and its gender will permit further close involvement with the female characters of the tragedy, although the *choros* makes no spoken contribution at all to the rest of this scene, until it sings and dances at its conclusion. Two general observations can be made: the carriage comes to the *choros* in the playing space, and the carriage cannot be placed directly in front of the doors of the *skene*, from which both it and the *choros* would have to be withdrawn hurriedly if the appearance of Agamemnon is not to be pointlessly obscured and obstructed. The engagement of the *choros* with the carriage as well as with its occupants is scripted purposefully, and different members of the *choros* are deployed to different tasks, in what must be intended to be a picture of excited activity, with actors/characters and the baby Orestes occasioning interest and attention.

Toward the end of the sequence both Clytemnestra and Iphigenia must become clearly seen and separated from the *choros* in order to meet Agamemnon, and members of the *choros* cannot (or are extremely unlikely to) leave to conduct the carriage and its horses out of the *orchestra* at any point, certainly not at the end of the scene, when all members of the *choros* must sing and dance. The male attendants, who have presumably driven and accompanied the carriage, are sent into the *skene* almost immediately, although Clytemnestra greets the *choros* and introduces her daughter as a bride initially from the carriage. The attendants go one way from the carriage, into the *skene*, while the action involving the actors/characters and the *choros* occurs on the other side of the vehicle, away from the *skene* facade and into the *orchestra*. The carriage may be led away into a second position in the *orchestra* by members of the *choros* as or just before Agamemnon appears, and the male attendants may reappear from the *skene* at some point unobtrusively to remove it completely from the *orchestra*, since they are most strongly associated with it.

This scene suggests that *Agamemnon* was a formative play and was influential on the mind and art of Euripides some fifty-five years after it was first produced.[125] Much is worked through reversals here, with Clytemnestra and Iphigenia (and, indeed, Orestes) coming to Agamemnon, in contrast to

125. This is not to say that vehicles were not used to a similar effect before *Agamemnon*, because even from our drastically limited view we know that they were (in *Persians*). But the vehicle associated with the household of Agamemnon in the tragedies of Euripides is most plausibly linked with the impressions created by Aeschylus's *Agamemnon*, unless Aeschylus was himself adopting a type scene from earlier tragedies. Modern opinion is divided on the question of whether the tragedies of Aeschylus were produced in revivals at the City Dionysia in the fifth century, and nothing certain can be concluded.

Agamemnon and Cassandra coming to Clytemnestra in Aeschylus's *Agamemnon,* and Iphigenia destined for death in Euripides much as Cassandra is in *Agamemnon.* The sequence as we have it exploits the activity of women welcoming and helping with the arrival, in contrast to the solemnity of the welcome afforded to Agamemnon by the *choros* of old men in the *Oresteia.* Agamemnon appears from the *skene* with concealed intent and in confusion in Euripides, which contrasts strongly with the resolve of Clytemnestra in Aeschylus, but no attempt is made to exploit the stepping down and progress on cloths from the vehicle into the *skene* that is essential to the scene in *Agamemnon.*

Euripides' *Electra* also contains a scene in which Clytemnestra arrives in a carriage, in this instance in answer to a summons from her daughter Electra, who is married to a farmer. The *skene* represents this farmer's house, and much is said that would characterize it in strong contrast to a palace. Clytemnestra has been lured to what will be her death by the false news of the birth of a child to Electra, and the allusion to the arrival of Agamemnon and Cassandra in *Agamemnon* is understandably attractive in a tragedy that transforms some part of the action of the *Oresteia.* The corpse of Aegisthus, killed by Orestes and Pylades while at sacrifice in the fields, has been carried into the *skene* by slaves of Electra or her husband (959–61). Some movement in the distance is noticed by Electra and identified by Orestes as the arrival of his mother (963–64). This approach is described by Electra as proud, since Clytemnestra is coming in a carriage and "dressed up" (966), which probably refers to her costume rather than to the grandeur of an escort. As Orestes and Pylades enter the *skene,* the *choros* chants a welcome for Clytemnestra, revering her like the goddesses for her wealth and great good fortune (994–95). Electra has apparently waited for her outside the *skene.*

On her arrival in the playing space, Clytemnestra addresses herself neither to Electra nor to the *choros* but to her attendant Trojan women slaves, who are with her in the carriage, in a telling recall of the arrival of Cassandra with Agamemnon. They are to step down and to lend a hand to help her do so (998–99).[126] She then adds an explanation, addressed explicitly to no one in particular, that most of the spoil from Troy was dedicated to the gods in their temples but that she kept these slaves, "the pick of the Trojan land" (1001–2), as an ornament for her palace, small compensation for the child she lost (1002–3). This disingenuous explanation might appear to be, if

126. There is no particular reason why we should (lavishly) imagine that they step down from their own carriage, and then help Clytemnestra down from hers: see Rehm (2002, 189, with 369n94 and references).

anything, an acknowledgment of the presence of the *choros,* but it also expresses part of the conflict between Clytemnestra and her daughter. Electra offers herself as a helping hand in response, because she is, as she says, after all a slave ejected from the palace to live in a less fortunate house (1004–6); but Clytemnestra rejects her help, insisting that her own Trojan slaves will do (1007). After an exchange, Clytemnestra agrees to enter the house and instructs her male attendants to take the carriage to the mangers and to return when they think the sacrificial rites are at an end, in order to proceed to meet Aegisthus in the fields (1135–38). Electra pointedly warns her mother to mind that the grimy house does not soil her clothing (1139–40). The *choros* is not explicitly addressed or acknowledged throughout the scene.

If this is one carriage, and the Trojan women slaves travel in it rather than walk alongside, the number of Trojan women is unlikely to be large, and there are plainly men driving or leading the horses. Clytemnestra must be finely costumed, and her eventual entry into the *skene* is the most important allusion to the scene in *Agamemnon.* Euripides is conscious of the wealth that adds substance to the scene in *Agamemnon* and here deploys it in the contrast between the clothing of Clytemnestra and the palace from which she has come and the state of Electra and the *skene* that is her home, a contrast on which Electra has dwelt bitterly earlier in the tragedy (300 ff.). The instruction to (re)move the carriage that comes at the end of the scene is a minor indication that it may not have been moved much before this point, and it is used by Euripides to make the entry of Clytemnestra into the *skene* more marked and final (fig. 16).

This seemingly contrasts with the purpose in creating bustling activity around the carriage in *Iphigenia at Aulis* (607 ff.), where the excitement of the women of the *choros* and their involvement is a careful prelude to the appearance of Agamemnon from the *skene.* Electra must come to the side or rear of the carriage, alongside the Trojan slaves who have descended from it, for the scene to have its full effect. We cannot tell where the *choros* is positioned, although it must withdraw sufficiently, during or after the greeting it offers, for the carriage to occupy a prominent and suitable place in the *orchestra.* We can hardly doubt, in any of these instances, the use of live animals, and it must be the case that what is prescribed in *Iphigenia at Aulis* (619–20) regularly happened, namely, that someone stood at the head of the animals once they had come to rest. It is, of course, the back or the side of the carriage, from which the figures descend, that must be presented to the audience.

Euripides' *Electra* is of unknown date, although it must obviously precede his *Iphigenia at Aulis.* His *Trojan Women* was produced in 415 BCE, and it con-

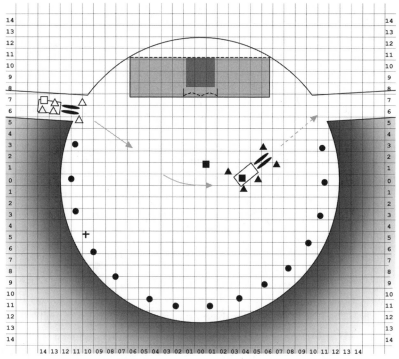

FIGURE 16 Euripides' *Electra* 1004–5. Clytemnestra has arrived in her carriage, attended by Trojan women slaves, and Electra has offered to help her mother descend from it. In the dialogue between them, Electra stands at some distance from the carriage and her mother.

tains another of these scenes, one in which Andromache, wife of the dead Hector, is brought into the playing space with their young son Astyanax. If the vehicle is in this case a war chariot, then the setting—which is the Greek encampment at a now captured Troy—would seem to make that appropriate. But the language used of it once again includes the term *apene,* which features in the other scenes from Euripides discussed above and is usually understood to mean a wagon or a carriage rather than a chariot.[127] In this se-

127. Halleran (1985, 97) is no more inconsistent than many when he writes confidently of a wagon in this scene from *Trojan Women* in contrast to the chariot that he would see for Aeschylus's *Persians* and *Agamemnon* and Euripides' *Electra.* Lee (1976, 174) is certain that Andromache rides in a "wagon": "Her conveyance is not a royal chariot, but a humble cart that she shares, chattel that she is, with the rest of the booty belonging to the son of Achilles." Lee also contrasts this scene with that in *Agamemnon.*

quence the armor of Hector is also piled on the vehicle, among other spoils from Troy (573–74). Our preference here may depend on what we conclude about the vehicle in Aeschylus's *Agamemnon,* which is also termed an *apene.*

Those who conclude in favor of the symbolic value of a chariot in that sequence may find attractive reasons for thinking of a chariot here, too. Since Andromache is now the slave of Neoptolemos, the son of Achilles, the climax of Homer's epic *Iliad* in which Achilles drags the body of Hector behind his chariot around the walls of Troy, a scene that Andromache had witnessed in the epic, would be called to mind. Similarly, Andromache would be, after Cassandra in *Agamemnon,* an image of another Trojan woman enslaved by a war leader and conqueror, and this interpretation might gain support from the fact that in the previous scene in *Trojan Women* Cassandra has been the center of attention. But practicability should make us pause, since in the sequences from Euripides the limited capacity and relative instability of a chariot make its use implausible.

The arrival of the vehicle in the playing space is recognized by the *choros,* in a chant that alerts Hecuba and emphasizes that Andromache is being transported in it to an unknown destination, although the *choros* knows that the spoils will be dedicated by Neoptolemos in Phthia, his homeland in Greece (568–76). In the other scenes at which we have looked, climbing down from the carriage is carefully scripted. Interestingly, there is no indication in the script of that event here, and it seems likely that the inevitable passage of Andromache out of the playing space and away to slavery is a strong component of this scene. Nor is there, here, any reference at all to the *skene,* which is a tent belonging to Agamemnon (138–39), and housing those enslaved Trojan women who have yet to be allocated to a master (32–33). The vehicle is, so to speak, halted in its passage through the playing space, presumably arriving from one *eisodos* and departing along the other.

Yet the actors/characters of Hecuba and Andromache sing closely together (577–607), and we should expect a dance from them both, which would be impossible with Andromache in the vehicle.[128] After this song, Andromache displays her state to Hecuba (610–11) and describes herself as "carried away as plunder with my child" (614). Later she refers to her previous descent from the vehicle to cover the corpse of Polyxena and to mourn her death by beating her breast (626–27), an event of which we hear but do not see. Her child, Astyanax, is also taken from her by Talthybius. Before that

128. The character of Andromache is played by the actor who sang and danced the role of Cassandra.

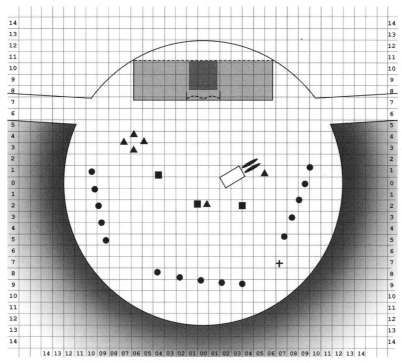

81

FIGURE 17 Euripides' *Trojan Women* 750–65. The Greek herald Talthybius has returned to demand that Andromache's son Astyanax is handed over to be killed, and Andromache clasps her son to her. Hecuba stands nearby, in silent grief and despair.

moment Andromache describes the child as clutching her and her clothes and nestling up to her (750–51), and she embraces him (756 ff.), bitterly inviting the Greeks with Talthybius to take Astyanax from her (774–75). Her final words are that she is coming to her wedding, and the concluding chant of the scene is shared between Talthybius and Hecuba (782–98), with Talthybius ordering Astyanax to be taken to his death (786) and Hecuba concluding that she cannot prevent what is happening but can only lament (figs. 17, 18).

Perhaps the most plausible interpretation of this extraordinarily powerful scene is that Andromache descends from the vehicle to sing and dance with her mother and that her child comes down from it afterward. This would repeat the descent to which she alludes when she dressed and mourned the corpse of Polyxena. She wonders whether the boy understands what is fac-

82

FIGURE 18 Scene from Euripides' *Trojan Women* 750–65.

ing him (749), and he might well come down from the carriage after the announcement made by Talthybius (709 ff.) or be taken by Andromache to
herself from the vehicle (740). Since she is compelled to accept what has
been determined for her and for her child, after she has relinquished him she
may climb back once again into the vehicle, to be drawn from the playing
space with the spoils and the armor, while her son is taken away, perhaps
down the opposite *eisodos,* to the chant of Talthybius and Hecuba.[129]

This interpretation would allow the actor of Andromache to perform
without restriction, which is surely necessary, while the lack of reference to
a descent can be explained by the lack of its ultimate significance: it is, bru-
tally, no more than a moment in her passing on to slavery, deprived of all she
ever had. The performance, not just of the song and dance, but of the whole
scene will take place on the side of the vehicle away from the *skene,* and
Talthybius will come to the actors/characters of Andromache and Hecuba in
the playing space. The *choros* is undoubtedly of considerable significance in
this tragedy; but in this scene we encounter composition for the playing

129. Halleran (1985) considers some of these issues about the closing of the scene but remains undecided; he does not discuss the substance of the scene, between its opening and
its ending (97–98).

space that is completely reliant on the actors/characters, the mute extra playing the boy Astyanax, and on the avowedly symbolic material presence of the trappings of war, defense, and conquest, without reference to a *skene* from which no one appears and which no one expects to enter.[130]

THREE KINDS OF VOCAL DELIVERY IN TRAGEDY

My final selection of material from the tragic scripts after Aeschylus will, once again, be related to the problem of the playing space, but it will also necessitate some brief considerations of other important issues in tragic performance at Athens. The selection is of sequences in the tragedies in which actors/characters are involved in coordinated movement and singing and dancing with the *choros* for the relatively simple reason that we know that the *choros* sings and dances in the open ground of the *orchestra*. Apart from its arrival in the playing space, which is regularly along an *eisodos* but which may be exceptionally from the *skene*, we may expect the *choros* to sing and dance in the *orchestra*, and we may be confident that the tragic *choros*, like the other theatrical *choroi*, comic and satiric, does both. All our accumulated evidence points to that conclusion, and it is worth noting that in early usage the word *choros* might refer to a dancing place rather than the dancers (see the early sections following here in chap. 2). This is also the meaning of the word "*orchestra*." But an apparently convenient division made by scholars between actors/characters who speak and a *choros* that sings and dances is a misapprehension that needs to be discarded. Before I discuss some of the more interesting and revealing passages from the scripts in relation to the playing space, I should offer some commentary on the scripts as indicators of kinds of performance.

So far in this chapter I have referred without question to three kinds of vocal delivery in tragedy, writing of speaking, of chant, and of singing (with dancing). There is nothing inherently misleading about this, but some further examination may well be useful. The tragic scripts are composed throughout in verse; there is no prose in them at all. The verse is of different kinds, and it is possible to assign certain characteristics to these different kinds of verse. So, for example, what I and others would term the "speaking" verse is

130. Kaimio (1988, 45–46) believes that the vehicle is a cart and concentrates exclusively on the physical contact between Andromache and her child, suggesting accordingly that "the long clinging together is interrupted by the sudden handing over of Eurysaces from the cart to the hands of Talthybius." (Note that Eurysaces here should be Astyanax; Eurysaces is the child of Ajax.)

largely assigned to the actors/characters, although the *choros* may make some small contribution to spoken exchanges. What is composed is a sequence of lines in the same verse pattern (meter, or measure), thus permitting the development of an argument or a "speech" by a character or an exchange between characters. For song, either by the *choros* or by actors/characters, a greater variety of verse patterns is used, and a curious form of dialect is present, notably in some vowels, further distinguishing the language from tragic speech.[131] The general term for verse that is sung is "lyric," which also applies to song outside tragedy, and is rather misleading in relation to tragedy, because the lyre did not accompany theatrical performances. The accompanying instrument was the *aulos,* a kind of pipe, on which I comment as I do on song and other matters affecting the *choros* in chapter 2. The third category, "chant," is a repeated verse line, as in the case of the meter or measure for speaking, but one of a different kind from that used in speaking. The speaking verse is known as "iambic" and the "chanting" verse is known as "anapestic," or more often directly as "anapests."[132]

It may be helpful to understand a Greek tragic script as a vocal rather than just a semantic script, a composition directing a variety of implementations of the capacities of the human voice. We should also acknowledge that even in the case of "speaking" we may be dealing with a phenomenon that is hidden from us. A repeated verse line that is to some extent discursive, which permits explanation, argument, and description, may be delivered in all kinds of ways, and we should refrain from assuming that such parts of tragedy sounded "natural" or used the voice simply in modes adopted from the everyday. But we may be relatively sure that the speaking verse was not usually accompanied by an instrument and that the use of the voice for this speaking verse was distinct from its use for chanting and for song.[133]

The sections of the scripts in anapests prompt different reflections. The starting point for most conclusions about this kind of verse in tragedy is the observation that the *choros* may arrive in the playing space with anapests composed for it, and this has given rise to the term "marching anapests." The

131. This is generally known as Doric or Dorian because it more closely resembles the dialects spoken by one of the broad ethnic groupings in ancient Greece. But it is, as it seems, an artificial creation, which became associated with song and so was used even in the composition of dramatic songs by Athenian composers.

132. Rehm (1992) offers some comparable comments on this general subject in his fifth chapter, 43–74.

133. Some passages of spoken verse were in a longer verse line, closely related to the iambic, and are known as trochaic tetrameters. These occur occasionally, and whether or not they were accompanied cannot be certain. On the question of how they were performed, see the subsequent note.

logic here is that if this kind of repeated verse line is different from the songs composed for the *choros,* and also distinct from the spoken verse, then it may or must represent a distinctive form of delivery.[134] In truth, the evidence we have for the performance of anapests is tenuous in the extreme, but their distinctive quality in comparison to the verse designed for speaking or for song has to be accepted, and the hypothesis that they were "chanted" in some fashion, accompanied by the *aulos,* and associated with movement is one that seems to satisfy their "situation" in the scripts. Anapests are also used by actors/characters and may mark a passage into song. Translations are often unconcerned to differentiate clearly between the different kinds of verse and delivery, and this is particularly true of the distinction between anapests and the verse of song.

MOVEMENT AND DANCING IN THE PLAYING SPACE

The close association of anapests with movement provides an obvious starting point. It is undoubtedly convenient to think of the movement implied by anapests as being motion in a direction (hence "marching") rather than dancing, and this may be correct. The arrival of a *choros* to anapests might justify this assumption, as it proceeds along an *eisodos* into the *orchestra.* But not all tragic *choroi* arrive in the playing space to a script composed in anapests; in many cases, their opening script is for song and dance. Commentators ask the reasonable question whether such *choroi* arrived and then sang and danced, or sang and danced as they approached, and there is no available answer to that.[135] Again, the length of compositions in anapests for the arrival of a *choros* varies considerably. So a simple approach to their function in relation to movement into the playing space is just not possible. But granted their use by the *choros,* and the clear distinction from the brief, spoken interjections by *choroi,* their association with movement of some kind seems highly plausible, and this should surely be a kind of movement that is not dancing. This may also remain the hypothesis for anapests composed for actors/characters, and it does seem the best general explanation of the phenomenon and of the purpose and intentions of composition.

134. Some few incidental references in ancient sources suggest that there was a form of delivery that was intoned, and the term "recitative" is often used in relation to it, although it must be acknowledged that none of these indications refers to anapests. A detailed account is given by Pickard-Cambridge (1988, 156 ff.), who unfortunately quotes passages in Greek without translation. Hall (1999, 102 ff.) discusses the unaccompanied and accompanied voice, including the recitation of anapests, providing a more accessible alternative.
135. Taplin (1977b, 64–65) summarizes these problems conveniently.

But even this hypothesis is subject to qualification, if not contradiction. Movement is not always easy to demonstrate from a bare script, and it may be much easier to demonstrate its lack. In Sophocles' *Women of Trachis* Heracles is carried into the playing space because he is racked by the pain inflicted by a poisoned garment. The actor/character who leads this dismal procession participates in a script composed in anapests, as does Heracles himself, but Heracles is carried and cannot himself move (974–1003). An even more striking example comes from *Prometheus Bound,* a tragedy that is probably not by Aeschylus, and that I excluded from the consideration of his work, but that probably does date from the fifth century. In the opening of the play Prometheus is pinned to a rock by the speaking character Power and the silent Violence under the supervision of the god Hephaestus. Once they have left, Prometheus mixes speech with anapests (88–127) and continues to respond in anapests to the arrival of the *choros* (128–92). Self-evidently, the actor/character of Prometheus cannot move. Why then were anapests used in the composition of these sequences?

If we wish to be straightforward in our explanation, we might comment that since the procession is moving in *Women of Trachis* then the composition for Heracles simply accompanies that movement. A related explanation for Prometheus would be that the composition for him in anapests is intended to be an anticipation and then accompaniment of the arrival of the *choros,* which will be moving into the playing space and dancing. But tragic composition may be more sophisticated than that. If the sound and delivery of anapests imply movement, to compose them for an actor/character who has been violently placed in a position in which he cannot move may be an impressive, performative effect. What the verse implies is the very thing the actor/character cannot do himself; the verse form itself points to the (in)action of the tragedy. If this is correct, then the exceptions would prove the rule about anapests and directional movement, which would need to be advanced as a general principle for any *choros* and for any actors/characters for whom they are composed.

The situation is a little more complicated even than that, because some anapests composed in a similar way make use of the dialect associated with singing, and the manuscripts that carry the scripts almost inevitably can become confused, as A. M. Dale has observed in a very helpful section of her study of the meters of tragic song.[136] Song for actors/characters plays a sig-

136. Dale (1968, 50 ff.). Even if some of the technical references to meter in that account may elude readers, the general situation may be clear.

nificant part in the composition of tragedy. But for the purposes of the inquiry in this chapter it is movement rather than singing that is important, and we should like to be as certain that dancing accompanied singing for actors/characters as we are that it did so for the *choros*.[137] As with so much of vital significance to our understanding of tragic performance in the fifth century, there are no direct and contemporary testimonials on this aspect, although few commentators would be inclined to doubt the presence of dancing altogether.

Anecdotal comments from late antiquity strongly suggest that the early tragedians were specialists in dancing, and scholars are confident that these earlier tragedians (including Aeschylus and Sophocles earlier in his life) were performers in their own compositions.[138] But we may also be helped in this respect by a passage from a comedy by Aristophanes, *Wasps* of 422 BCE, in which an actor/character conceives a drunken mania for tragic dancing and comes out of the *skene* to engage in a contest with some tragic, solo dancers. Taking "evidence" from comedy about any "reality" is a hazardous and often deeply misconceived activity, but it would be hard not to conclude from this that dancing by individual actors/characters was a part of tragic performance.[139] The question that then arises is whether actors/characters are always dancing when they are singing. Once again, the verse patterns of the script can inform us about the singing, but they do not provide us with indications of (danced) movement. Yet, if dancing was an accomplishment for the tragic performer, is it not likely that a script composed for singing was also composed for dancing, as we know it to have been in the case of the *choros*?[140]

Curiously, it is once again the exceptions that may prove the rule. Perhaps the most absolute of these comes from indications in another comedy of

137. Dancing unfortunately features very little in Hall's studies of actor's song (1999, 2002), but the few examples for which she does allow do not seem to be exceptional (2002, 28).

138. See, for example, Csapo and Slater (1994), sec. 4, no. 3b, 225, and nos. 303 and 304, 359–60.

139. The sequence concludes the comedy *Wasps*, at 1474 ff. It is, however, just possible that the dancers here are individuals presenting what they might dance in a *choros*. In a story about some bizarre solo dancing at an aristocratic wedding in the sixth century BCE, which he interprets in terms probably familiar from tragedy to his fifth-century audience and readership, the historian Herodotus also seems to envisage individuals dancing. I present and discuss this passage in chap. 2 in some detail in the section on dancing.

140. Wiles (1997) seems to assume that actors danced as well as sang *before* the arrival of the *choros* and wonders whether the *choros* danced *while* actors sang (and danced?). But he does not argue the case for actors dancing (104–5).

Aristophanes, *Women at the Thesmophoria,* dated to 411 BCE, in which a tragedy of Euripides is parodied. This is the lost tragedy *Andromeda,* and what is evidently parodied by Aristophanes (at 1008 ff.) is a song by the actor/character Andromeda. With all the reservations that one might apply to "evidence" drawn from Aristophanes, it is clear that the model for this must have been a solo song by Andromeda, who has been fastened to a rock on the seashore, from which she will be rescued by Perseus. In this case, Andromeda must have sung but not danced, but we might note the parallel with what was observed of anapests above. There is a considerable purpose in composing a song for a character who is constrained from the (danced) movement normally associated with song, and restraint and constraint become interesting in this respect, for the use of anapests or of song.

Similar questions might be asked of other actors/characters in surviving tragedy. Heracles sings of his agony and misery in *Women of Trachis* (1004–42), immediately after he is brought into the playing space, although he speaks for the rest of the tragedy until he is finally carried out of the playing space. Characters who are physically disabled raise further questions. In Sophocles' *Philoctetes,* Philoctetes is severely disabled by a poisonous wound to his foot, which impedes his progress and mobility even when it is not causing him exhausting agony. Yet the actor/character of Philoctetes sings alongside of and to the *choros* in an extended sequence in the tragedy (1081–1217): does he also dance? There may be no good reason to assume that the actor/character does not, and those portrayed as old and frail certainly do dance, since *choroi* in such characterizations are an established part of tragedy. Assumptions reliant on any concept of "the natural" are of no value here, and the separation of actor from character is most important.[141] The portrayal of the old and infirm, as well as the tormented or despairing, by singing and dancing is an accomplishment in tragedy.

But there are other problems, which may present themselves to us because we misread the script in a rational manner or simply cannot interpret the activity in the playing space confidently from the available indications. I

141. Comparative thoughts may be useful here, as a guard against assumptions. Greek tragedy may have been similar in this respect to the Japanese *noh,* in which the portrayal of the old in dancing and song was a major accomplishment. The treatises of the major composer and performer Zeami Motokiyo are concerned with the skills involved (Rimer and Masakazu, 1984; Ley, 2000). In concentrating on Aeschylus's *Persians* in an extended structural and stylistic comparison with a *noh* composition by Zeami, Smethurst (1989) does not address this topic directly, although she is highly conscious of the importance of dancing to both forms.

have suggested above that Andromache may descend from the chariot in *Women of Troy* to dance as well as sing, but there is nothing that can firmly prove this. In Sophocles' *Oedipus at Colonus* there is a similar problem about the stance of the actor/character. Toward the end of the relocation of Oedipus away from the grove, Oedipus asks if he can sit down and is directed, it seems, to a place where this is permissible by the *choros*. We might ask when does he sit down in this sequence, and does he remain seated in later parts of the tragedy when he is singing?[142]

Again, in Sophocles' *Electra,* Electra states her intention to "let myself sink down by this door and waste away my life, without a friend" (818–19). But what immediately follows is an extended sung exchange between her and the *choros* (823–70), in which we should expect the *choros* at least to be dancing. Would we be guilty of too literal an interpretation of her words as a "stage direction" if we thought that she sang, collapsed, by the *skene* doors? Might we alternatively see this as an expression of what she sees in store for herself, now that she believes that Orestes is dead and all hope of revenge and restoration extinguished, and that she is drawn away from adopting this posture into song and dance (by and) with the *choros*? There is no later reference to Electra lying down collapsed, or to her standing up, when her sister arrives with remarkable news and eventually provokes Electra to plot the active course of revenge.

In Euripides' *Alcestis* the issues of stance and of debility are combined when Alcestis appears from the *skene* with Admetus, presumably supported by him, in accordance with what the *choros* has heard from the woman Slave (136–212). Alcestis is dying, but the *choros* sees her "coming from the house" initially with Admetus (232–33), and she then sings while Admetus speaks and chants. At the end of her singing Alcestis asks to be let down, "lie me down, my feet have no strength" (267); but would we be justified in believing that the actor/character has not been dancing as well as singing?

There are two similar scenes in Euripides' *Hippolytus.* In the first, the old Nurse appears in front of the *skene* doors bringing Phaidra out of the palace (170–71), and in her chant the Nurse refers to the sickbed that has been brought outside (179–80). Phaidra herself may be singing or chanting, in response to the Nurse's chanting, and she asks her attendant women to sup-

---

142. Arnott (1989) draws attention to this passage in observing how rarely actors/characters sit down, or sit down for long, in the surviving tragedies. Our counterbalance to this shrewd observation is the accusation from the character of Euripides in Aristophanes' *Frogs,* who mocks Aeschylus (905–6) for keeping leading actors/characters such as Niobe and Achilles (in tragedies now lost) seated and silent for much of the play.

port her head and her arms (218–22).[143] But there are no indications that she lies down on her bed, either in this sequence or in the spoken exchange with the Nurse that follows, in which the Nurse grasps Phaidra's knees in supplication (326) and after which Phaidra addresses the *choros*.[144] Toward the close of the tragedy the fatally injured Hippolytus is brought into the playing space, supported by men slaves, whom he instructs in his chant to take extreme care (1358–59), and he dies only at the end of the play, apparently in his father's arms. It may be that when he asks his followers to "let go" of him (1372) that he collapses, but he has started to sing at this point (1370–88), so we should not necessarily assume a "natural" and gradual disintegration. He is clearly lying down toward the close of the tragedy, as darkness descends on his eyes, but his chanted approach at the beginning of the sequence confirms the announcement by the *choros* (1342) that he is making his way into the playing space rather than being carried.[145]

My feeling about these problems is that composition is purposeful both in relation to chanting and movement and to singing and dancing. Solo dancing, like group dancing, would be a considerable skill, and an enhancement of the performance of a tragedy. We are more likely, I would contend, to be correct if we adopt a constructive rather than a restrictive view of dancing by actors/characters, one that understands a composer to compose in order to create appropriate opportunities for this kind of performance and to

143. Bain (1981, 21–22) regards the instructions as typical of those that are not carried out by servants, against his assertion of a general rule that such instructions are executed; but he believes that Phaidra is "carried on to the stage on a litter" (23n3). Taplin (1978) tries to reconcile an assumption that Phaidra is brought on "lying on a bed" with his sense that "somehow she rises and expresses in an anapestic chant her longing to be elsewhere" (135). Kaimio (1988) has Phaidra "carried out in her bed by attendants in the care of the Nurse," and "lying prostrate on her bed," but believes that Phaidra must then "struggle to a sitting position or at least raise her head" (19).

144. Barrett (1964, 194–95) has Phaidra carried out on her sickbed, back onto which she collapses after being raised up (210). He would also see her still lying down as the Nurse clasps her knees, since Phaidra "has presumably left her bed" (227) only after the song from the *choros* at 362–72. Halleran (1985) remains uncertain about the appearances from the *skene* of Alcestis and of Phaidra, although he inclines without explanation to believing that Phaidra was carried in and Alcestis was not (28n30). But he is interested in "the processional quality of the entrances" rather than in questions concerning the singing and associated movement or dancing.

145. Halleran, following Barrett, believes that Hippolytus is "supported by his companions" (1985, 15). Taplin has Hippolytus "supported by his followers" for the "chanted anapests" of his arrival and lying down for his subsequent song (1978, 135–36). Kaimio (1988, 18) follows Barrett in a reading that has Hippolytus asking his father to take hold of him and to lay him down (1445), with the sequence leading, through the guidance of the goddess Artemis (1431–32), to this physical contact between father and son.

have a distinctive purpose when he constrains the actor/character from either movement or dancing.[146] We should expect movement in connection
with anapests or chanting, and dancing in connection with song by actors/
characters, while allowing any firm indications from the script to control or
adjust our understanding of a given sequence.

It must also be important, as I hope some of the examples above demonstrate, to exercise considerable care in interpreting such indications, not seeing a blanket cancellation of movement in every suggestion of collapse or
rest apparent in the script. Above all, we should not presuppose that infir-
mity, indisposition, trauma, or old age preclude the composition of song and
dancing for actors/characters in tragedy.[147] Movement and dancing are no
more or less "inappropriate" than chanting or singing, since all these states
are representations achieved in performance. To conclude against movement and dancing would be to insist on the verbal apart from the physical
without good reason and, perhaps, to contradict the express purposes of
composition for tragic performance by *choros* and actors.

ACTORS/CHARACTERS AND *CHOROS:* CHANTING, SINGING, AND DANCING IN THE PLAYING SPACE

I turn now to sequences in the tragedies after Aeschylus that involve both
choros and actors/characters in the playing space, starting with sequences
from Sophocles, but not taking them in chronological order or trying to classify them by any formal criterion.

An involvement of actors/characters and *choros* in the playing space that
includes singing and/or chanting is apparent in the earliest surviving tragedies and continues in the *Oresteia.* Exchanges in which an actor/character
speaks while the *choros* sings and dances (Eteocles and the *choros* in *Seven against
Thebes* 207 ff., Pelasgus and the *choros* in *Suppliants* 348 ff.) are accompanied in

---

146. The theatrical commentaries in the series edited by Ewans regularly assume that ac-
tors/characters danced. It would seem that Arnott (1989, 56–57) believes that the actor
also danced, while Rehm (1992) intermittently assumes dancing for an actor/character
(57 of Ion, and 86 of Cassandra in *Agamemnon*). Kaimio (1988, 64) mentions Polymestor's
"frenzied song and dance" in Euripides' *Hecuba.*

147. This, inexplicably, seems to be the view of Gardiner (1987) in her book on the *choros*
in Sophocles: "But no matter how common dancing may be in a culture, there are numerous occasions which are hardly suitable for dancing. The old would seldom dance except
for religious reasons" (7). There is no indication here that Gardiner is distinguishing between theatrical and nontheatrical dancing, since she is doubtful whether dancing existed
without exception in all tragic choral songs.

the earlier tragedies by a sequence involving both chanting and singing with Xerxes and the *choros* in the conclusion of *Persians*.[148] In *Agamemnon,* the sequence with the *choros* and Cassandra starts with the *choros* speaking and Cassandra singing and dancing, and proceeds to share the singing and dancing between actor/character and *choros*.[149] Later in the tragedy the *choros* sings and dances as Clytemnestra speaks, and the sequence continues with song and dance from the *choros* embracing chant from Clytemnestra. In the conclusion to *Eumenides* a similar pattern is found, between the actor/character of Athena and the *choros,* while in *Libation Bearers* in the remarkable sequence at the grave of Agamemnon the *choros* begins by chanting, and continues to do so, but also joins in singing and dancing with both Orestes and Electra.[150] So the involvement of actors/characters and *choros* in sequences of this kind in tragedies after Aeschylus represents a continuity, as does the variety of those sequences, which is already apparent from their composition by Aeschylus.

Throughout the action of Sophocles' *Antigone* the character of Creon has been associated with spoken verse, with the exception of one moment where he switches to chanting and insists that Antigone must proceed from the playing space to her death (931–32, 935–36). But at the close of the tragedy Creon returns to the playing space carrying the body of his son, Haemon, and his personal trauma leads him to sing in self-accusation. The *choros* chants as he returns (1257–60) and prompts the continuation of his song with a spoken line (1270). Whether Creon continues to hold the body of Haemon while he sings we cannot tell. The Messenger who appears from the *skene* at the close of the first part of Creon's song contrasts what Creon is carrying with what he shall soon see, which is the body of his wife, Eurydice (1277–80). Toward the close of the second part of his song, Creon sings that he was holding the body of his son "in my arms just now" (1298). Our own sense of pathos may dictate that we see the references to his arms as literal. But we

148. Ewans (1996, 183–85) considers dancing as well as song in his discussion of the close of *Persians.*
149. Ewans (1995, 149–50) and Rehm (1992, 86–88) offer suggestions about the nature of Cassandra's dancing.
150. Ewans, in discussing this extraordinary sequence, does not appear to envisage dancing from Orestes or Electra (1995, 171–73) but, instead, "movements and gestures" (173). Yet the only suggestion of a static posture comes in the spoken section after the song, when Electra refers to "these fledglings seated at your tomb" (501), and this might describe a symbolic rather than a precisely physical state: it is language that signifies supplication, as it does in *Eumenides,* when Orestes describes his supplication of the image of Athena (409). I cannot see any good reasons for discounting dancing as well as singing from the actors/characters here.

should not completely dismiss the possibility that the body of his son may be carried by others, nor the possibility that he has laid the body down before he starts singing.[151] With either of these latter possibilities, the actor/character of Creon would be free to dance as well as sing, whereas even just singing while holding or carrying a body might be thought to be a most difficult performance for an actor at the close of a long and demanding role.[152]

A similarly awkward question arises over the display of the dead body of Eurydice from the *skene*. At 1293 the *choros* states that Eurydice's body is now visible, and commentators are inevitably divided over whether the *ekkuklema* is used to display the corpse or whether the body is carried on. But what is clear is that Creon sings of the one body (of his son) that is near to him and the other body (of Eurydice) that he can now see (1295–1300), and this confirms the Messenger's harsh announcement earlier (1277–80).[153] Creon's ecstasy of grief continues in song, and there is no reason why we should not believe it to have continued in dancing as well, and he insists that he himself must be taken away. To these third and fourth parts of his song (1306–27, and 1328–46), first the Messenger and then the *choros* contribute with spoken lines, the Messenger describing Eurydice's death and the *choros* counseling Creon. Throughout the sequence, Creon is closely associated with the *choros* in the playing space, to which he brings the body of his son, and he is additionally confronted by appearances from the *skene,* which provoke a continuation of his song and, as I would propose, his dancing.

This relationship with the *choros* in a traumatic conclusion to the tragedy is even more marked toward the close of Sophocles' *Oedipus the King,* when Oedipus forces his way out of the *skene* doors toward the *choros* and away from everything that the *skene* holds at this moment. The Messenger who has come from the *skene* to report Oedipus's self-blinding and the murder of Jocasta to the *choros* has warned that Oedipus is calling for the doors to be opened (1287–88), and the *choros* chants in horror as Oedipus appears and comes toward it (1297–1306), appalled at the sight of him. The initial anapests composed for the actor/character of Oedipus on his appearance

---

151. Seale simply considers both possibilities (1982, 105), while Gardiner does not consider how the sequence is conducted in the playing space (1987, 96–97).

152. Singing and dancing at the same time might be thought in modern terms to be taxing; yet it is what the members of the *choroi* were trained to do, and the actors were more experienced. But lifting a body weight at the same time might be thought to be asking rather too much even of an experienced and committed performer.

153. Seale is impressively aware of this contrast, and its implications for what he calls "the scenic arrangement" (1982, 106).

(1308–12) are in the dialect form that is associated with song. After a spoken line from the *choros*, Oedipus sings, and if we accept the existence of solo dancing in tragedy it would be perverse not to see this sequence as a composition for song and dance.

In that case, we would have the chanted anapests of the *choros* for the initial appearance and progress of Oedipus from the *skene*, Oedipus's sung anapests as a transition into song from chant, and then the song and dance of the actor/character of Oedipus.[154] The first two parts of his song are relatively short, and in the second part Oedipus addresses the *choros* as his friend, his only remaining attendant, caring for him in his blindness by not turning away from him (1321–23). But in the third and fourth parts of his song, the *choros* gradually determines that it would have been better for Oedipus to die than to live and be blinded. The contribution of the *choros* to the song is brief and may include speech. At the close of the song, Oedipus addresses the *choros* and, finally, appeals to it to touch him (1413), before Creon returns to the playing space, into which Oedipus's young daughters are eventually brought for him to touch them.

Sophocles' *Oedipus at Colonus* presents an interesting series of sequences involving actors/characters and the *choros*, and the first of these I have already introduced, as Oedipus is drawn away from the grove with the support of Antigone to a position in the playing space. This sequence opens with singing and dancing from the *choros* as it arrives searching for the transgressor (118–37) and continues with chant from Oedipus and the *choros*, as Oedipus reappears from the grove (138–49). The second part of the danced song from the *choros* follows, as the *choros* expresses its horror at the contrast between the sight of the transgressor and the sanctity of the grove, urging Oedipus to move away. The actors/characters of Oedipus and Antigone then chant as they prepare to move (170–75), and both actors/characters and the *choros* sing and dance together as Oedipus and Antigone respond to the demands of the *choros* (176–87). Oedipus briefly chants his respect for these pious wishes (188–91), and in the second part of the shared song and

---

154. Rehm passes relatively quickly over the reappearance of the actor/character of Oedipus and his song (1992, 119), and Seale, after mentioning that Oedipus "stumbles on" (1982, 248) does not discuss the song or the playing space. In contrast, Taplin (1978) considers that Oedipus may be brought forward on the *ekkuklema*, "fallen, polluted, blind, bloody" (110), although later he writes that Oedipus "once more stands in the palace doorway" (131); he does not discuss the song or the playing space. McCart takes account of song, movement, and the playing space in his workshop commentary (in Ewans 1999, 298–99).

dance he and Antigone finally reach the place where he hopes he may rest (192–206). In the concluding parts of the sequence, Oedipus and the *choros* join in song (208–36), and we should expect the *choros* to be dancing. The song is the forced declaration of the identity of Oedipus, which is traumatic for Oedipus and hardly less horrific for the *choros*, which returns to insisting that Oedipus leave the sanctuary and the country. We might conclude that Oedipus has not sat down but that his dance as well as his song expresses his agitation in rising conjunction with that of the *choros*. In the final part of the sequence, the actor/character of Antigone sings in an attempt to placate the *choros*, entreating its members with her eyes that see, looking at them eye to eye (237–54). It is an appeal to the *choros* in the playing space for which dancing would be most appropriate in addition to her song.[155]

If the actor/character of Oedipus is indeed seated by the close of this sequence for the spoken exchange with the *choros* that follows, he must surely rise to be embraced by Ismene on her arrival in the playing space (324–25, and 329 in particular). Oedipus renews his address to the *choros* at 457, and after his exchange with the *choros* and its instructions to him, his daughter Ismene leaves to make offerings to the Eumenides. Oedipus declares that he has not the strength to walk on his own and without someone to support him, and this encourages Ismene to tell Antigone to stay with their father (500–501). In the sequence that follows, the *choros* sings with Oedipus (510–48), relentlessly pursuing its curiosity despite the misery to which it subjects him, and this provokes the question of whether Oedipus also dances with the *choros*, or sings, perhaps sitting.[156]

Once again, the sequence has been composed principally for the agitation it contains and shows. A firm conclusion about its performance is impossible, but we should note that the separation of the sisters, with one remaining, is purposeful in that it permits the composition of a later sequence involving the *choros* in which Antigone is seized by Creon. This purpose may explain the composition of the lines in which Oedipus insists he cannot walk without help, which justify one of the two sisters remaining with him, while they also anticipate the wonder of him walking unaided into the grove at the climax of the tragedy. So we might choose to consider a tragic performance

155. In his commentary, McCart (in Ewans 2000, 261–62) seems to envisage that Oedipus does sit down for his singing but that Antigone leaves his side "to dance an approach to the Elders [the *choros*] each in turn"; Seale (1982) does not discuss either the singing or the playing space (122–23).
156. McCart (in Ewans 2000, 267–68), consistent with his earlier inclinations, has Oedipus seated while the *choros* sings and dances.

in which the mobility of a character is understood to be impaired, but his agitation may be danced. Alternatively, the composition of those lines might be explained as including a justification of the fact that Oedipus will sing but not dance, while the *choros* both dances and sings.

96   The close involvement of the actors/characters of Oedipus and Antigone with the *choros* in the playing space continues with the arrival of Creon, who first argues his case with Oedipus and then proceeds to attempt to seize Antigone. As the argument between Oedipus and Creon degenerates, Oedipus claims to speak for the *choros* as well as himself in ordering Creon to leave, while Creon responds by calling on the *choros* as witnesses to Oedipus's reaction (811–14). Oedipus regards the *choros* as his ally in any act of violence (815), and when he hears that Creon has already seized Ismene he calls on the *choros* again to act, to drive the impious intruder Creon out of the land (822–23). At this point the *choros* responds, but Creon issues his orders to his guards to seize Antigone, who wonders where she should run to escape from them (824–29).

The action is increasing in vigor, and the spoken lines fragment between Creon, the *choros,* and Oedipus, culminating in the first part of a song involving all of them (833–43). The action in the playing space and during the song is an occasion for dancing, and the sequence is surely composed for both dance and song as Antigone is seized and the *choros* opposes Creon. Without Antigone, Oedipus is helpless, and his involvement is small in the script, but vital in the turmoil. Immediately after this first part of the song, Antigone exclaims that she is being dragged away, pulled away by force, as Oedipus calls on her to stretch out her hands and she protests she cannot (844–46). Creon then bluntly orders the guards to "take her away" (847), which will be down an *eisodos.*[157] In this spoken part of the sequence, the *choros* attempts to restrain Creon physically, which Creon resists, threatening to remove Oedipus as well (856–60) and, finally, resolving to do so, even though he has now no guards to assist him (874–75).[158]

In the second part of the song Creon, Oedipus, and the *choros* are all involved, with the seizing of Oedipus and the opposition of the *choros* the central themes (876–86). One of the curious features of the whole sequence is

---

157. Bain (1981), in a complicated analysis (48–55) that is part of his consideration of orders from masters to servants in Greek tragedy, believes that Creon has first seized Antigone himself and then transfers her to his guards only at this point.

158. Seale has Oedipus sitting, "feeble and immobile," up to this point (1982, 132); in contrast, McCart (in Ewans 2000, 272) has Oedipus on his feet from the start of the sequence, in response to the insults from Creon.

the apparent fact that physical opposition occurs in the speaking section as well as in the song, both parts of which are short.[159] It is as if the particular moments of the seizing of Antigone and then of Oedipus are seen by Sophocles as themes for the creation of a song and dancing, rather than purely as actions, which might have been encompassed through the means of spoken verse. This sequence, in common with most of the tragedy, happens well away from the sacred grove, which is almost certainly to be identified with the *skene,* with the action in the playing space extending to both *eisodoi,* down one of which Antigone is dragged while along the other Theseus arrives in haste, to prevent the abduction of Oedipus and in answer to the final cry of the *choros* for aid (884–86).

97

At the climax of the tragedy, Oedipus walks unaided toward and into the sacred grove (1540), but he has instructed both Theseus and his daughters to follow him there, leaving the playing space to the *choros* for the first time in the play. What has happened inside the grove is brought to the *choros* by the Messenger, but Antigone and Ismene subsequently reappear from the grove, both mystified by the final moments of their father's life and bereft, isolated in a foreign country. The *choros* expects them to return to the playing space (1667), as it also expects Theseus to do, and the daughters are heard weeping before they are seen (1668–69). The actors/characters join with the *choros* in a song, with the *choros* briefly prompting responses (1677 and 1678, 1704 and 1705) and also offering consolation at the close of each of the first two parts of the song (1693–96 and 1720–23).

In the third part of the song, the sisters respond to each other, with Antigone sensing the urge to rush back to the grove and to see their father's final goal, Ismene aware of the potential sacrilege, Antigone contemplating her own death, Ismene ultimately despairing, and the *choros* not involved, in a sequence that was surely designed with individual dancing firmly in mind (1724–36). In the final part of the song the *choros* attempts to provide consolation, with apparently just the actor/character of Antigone singing of her hopelessness and desolation in response to the *choros* (1737–50). The singing and the dancing are brought to an end with the reappearance of Theseus from the grove, who addresses the daughters and is answered by Antigone in the chanted anapests of movement, a movement that terminates with the *choros* and may bring actors/characters and *choros* finally out of the playing

159. Kaimio, like Bain, worries over whether Creon or his guard drags Antigone away, and discusses the conflict between Creon and the *choros,* but avoids any consideration of the implications of the whole sequence for our understanding of the playing space (1988, 76–77).

space. Throughout the tragedy, Sophocles conveys a sense of the sacred and of human violation through movement and action on the ground.

98

My final sequence taken from the tragedies of Sophocles is from *Antigone*, when Antigone is led away to be immured, and I have left it until last because sequences of a similar kind are also found in Euripides. In *Oedipus at Colonus*, as we have seen, the actor/character of Antigone is led away and out of the playing space under compulsion by the guards of Creon as part of an integrated sequence of song, dancing, and speech, involving three actors/characters and the *choros* in the playing space away from the *skene*. In *Antigone*, Antigone is brought under guard from the *skene* into the playing space. The *choros* has danced and sung (781–800) and, as she reappears from the *skene*, it chants its dismay and distress (801–5). Antigone's song then addresses the *choros* directly, calling on the *choros* to see her "going on my last journey" (807–8, literally "path/way"), "looking at the last light of the sun" (808–9). The *choros* responds to her song with chant, offering her praise and fame after death (817–22, and 834–38). In the third part of her song Antigone responds sharply to this last idea, claiming that the *choros* is mocking her and calling on sacred sites to witness that she goes alive and unlamented to her tomb (838–52). The *choros* is now drawn into the song (853–6), as it is again in the fourth part (872–75). In the final part of the song Antigone protests that she is being "led away on the journey that has been prepared for me" (877–78).

At this moment Creon reappears from the *skene* to insist that no one would ever cease "singing and wailing" before death unless compelled to do so (883–84) and to urge the guards to "take her away as quickly as possible" (885).[160] He does not address Antigone, nor does Antigone respond to him. But she speaks of him in the third person as one who now "leads me away, after laying hands on me like this" (916). The words refer not just (as repeatedly throughout the sequence) to the progress of Antigone through the playing space to death but to compulsion and how Antigone has been treated like a criminal. Creon's power is such that his guards are almost the equivalent of his own hands, and the phrasing and the idea might make us reflect on the references to his hands and arms in the closing sequence of the tragedy. In the final part of the whole sequence the *choros*, and the actors/characters of Creon and Antigone are given the chanted anapests of movement, with Creon threatening the guards for their slowness in removing Antigone (931–32), and Antigone finally appealing to the gods, the city of Thebes, and its leaders that she is "taken away, and there is no more delay" (939) because .

160. Bain's discussion (1981, 23–29) is largely concerned with the fact that the guards do not obey Creon immediately.

she revered what deserved reverence. The chanting will accompany her as she is marched off down an *eisodos* by the guards, leaving the playing space for the subsequent danced song of the *choros*.[161]

There are two similar sequences in the tragedies of Euripides, which contain the involvement of actors/characters with the *choros* in the playing space and the "leading off" of a character to death. Toward the end of *Iphigenia at Aulis* the actors/characters of Clytemnestra and Iphigenia are left in the playing space by Achilles, after Iphigenia has resolved to offer herself for sacrifice so that the Greek fleet can sail against Troy. As she prepares to leave for the altar of Artemis before she is taken there by force, Iphigenia insists that her mother does not come with her and expects one of the attendants of Agamemnon who are present to accompany her (1458–59). Iphigenia then calls on the *choros* to sing to Artemis, and herself starts to sing with the instruction to "take me away" (1475). The *choros* adds its part to her song (1500–1501, and 1504), as she invites it again to join with her in singing of Artemis (1491–93), and the sequence ends with a song and dance from the *choros* (1509–31) as Iphigenia moves away down an *eisodos*. In *Antigone,* chanting brought Antigone into the playing space and accompanied her out of it, and as the actor/character of Antigone sang, the *choros* at first chanted, then joined with her in the song and the dance. Antigone may have danced alone at first, and the actor/character of Iphigenia may do so here, with the *choros* eventually taking over the singing and the dancing as the actor/character of Iphigenia moves out of the playing space and away.

In Euripides' *Andromache* Menelaus forces Andromache from her refuge at the shrine of Thetis, instructs his attendants to bind her hands, and takes her and her son away from the shrine in the playing space and into the palace (425–34). The danced song from a sympathetic *choros* that follows ends as the *choros* sees Andromache and her son reappearing from the *skene* condemned to death, and both are addressed directly in the chant (494–500). Andromache and her son join in a desperate and pathetic song (501–14), with Andromache leading with a reference to how her hands are bleeding

161. In comments on the movements that accompany this sequence, Seale (1982) envisages that "Antigone is first led forward from the palace," that "progress is arrested by the long lyrical lament," and that Antigone finally "proceeds towards the *parodos*" (100–101). He does not discuss the song between the actor/character of Antigone and the *choros* in any detail (99–100); in contrast, Gardiner (1987) does not consider movement in the playing space at all (91–93). Evans (1999) has Antigone both singing and dancing and has recommendations for movement in the playing space throughout the sequence (230–33). Rehm (1994) emphasizes the connotations of the combination of the bridal procession and the carriage of the corpse to the grave, so providing a substantial cultural reference for movement through the playing space (63–64).

from the bonds (501–3). The song is closed by a ruthless chant from Menelaus (515–22), who has also reappeared from the *skene* to supervise their progress to death and the underworld, as his first words emphasize (515). The second part of the song (523–36), which is again shared by Andromache and her son, includes a supplication from the boy to Menelaus (529–31), which Menelaus scorns in his chant, repeating his insistence on their progress down to the underworld (537–44).[162]

But that progress is curtailed. The *choros* speaks two lines, identifying Peleus as he arrives from an *eisodos,* while Peleus seems to address the henchmen of Menelaus and Menelaus himself, who has a drawn sword (547–50), before urging his attendant to lead him forward more quickly (551–52). Once the actor/character of Peleus has arrived in the playing space, he speaks to Andromache, asking her why her hands are bound and why she is being led away (555–56). Andromache confirms that the men standing by her are leading her away to death, and she falls to the ground in front of Peleus in supplication, since she cannot touch his beard with her hands bound as they are (572–73). Peleus's reaction is to order her hands to be freed from the bonds, but Menelaus forbids this, and the quarrel then develops, with Peleus threatening to strike Menelaus with his stick and Menelaus threatening in turn, since he has a sword. The extended spoken argument culminates in Peleus ordering the henchmen to stand aside from Andromache (715–16) and instructing Andromache herself to stand up, so that he may untie her hands himself (717–18).[163]

Two further sequences from *Andromache* add to our sense of composition for the playing space. Once Menelaus has left, and Peleus has conducted Andromache and her son away, the *choros* sings and dances, partly in honor of Peleus (766–801). At the end of the song the Nurse rushes from the *skene* toward the *choros,* calling on the women of the *choros* to help in an emergency: Hermione is now trying to kill herself. She invites the women of the *choros* to go into the palace, in the hope that Hermione might listen to them (817–19), but the *choros* responds that Hermione is coming out, escaping from the restraining hands of the slaves (820–24). In her distraction Hermione tears off her veil, and her gown is loose over her breasts, perhaps from the moment when she was about to stab herself with the sword that was taken from her. She sings and dances, while the Nurse tries to calm her in speech and to in-

---

162. The son must be played by a child actor, since all three adult actors are together in the playing space at the close of this scene.
163. For Halleran, Andromache and her son are one example of a "moving tableau" (1985, 54), but his short discussion of the whole sequence does not refer to movement in the playing space.

duce her to remove herself from the playing space. At that moment, the actor/character of Orestes arrives, addressing his questions to the *choros* and identifying himself, asking after Hermione. She suddenly falls to the ground in front of him, grasping his knees in supplication (891–95). In the exchange that follows Hermione repeats and reiterates her horror of the palace and her fear of death at the hands of her husband: the palace itself seems to take voice to drive her out (923–24), and Orestes must send her away as quickly as he can, before Neoptolemos returns (989–90).

The end of the play begins when Peleus returns to the playing space to address the *choros* (1047 ff.). He barely has time to hear of the danger to his grandson and act on the news before a Messenger arrives with the report of the murder of Neoptolemos at Delphi by Orestes. The final sequence begins with chanting from the *choros,* identifying the body of Neoptolemos as it is carried into the playing space toward Peleus, who sings a lament, with two brief lines of spoken comfort from the *choros* (1184–85). The *choros* then joins in lamentation with Peleus, leading off their joint song and dance (1197–99), with Peleus responding to the *choros.* The sequence of singing and dancing closes as Peleus appeals to Thetis to see him falling to the ground, and Thetis arises, "transported through the air" (1228–29), while the *choros* chants in astonishment (1226–30). The tragedy ends without further reference to the *skene,* since Peleus is instructed to carry the body of his grandson Neoptolemos out of the playing space and away to Delphi for burial (1263–64).

The transport of dead bodies into the playing space is an aspect of tragic composition that did not end with the introduction of the *ekkuklema.*[164] In Euripides' *Suppliants* the carriage of bodies into the playing space provides the occasion for two sequences, the first with the return of the dead war leaders to their mothers in the *choros,* the second with the return of their ashes after cremation to the playing space and to the mothers. The first of these sequences is expected after news of the victory of Theseus on their behalf has been brought by a Messenger to the mothers of the *choros* and to Adrastus (634 ff.). The dead war leaders are to be brought in on biers (766), and Adrastus honors them in advance by raising his hand in greeting and dedicating to them "tearful singing" (772–73). The *choros* sings and dances briefly in anticipation (778–93) before chanting in recognition of the carriage of the bodies into the playing space (794–97).

---

164. After Aeschylus, the *ekkuklema* is certainly used in Sophocles' *Ajax,* generally believed to be the earliest of his surviving tragedies, and also by Euripides, the earliest example in the surviving tragedies probably being that in *Hippolytus* (of 428 BCE).

Adrastus and the *choros* then share a lament, with Adrastus voicing his guilt and the mothers their sorrow, and the *choros* asking to hold and embrace the bodies (815–18). Adrastus leads off the lament (798–801), inviting the *choros* to respond to him, and the integration of actor/character with *choros* is constant and close in what must surely be a danced song.[165] After the cremation, the remains of the war leaders are returned to the playing space and to the women of the *choros,* who chant as they are brought in by their grandsons (1114–22).[166] At the end of the sequence, Theseus observes that the grandsons are carrying the remains themselves, in their own hands (1166–67), although at the end of the song the *choros* asks to hold the ashes or, at least, to clasp them (1160). The song (1123–64) is shared between the *choros* and the grandsons in different patterns of response as it evolves, and an elaborate choreography would be required, quite different in kind from the earlier sequence, since the grandsons effectively form an additional *choros.*[167]

102

The body that is carried into the playing space at the end of Euripides' *Bacchae* is that of Pentheus, and the sequence is grim in the extreme because his body has been torn apart. The narrative of Pentheus's death in the mountains is given to the *choros* of worshippers of Dionysus by a Messenger, and at its opening the *choros* celebrates the news of his death with outbursts of song and dancing (1024–42, with song at 1031, 1034–35, 1037–38, and 1041–42), at which the Messenger is appalled. The mother of Pentheus, Agaue, began the tearing apart of her son, and the *choros* is told that she is coming back to the city, with her son's head stuck on the end of her ritual rod, the *thyrsos* (1139–40). The Messenger cannot face this sight and is determined to withdraw before she arrives (1148–49). The response of the *choros* is to sing and dance in honor of Dionysus and of the Theban bacchants and their victory, especially in honor of the mother who has dipped her hands in her son's blood (1153–64). At the close of the song the *choros* speaks as it sees the ac-

165. Rehm (1992) writes of the "procession" conducted by Theseus and comments that, after the carriage of the bodies "into the theatre," "the *orchestra* fills with corpses and lamentation," but he does not discuss the chanting or the singing of Adrastus and the *choros* (128–29). His commentary on the whole of the tragedy here is extended from his particular study of the altar in the opening of the play (Rehm 1988). For Halleran, the procession is another example of a "moving tableau," and he comments briefly on the "solemn movement that might accompany the entrance of a corpse" (1985, 11) in connection with the announcement of the procession.

166. Halleran (1985) notes the reasonable proposal that Theseus and Adrastus should accompany this subsidiary *choros* of the grandsons rather than arrive after the event of lamentation (21).

167. Rehm (1992, 131) sees the second part of the song, from 1139 to1152, as sung by individual sons, and if this were the case then surely the third part must be also.

tor/character of Agaue approaching, her eyes rolling, and asks for a welcome to the god's celebrants (1165–67).

The *choros* is immediately hailed by Agaue, and the first part of their joint song is ecstatic, as Agaue displays her trophy, celebrating the place and her leading part in the hunt. The second part of the song has the *choros* mixing continuing praise with its awareness of Agaue's delusion, but the Dionysian ecstasy must be danced throughout. The anticipatory reference to the rolling eyes of Agaue (1166–67) cannot be literally represented, as the actor is wearing a mask, but it indicates what might be expected of the dance, throughout which the head of Pentheus on the *thyrsos* is prominent.[168] The dance ends, and the *choros* tells Agaue to show her prize to the citizens of Thebes, prompting Agaue to shout for the Thebans and to ask for the presence of her father Cadmus and her son Pentheus. The actor/character of Cadmus has been approaching and now arrives in the playing space with attendants carrying what remain of the torn and scattered limbs of Pentheus. He recounts his sad experience, knowing that Agaue has come back into the city, and finally he sees her (1232). In the exchange that follows, Agaue comes to learn whose head she is holding.

In Euripides' *Trojan Women,* it is the body of a child that is carried into the playing space on his father's shield and laid on the ground (1156 ff.). As the dead child is clothed in the little that remains of Trojan magnificence by his grandmother, Hecuba, the *choros* sings, first to accompany her spoken lines (1216–17) and, then, with her (1226–39). She releases the body and it is carried out of the playing space for burial, but the chanting of the *choros* moves from condolence to alert her that flames are being set on the high places of the city of Troy (1251–59).[169] The Greek herald Talthybius returns for the

---

168. The head rather than the song and dance occupies Taplin (1978, 98–100). It is not possible to say whether Agaue was accompanied. The instruction the *choros* gives to welcome the god's followers (*komos,* 1167) might be taken to embrace the union of Agaue with the *choros* itself in the playing space, since she is welcomed by the *choros* as a fellow celebrant (*synkomon,* 1172), and the Messenger has earlier stated that Agaue has left her sisters behind (1143).

169. Wiles (1997) insists of this moment that we must either imagine that the *skene* has been redefined from the tent that it is at the opening of the play to the walls of Troy or that the "space occupied by the audience is taken to be Troy" (119). In the first case, Hecuba would rush "towards the door of the *skene*" (120), but Wiles does not propose movements for the alternative. The established range of speculation envisages either actual or imagined torches, and Halleran favors the latter, with Talthybius giving orders "to those beyond the audience's vision" (1985, 22). Lee, contrastingly, sees no need for a "change in scene" but suggests that the fire "is to be imagined . . . as burning . . . in the background" (1976, 274).

last time to order the burning of Troy and the collection of the enslaved Trojan women, including Hecuba and the *choros,* for transportation to Greece. When Hecuba calls on the Trojan women to run into the flames (1282–83), Talthybius comments that she is out of her mind with grief and instructs the soldiers with him to take her away into slavery for Odysseus, whose prize she is (1284–86). The sequence that follows bears final witness to the existence of Troy, in the moment of its material destruction and of the dispersal of all who remain of its population, who are present in the playing space. The *choros* and the actor/character of Hecuba join in the lament (1286–1332), which acknowledges the ground on which they are singing and dancing in the second part of the song (1302–16) as Hecuba kneels on the ground and strikes it with both hands (1305–6), and the *choros* follows her movement (1307–8). The singing and the dancing end with the tragedy, in a reaction to the sound of the citadel crashing in the third part of the song (1325–26) and in the self-instruction of the last lines to move forward and away to slavery.[170]

The close relationship between the actor/character of Hecuba and the *choros* in the playing space has been constant throughout the tragedy, although *Trojan Women* opens with first one god, Poseidon, and then two gods, Poseidon and Athena, in the prediction of disasters awaiting the Greeks on their return voyages. But the actor/character of Hecuba is already present, identified by Poseidon as "lying in front of the doors" of the *skene* (37). In this position she begins her chant once they have left, telling herself to raise her head and her neck (98) and lamenting the physical dejection, the hard place on the ground where she weeps, that has racked her body from her head to her ribs, her back, and her sides (111–12). Hecuba then sings, turning in the song to the thought of her own position at the tent of Agamemnon, to which she has been led after the sack of the city and her own palace (138–42). The final part of her song calls on the wives of the dead Trojans to come to sing a lament for Troy, which she will lead (143–52).

The song and dance that the actor/character of Hecuba executes jointly with the *choros* is in two parts, both of which open with what appears to be the arrival of members of the *choros* and an address to Hecuba (153–38, and

---

170. Halleran (1985, 101) has Hecuba rising from the ground at 1327, but he does not discuss movements in the lament itself. Bain (1981, 25) notes that Talthybius's order to his soldiers at 1285–86 to conduct the women to the ships is not immediately obeyed, observing that the content of the lament that follows "hardly suggests that we are faced with a slow procession off stage," drawing attention in this respect to 1305 ff. Kaimio (1988) contradicts Bain, acknowledging that Hecuba "may be allowed some freedom of movement as she kneels down and beats the earth," but does not consider the implications of the sung lament for the playing space (63).

176–81). One possibility is that the *choros* is initially divided, and it seems very likely that we find each half of it referring to the *skene* as it comes into the playing space. The first half of the *choros* refers to the fact that Hecuba's cries have penetrated through into "the shelter" and that, as a consequence, fear dashed through the hearts of the "Trojan women who lament their en-   105 slavement inside this dwelling" (154–58). The second half of the *choros* sings that it "left these tents of Agamemnon" after hearing Hecuba (176–77), and the cumulative impression is that both references are to the *skene*, rather than to a set of tents imagined to be stretching off down either of the two (or both) *eisodoi*.

If the first half of the *choros* came out of the *skene* to join Hecuba in the playing space for the danced song, then this would make good sense of Hecuba's reference to Cassandra and her fearful order not to send Cassandra outside (169–70).[171] It is noticeable that the *choros* does not bring any news to Hecuba but, rather, asks Hecuba if she has heard news; and since any news would come from the Greek camp it seems most convincing that the *choros* has not arrived from there. Hecuba might dance first with one half of the *choros* and then with the other or, alternatively, she might dance first with one half and then with the complete *choros*. The *choros* then sings and dances the final part of the song by itself (197–229), and the song is self-referential, after the first lines referring to Hecuba, its theme uncertainty. The *choros* had expected Hecuba's cries to signal the decisions about the allocation of all the enslaved Trojan women to masters and to destinations.

As the Greek herald Talthybius approaches, he is identified by the *choros* in a chant (230–34), and the expected moment has arrived. In the exchange that follows between the actors/characters of Hecuba and Talthybius, Talthybius initially addresses the former queen, while Hecuba initially addresses the *choros* in apprehension (235–38 and 239). Hecuba's responses to Talthybius are sung, while the actor/character of Talthybius has spoken verse that may, in an extended alternation with Hecuba's song, be given a more heightened

---

171. Wiles, without any discussion of the opening scene, asserts that an "entry from two sides is used in *Trojan Women*" (1997, 112). Halleran comments that "the chorus enters in two groups" (1985, 94) after a long discussion of Hecuba's silence, but he does not expand on this or on movement in the playing space. Hourmouziades (1965) assumes that the two halves of the *choros* appear from the *skene* in an inconclusive discussion on the number of doors that the *skene* might contain (24–25). Lee (1976) believes that the *choros* arrives ("in two halves") from the *eisodoi* (90) but notes later that the reference to her cries penetrating through into the shelter "must mean that the chorus was inside when Hecuba's cries were first heard." (93). Of the reference to "this dwelling," he comments that "the leader probably points to the parodos through which the other semi-chorus is shortly to enter" (93). It is not a convincing presentation.

form of delivery. Talthybius's subject is the allocation of all the Trojan women, but Hecuba is largely concerned with her daughters Cassandra and Polyxena and with Andromache, the wife of Hector, before she turns to asking about herself. Her response to the information that she is allocated to Odysseus is a more extended song, which starts with reference to the self-laceration of grief and may well be danced (278–91). She also invites the *choros* to join with her in lamentation for herself (288–89), since she has the worst allocation of all. The *choros* neither sings nor dances but, instead, speaks, informing us that Hecuba's allocation is known, while the allocation for those in the *choros* is as yet undeclared (292–93). Talthybius proceeds to order his attendant soldiers or slaves to "bring Cassandra out here as quickly as possible" (294–95), adding that the rest of the women will also be taken away and distributed (296–97). At this point the actor/character of Talthybius shouts that he sees the flame of a torch inside the *skene* (298) and fears that the enslaved Trojan women are intending to burn themselves to death at the moment that they are due for transportation (299–303). He calls for the doors of the *skene* to be opened (304–5), but Hecuba insists that what he has seen is her daughter Cassandra "rushing out here like a bacchant" (306–7), carrying a torch.[172]

Cassandra dashes into the playing space, and it is clear from her song and dance that she is celebrating, as a priestess, in a manic parody the rites of a wedding, her "marriage" to Agamemnon, who we have been told has conceived a lust for her (255). In the first part of her song she briefly addresses her mother (315), whose misery she chooses to contrast with her supposed happiness at the prospect of her glorious wedding (315–16). But in the second part of her song she insists that there must be a choral dance (325–26) and that this choral song and dance will be holy (328). She appeals to Apollo, whose priestess she is, to lead the dance, to her mother to join in the *choros* (332), to join with her in a whirling dance (333–34), and finally to the *choros* to dance and sing with her in honor of her wedding (338–41). What the *choros* has to say at the end of this song is that Hecuba should put a stop to it, and it should be clear that neither the *choros* nor Hecuba has responded to Cassandra's invitations.[173] But the language is explicit, and Cassandra must

---

172. Halleran (1985) describes Cassandra as "running out in a frenzied state" (96), and his n57 (114) draws attention to the language.

173. The emphasis in most criticism is inevitably on Cassandra's wedding song and dance: see, for example, Rehm (1994, 129–30). Halleran is interested in Cassandra's "control not only of her entrance from the *skene*, but also of the ensuing scene," which he understands to incorporate both "song and dance" (1985, 96).

occupy the open ground of the *orchestra* for her invitations, with the *choros* withdrawing in shock and pity or standing motionless, and Hecuba standing aside. Hecuba then moves to take the torch away from Cassandra (348–49), and she instructs some figures to take it back inside the *skene,* and the Trojan women to change the wedding song to one of sorrow.[174] The *choros* does not respond to Hecuba's invitation to change the song immediately, since a long spoken sequence follows, but its song and dance at the close of the scene, after Cassandra has been taken away, is very much what Hecuba demanded (511 ff.).

In Euripides' *Hecuba,* the actor/character of Hecuba initially appears from the *skene* and comes forward into the playing space, helped by Trojan women (59–60), leaning on a stick. The tent is that of Agamemnon, and when the *choros* arrives in the playing space it refers to how it has crept away from the tents of the masters to whom its members have been allocated in order to come here (98–99), which seems to mark a distinction between the *skene* and other notional shelters away down the *eisodoi.* Hecuba chants as she appears from the *skene,* and in the opening song of hers that follows there is no cry to others to come to her. Instead, in this play the *choros* does bring news to Hecuba, which is the motivation for its arrival in the playing space, and it chants that news, in an account of the Greek decision to sacrifice Polyxena at the tomb of Achilles. Hecuba's response to this is a song of dejection (154 ff.), in which she turns on the *choros* as the bringer of bad news (165–66), demands of her own legs that they move toward the *skene* (169–71), and calls for her daughter Polyxena to come out of the *skene* to join her in the playing space. The actors/characters of Polyxena and Hecuba then share a sung exchange (177–96), which is followed by a song from Polyxena (197–215), largely addressed to her mother.

Later in the play, the ritual murder of Polyxena is reported by Talthybius, but the corpse of Hecuba's son Polydorus is brought into the playing space. It is carried by attendants but led in by the old Woman who had been sent to the shore to draw water with which to wash the body of Polyxena (609–10). The old Woman first addresses the *choros,* asking for Hecuba (657–58), and when Hecuba reappears from the *skene* she is puzzled about why the old Woman has brought the body of Polyxena to her (670–74). She then fears the body is that of Cassandra (676–77), and only when the old Woman uncovers the corpse for her to see the face does Hecuba realize that it is her son

---

174. It is likely that the first instruction is not meant for the *choros,* since there may be additional women attendants, as Bain notes (1981, 10–11, 13n5).

Polydorus. Hecuba then speaks briefly before singing, and in the exchange that follows, the actor/character of Hecuba sings, while the actor/character of the old Woman speaks to her, with the *choros* interjecting some consolation (693). The *choros* also asks Hecuba whether the dream that had brought her from the tent at the opening of the tragedy can reveal the murderer of her son (709), and Hecuba confirms that it can. The murderer was the Thracian king, Polymestor, to whom she and Priam had entrusted their young son (710–11). The song is ended by the approach of Agamemnon, who arrives in the playing space to ask Hecuba when she is coming to bury her daughter but then sees the body lying near his tent (733–34). Hecuba kneels to Agamemnon, in an appeal for the freedom to take vengeance, with the help of the Trojan women that the *skene* contains (880).

The body of Polydorus must be removed from the playing space at the end of the scene, since a danced song from the *choros* is followed immediately by the arrival of the Thracian king Polymestor with his young sons to a summons that had been sent by Hecuba (888–89). Polymestor addresses Hecuba directly, and he is asked to send his attendants away from the playing space, since Hecuba claims to have something confidential to disclose to Polymestor and his young sons alone (978–80). The lure of gold is introduced to draw him into the *skene,* and Hecuba invites him to walk into it (1018–19). Once he and his sons have done so, the *choros* sings and dances of the revenge that will now come (1025–33), and Polymestor's cries in spoken verse are heard from the *skene*. These cries successively communicate that he himself is blinded, that his sons have been killed, that he is threatening to break apart the inside of the tent, and that his attackers may run but they cannot escape from him (1035, 1037, 1039–40). For its part, the *choros* finally asks itself whether it should run into the tent and act as an ally to Hecuba and the Trojan women inside it (1042–43). Hecuba reappears from the *skene* speaking back into it to Polymestor, and she responds in gruesome detail when the *choros* asks her to confirm that she has done what she intended (1049–50). Polymestor will be seen immediately, outside the *skene,* blinded and staggering (1050), and the *choros* will also be able to see the bodies of his two dead sons; all of this Hecuba and the Trojan women did inside the *skene*. Hecuba then comments that Polymestor is coming out of the tent and that she will move out of his way, since he is raging and extremely violent (1053–55).

The actor/character of Polymestor emerges from the *skene* apparently on all fours, uncertain where to go, although these are questions that he poses to himself, not descriptions by another character (1056–57). He is also singing, and his theme and objective is the hunt, with a blind search requiring either movement or dancing, with changes of direction (1059–60).[175] He soon believes that he has heard the footfall of the women and longs to catch them and tear the flesh from their bones and eat it (1070–71). His song includes no reference to him carrying the dead bodies of his sons, and it seems as though he feels that he is caught between his hunt and the horror of leaving his sons behind (1076–79). The corpses may have been brought out from the *skene* as he moves away from it, or they may have been displayed on the *ekkuklema*.[176] The footfalls he believes he hears will almost certainly be those of the *choros,* which must move away or around him as he dances his desperate hunt in the playing space; Hecuba, who is less mobile, has clearly indicated that she is getting far away from anywhere he is likely to move.

So it seems likely that the *choros* here substitutes, in the playing space and in the blinded awareness of Polymestor, for the unseen Trojan women who have been said to be in the *skene* and who have perpetrated the violence. This is a stratagem that is developed in *Bacchae,* in which a *choros* in the playing space expresses the savage ecstasy of the women with Agaue on the mountain. The *choros* risks two spoken lines of small comfort to Polymestor, and in the second part of his song (1089–1108) he calls for help from Thracian warriors, while his frustration at his impotence, his inability to master the playing space as the field of his hunt, continues until the end of the danced song. Agamemnon's arrival in the playing space brings him up against Polymestor, and he sees the dead children; he also speaks to Hecuba, which prompts Polymestor to savage excitement at the thought that she might be near enough to him for him to get his hands on her (1122–26). The script suggests that Agamemnon, or his attendants, restrain Polymestor physically and compel him to speech rather than assault (1127–31).[177]

The last of the sequences I shall consider here come from Euripides' *Orestes* and are of interest because an actor/character is given the task, by the composer, of supposedly directing the *choros* in the playing space. The *skene* represents the palace of Agamemnon at Argos, but the playing space is initially defined by the presence of a sickbed in it, with a figure lying on it who is identified as Orestes by his sister Electra. Electra claims that she can look down the roads that lead to the palace (67), but apart from that we have no

175. Kaimio (1988), as I mentioned earlier, writes of Polymestor's "frenzied song and dance" at this point.

176. Hourmouziades (1965, 98 ff.) believes this is on the *ekkuklema;* Collard remains undecided (1991, 190).

177. Kaimio (1988) briefly discusses this moment of restraint, but she does not place it in the playing space (72, 82).

explicit indications of where the bed might be. The appearances of Helen and Hermione from the *skene* must make it unlikely that the *ekkuklema* has been used, as if to show an interior scene, or that the bed is located immediately in front of the *skene* doors. The arrival of the *choros* is seen by Electra, who describes its members as friends who have come to join her in laments (132–33), and she fears that the *choros* will awaken her brother (133–35). The *choros* does sing and dance when it arrives, and it does so in conjunction with the actor/character of Electra throughout, but the song is concerned with the immediate situation of the arrival of the *choros* and the fear of awakening Orestes.

Initially Electra commands the *choros* to move further away, over there, away from the bed (142), and to be quiet (145–46). But she then appears to invite it to come closer to her (149), and one explanation of this might be that the actor/character of Electra moves away from the bed in the dance and song and herself comes closer to the *choros* in the open ground of the playing space. It is, indeed, the *choros* that draws Electra's attention to the fact that Orestes is moving his body (166). The sung exchanges continue, and the actor/character of Electra concludes the song with the kind of lament that had been anticipated, but she sings and dances on her own (194–207). It is interesting that, at the close of the sequence, once again it is the *choros* that draws the attention of the actor/character to the prone body of Orestes. The speaker calls Electra to the body, expressing concern that Orestes might be dead since he is not moving at all (208–10). Paradoxically, Orestes then speaks for the first time, and Electra comes to him.

The climax of the tragedy is the plot to take the life of Helen, which is hatched by Orestes, Pylades, and Electra. Before Orestes and Pylades enter the *skene,* concern is expressed about the return of Hermione to the palace (1211 ff.). Electra is to remain in front of the palace, keeping watch, and to bang on the door or to send word inside if anyone looks likely to come inside (1216–17). Orestes and Pylades then prepare to go into the *skene,* but before they do, all three join in a spoken invocation of the spirit of Agamemnon, which recalls in purpose the invocation in Aeschylus's *Libation Bearers.* Once Orestes and Pylades have entered the *skene,* the actor/character of Electra starts to sing in conjunction with the *choros,* addressing it formally and gaining an equally formal recognition of her status from it (1246–50). Her orders are that the *choros* should divide, with some members of it standing on guard by the one cart track, and some by the other path, the references clearly being to the *eisodoi* into the playing space (1251–52). This precaution is to prevent someone approaching close to the *skene* (1255–57), and the *choros* divides accordingly, to the west and to the east (1258–60).

Both divisions, it seems, are then instructed by Electra to look around, and they respond by looking behind them. The song is clearly danced to this effect, with even an instruction from Electra to the members of the *choros* to "turn and look everywhere, through your hair" (1267–68), which suggests some play not only with movement of the heads but also with the masks. There is then a false alarm (1269–70), which certainly agitates Electra (1271–72), but it is quickly resolved. Toward the close of the second part of the joint song and dance, the actor/character of Electra sings that she will now listen at the doors (1281). Nothing is heard, and in the final part of the song Electra once again urges the two divisions of the *choros* to "keep watch now even better, running around, some of you over here, and some over there" (1291–92). A cry from Helen breaks from the *skene,* and the song and dance conclude with Electra's celebration of her murder.

Only at this point, as speech resumes, does the *choros* call for silence in the belief that it has heard someone approaching (1311–12), and Electra instructs the *choros* to take up the position that it held before in the playing space, away from the *eisodoi,* and to appear relaxed (1314–15). When the actor/character of Hermione returns, she says she heard a cry while she was still some way off from the palace (1323–25). It is now in the interests of the conspirators that Hermione should enter the *skene,* and Hermione states and demonstrates her willingness to hurry into the house (1344). In this play of silence and excited noise, the *choros* follows Electra's reaction to Hermione's entrapment with an encouragement to itself, in song and dance, to raise a racket (literally a "noise" and a "shout" [1354]) in front of the palace, to cover the sound of the murder and prevent the citizens of Argos rushing to interfere (1353–54). What the *choros* expects to see is the dead body of Helen, but what it does see is a Phrygian slave escaping from the house to sing and dance in the playing space his extraordinary account of the murder of Helen, with the *choros* briefly prompting its continuation.

Close analysis of these scenes and sequences from the tragedies after Aeschylus confirms the continuity of composition for the full ground of the playing space and demonstrates its extent and diversity in the combination of action, movement, speech, dance, and song from actors and the *choros,* most notably in interaction between them. Our understanding of tragic performance must rely on the evidence that such scenes provide and combine it carefully with an appreciation of the use made of the material resources of ancient production, of which the most imposing from the time of the *Oresteia* forward is the *skene.*

Appendix A

CHRONOLOGY OF THE SURVIVING PLAYS

TABLE A1   *Chronology and Authorship of Plays*

DATE	TITLE OF PLAY	AUTHOR
472 BC	*Persians*	Aeschylus
467 BC	*Seven against Thebes*	Aeschylus
463 BC	*Suppliants*	Aeschylus
458 BC	*Agamemnon, Libation Bearers, Eumenides* (the *Oresteia* trilogy)	Aeschylus
?	*Ajax*	Sophocles
?	*Antigone*	Sophocles
438 BC	*Alcestis*	Euripides
?	*Women of Trachis*	Sophocles
431 BC	*Medea*	Euripides
?	*Oedipus the King*	Sophocles
?	*Children of Heracles*	Euripides
428 BC	*Hippolytus*	Euripides
?	*Andromache*	Euripides
425 BC	*Acharnians*	Aristophanes[a]
424 BC	*Knights*	Aristophanes
423 BC	*Clouds*	Aristophanes
?	*Suppliants*	Euripides
?	*Hecuba*	Euripides
422 BC	*Wasps*	Aristophanes
421 BC	*Peace*	Aristophanes
?	*Electra*	Euripides

?	*Heracles*	Euripides	
415 BC	*Trojan Women*	Euripides	
414 BC	*Birds*	Aristophanes	
?	*Iphigenia in Tauris*	Euripides	
?	*Ion*	Euripides	113
412 BC	*Helen*	Euripides	
411 BC	*Lysistrata, Women at the Thesmophoria*	Aristophanes	
?	*Electra*	Sophocles	
?	*Phoenician Women*	Euripides	
?	*Cyclops*[b]	Euripides	
409 BC	*Philoctetes*	Sophocles	
408 BC	*Orestes*	Euripides	
405 BC	*Frogs*	Aristophanes	
?	*Bacchae, Iphigenia in Aulis*	Euripides	
401 BC	*Oedipus at Colonus*	Sophocles	
391 BC	*Women in Assembly*	Aristophanes	
388 BC	*Wealth*	Aristophanes	

Note. The known dates are those of production. The positioning of other plays remains uncertain. *Prometheus Bound,* formerly attributed to Aeschylus, is of unknown authorship and date, as is *Rhesus,* attributed to Euripides.

[a]All the plays of Aristophanes are comedies.

[b]*The Cyclops* by Euripides is a satyr play, and his *Alcestis* is a play composed to take the place of a satyr play.

The Chorus

The problem of the chorus (*choros, choroi*) is central to our contemporary understanding of Greek tragedies, and it is deeply frustrating. On the one hand, we sense that here is something vital, perhaps almost mystical, operating powerfully and evocatively throughout the action and theatricality of the plays. On the other hand, our initial fascination and excitement can gradually dissolve into resignation. The prefatory comments of Golder, one of the editors of an important collection of essays, although perhaps unduly pessimistic about the achievements of modern production, acknowledge this feeling: "The non-specialist who knows nothing else about Greek drama knows it had a 'chorus.' But as almost anyone who has ever seen a Greek play can attest, the chorus is every director's nightmare. It almost never 'works.' More often than not, its spectral presence proves the impossible otherness of the Greeks."[1] Similarly, everyone who has trained for the theater will have experienced the choral workshop, in one form or another, which is usually based on movement and seen as an almost philosophical starting point for generic exercises in group movement, voice work, and the anonymous ensemble. Workshops of this kind may provide an exhilarating experience. But few participants would feel confident that they have come close to anything authentic, and many would feel that their actual understanding has made very little progress toward Golder's "impossible otherness" of the Greek chorus.

A good starting point in tackling this awkward problem might be with the concept of choreography, which in the context of the Athenian theater involves both music and dancing, and problems associated with these topics will occupy much of the central part of this chapter. The institutional and ideo-

[handwritten margin note: see Arion]

---

1. Golder and Scully 1995, 1.

logical context of the great festival of Dionysus at Athens, the City Dionysia, has been well documented and reviewed elsewhere, and I shall not repeat or summarize those modern studies here.[2] But there is the diversity of *choroi* to consider, as a central component of ancient Greek culture, both before and outside the Athenian theater and within the Athenian theater itself. Placing the tragic *choros* in that cultural spectrum of activity will be constructive.

So I shall review the problem of the tragic *choros* in this chapter by considering the *choros* as it first appears, in the narrative of the Greek epics, and tracing the diversity of *choroi* and composition for them. I shall then consider music and dancing in some detail, before turning to the theatrical *choroi* of the dithyramb, the satyr play, comedy, and tragedy.

THE *CHOROS* IN EPIC

I refer here to Homer and other composers from a similar period who make use of or adapt epic diction. The relevant period is before and after 700 BCE, and the composers are singers, *aoidoi* (singular, *aoidos*), if that is what *aoidos* means at that time. The recitation of verse to a repeated rhythm, with formulaic language and a tradition that did not involve written texts is, of course, a form for which we have no obvious or near equivalent in modern Western culture. So hoping to find a good translation of the key term is missing the point; even if we conclude that singing is indicated, we cannot be sure what that singing sounded like.[3] But the *aoidos* was associated in the Homeric poems with the *phorminx*, an early version from the group of instruments that we would most usually call lyres. Instruments from this group form one of the two major accompaniments to the human voice in the Greek musical tradition, and their distinguishing characteristic is that they can be held and played by a singer. In contrast, the second significant instrument is the choral accompaniment par excellence, the *aulos*, or more accurately—since they are normally paired—the *auloi*, which are pipes; since these are blown, the player himself cannot sing.

The Homeric poems, the poems of Hesiod, and the so-called Homeric

---

2. Sources are presented and discussed in Csapo and Slater (1994) and Pickard-Cambridge (1988), with much subjected to a fresh analysis in Wilson (2000). There are extremely helpful essays collected in Winkler and Zeitlin (1990), with that by Goldhill of great relevance. The *choros* might also be assessed as a given *choros* in any specific tragedy: commentaries and books regularly offer us critical and thematic interpretations of the surviving verbal scripts, and I shall not be duplicating that activity here.
3. West 1981.

Hymns are tempting because they may appear to offer us evidence, to contain strata like an archaeological site that we can gently free from surrounding material and then isolate for discussion. So, if we are not cautious, we may feel that they give us a privileged first glimpse of the reality of the *choros*. Plainly they do testify to its existence, but it is important to register that we are visualizing under the permission of the narrative, that is, of a cultural vehicle that is driven by a proud owner or owners. A good example of this is a famous passage that relates to skilled singing to the *phorminx* itself. At one point in the *Iliad* Achilles is "discovered," in his withdrawal from the fighting, by the narrative and by some Greek leaders who are making a tentative approach to him:

> They found him soothing his heart with a clear-voiced *phorminx*,
> one of beautiful workmanship, which had a silver cross-bar to it;
> he had won it from the spoils when he destroyed the city of Eetion.
> With it he was soothing his spirit, singing of famous actions of men.
> (*Iliad* 9:186–89)

That Achilles should choose a *phorminx* from among the available spoils is a compliment to the art of the *aoidos*, as is the fact that, although preeminent and fixed in his role as a warrior, he has acquired the skills of playing and singing. He has also, presumably, found time to listen to the work of composers, and so he himself becomes part of the fraternity of composers/reciters. The activity is said to please both his *phren* ("heart" [above]) and his *thumos* ("spirit"), words for which there is no adequate translation but which represent vital elements of heroic motivation, impulse, and feeling. In that respect, singing/playing can hardly be seen as idle; it has the highest heroic valuation it might have.

From the first moment, then, if we take the *Iliad* to be that first moment, nothing comes to us from art as "evidence" that is not already artistically conceived. For our immediate purposes another passage from the *Iliad* must feature, which again concerns Achilles. It is the description of the shield that is brought to him, fashioned by the god Hephaestus, and is what is known in technical jargon from a later period as an *ekphrasis*, an artistic description notably of a work of art (*Iliad* 18, 490–606). It is inevitably tempting to treat the pictures presented to us here by the composer as if they were a site of cultural archaeology, as if, unwittingly or in order to release an additional vitality, the composer was revealing to us aspects of his own society. This inclination to read in "reality" may even increase (paradoxically) if we explore the artistry or the design of the description. Such aspects as the selection of detail or the significance of construction may enhance our feeling that the core components of composition must be drawn from a real world, if only in the same way as the clay from which a pot is artfully made.

The singer/composer grants us a vision of *choroi,* but one in which this entertainment is implicitly subordinated to his own art form of narration.[4] In the first of the vignettes from the shield, the context is that of weddings and a loud wedding song, and a dance of young men is mentioned, with both *auloi* and *phorminges* among them, and women watching from doorways. In the second, the vintage is the context, and a boy plays on and sings a song to the accompaniment of the *phorminx* in the middle of girls and boys carrying home the grapes:

> while they, beating the ground together
> with song and shout, leaping with their feet, followed.
> (*Iliad* 18:571–72)

Not an appealing translation, but the literalism may be helpful. It is interesting for our purposes that the song of the boys and girls remains obscure, while that of the young *phorminx* singer is placed in the foreground. There is some kind of coordination intended in the dancing, as almost certainly in the singing, but the physical relations are impossible to construe, not really through oversight or omission as such: the narration chooses to mention "in the middle of" first, but then ends with "followed."

In the third vignette, Hephaestus (the divine maker of the shield) has cast on the shield a *choros,* which may mean either a group or a dancing place.[5] The narrator here likens Hephaestus's *choros* to that which Daedalus fitted or formed or trained in Crete for Ariadne (the meaning of the verb *askein* might just stretch to any of these); since Daedalus is notably a craftsman and architect, a dancing floor is more likely than very early chorus training.[6] In this picture Hephaestus—and how can we doubt the veracity of a god?—has, the

---

4. There is a good collection of passages in translation in the first volume of Barker's *Greek Musical Writings* (1984), many of which are relevant to our study of the *choros,* because they attend in various ways to music. The Achilles passage appears as his no. 4, 21, while extracts from the shield description form his no. 7, 22–24. Readers may find it helpful to obtain a copy of Barker and run through it in conjunction with my account, although I also indicate the location of passages in the original works, which may be followed in translation
5. In his excellent book on *Dance and Ritual Play in Greek Religion,* Lonsdale reviews the instances of the adjective *euruchoros* (with wide dancing floor) in the Homeric poems and notes that the Spartans, even into the Roman period, called their *agora,* their central civic and religious space, the *choros* (Lonsdale, 1994, chap. 4, esp.117, 117n31, 118, 118n37). The discussion by Boedeker (1974, 52–57) is also valuable.
6. Barker (1984, 23n13); this is also Boedeker's conclusion (1974, 56).

narrator informs us, shown young men and girls dancing with their hands on each other's wrists, running round in a circle and in lines toward each other, watched with pleasure by a crowd, while two tumblers whirl in the middle as *exarchontes molpes*, "leaders of the song/dance." *Molpe* is a problem, since it is capable of carrying the connotations of song and of dance, and although the choice of meaning is made clear in some passages by other aspects of the context, it is not so here. The same difficulty, incidentally, applies to the first passage above, in which I have translated *molpe* as "song."[7]

Now it might be argued that a detailed commentary that elucidated all these issues would clarify the picture, but I think this is missing the point. Even if we accept, as I have above, that *molpe* refers to singing, we still have only the vaguest picture of the relationship between *phorminx* player/singer and group in the second of our vignettes. If (on the same translation) there is singing in the third, we can hardly be sure who is doing it: tumblers, *choros*, the *aoídos* who may or may not belong here? In the first vignette there is a loud wedding song, but who is singing it or how it relates to the dances of the young men or to the instruments are matters that are quite unclear. Rationalist critics may question how an inanimate object can be expected to render sound. I should comment in reply that this is an object made by a god, and what we are reading (originally hearing) is a description (in fact, an invention) of it by the composer. If he can state unequivocally what an *aoídos* is singing, the very type of the song, then he can manage other indications if he chooses. But my own feeling is that we can conclude very little in any detail, with the possible exceptions that dances with linked hands, circular dances, and line dances may have been familiar images.[8]

The *Odyssey* has a more pronounced or explicit interest in the *aoídos* than the *Ilíad* and is not a battlefield epic; it may be reasonable to suppose that those two things go together. I shall concentrate on two of the passages of most relevance. At Ithaca, the *aoídos* is named, Phemius, and in this first passage he plays a *kitharis*, which is either a synonym for the *phorminx* or is a related stringed instrument. The scene is set among the suitors of Penelope, in the hall of Odysseus, and the thoughts of the suitors turn to *molpe* and

---

7. There is a further complication in the question of whether an additional line referring to an *aoídos* playing on the *phorminx* also belongs here, since it is joined to the same lines about the tumblers in a passage in the *Odyssey*: see Barker (1984, 24n16) and commentators on the *Ilíad* for further discussion

8. For images on vases from this period, see Webster (1970, 4–8, 46–55); Webster accepts the Homeric descriptions as authentic, although he notes that we cannot be sure "how much memory Homer has enshrined of earlier choruses" (46).

dancing.[9] We have the same problem here with the meaning of *molpe*, but the pairing with *orchestus* (dancing) makes a reference to singing plausible, since tautology is unlikely.[10] Phemius is handed his *kitharis* and begins a fine song. Unfortunately for our inquiry, he is interrupted by the narrative turning its attention to Odysseus's son Telemachus having a conversation with the god- 119
dess Athena. Their exchange is an extended one, and at its conclusion the narrator returns to the larger scene in the hall:

> The famous singer was singing to them, and they
> sat listening in silence. He sang of the bitter homecoming
> of the Achaeans from Troy, which Athene had imposed on them.
> (*Odyssey* 1.325–27)

The narration is interested in his song because Phemius is singing what the *Odyssey* itself is narrating, and a collection of leaping dissolutes is hardly a match for him. But it is sad that the promise of singing and dancing ends in immobile silence, giving us just the vaguest of hints and nothing more. During Odysseus's stay in the country of the Phaeacians, we are offered a little more de- tail after the competitive games, when a *choros*—a dancing place—is smoothed and a wide place for the gathering (*agon*) is created. The *aoidos* Demodocus is placed in the center with his *kitharis,* and male youths who know how to dance gather round him: "They struck a godlike *choros* with their feet" (*Odyssey* 8.264). The song that the *aoidos* sings is a narrative of the infidelity of Aphrodite with Ares, and the narrative and the song includes direct (that is, "quoted") speech from the gods. After it, two named youths are ordered by their king to dance alone, while the rest of the young men beat time, creating a loud noise.[11]

The Homeric narratives have no place for any vocal accomplishment in the *choros,* even if we sense at times that singing might be a part of it were the *aoidos* not so foregrounded. Indeed, there is nothing really to prevent us from forming the view that the *choros* was in essence a dancing group and that youth (both male and female) was a prominent feature of its constitution. Yet there are some specific references to the group as a vocal entity, which occur notably at the death of the Trojan Hector in the *Iliad.*[12] First, Hector's parents Priam and Hecuba cry aloud, and their cry of lamentation is taken up throughout the city. Then Priam expresses his desire to go and plead with

9. Barker (1984), no. 9, 25; *Odyssey* 1.150–424, in excerpts.
10. This is fundamentally the argument of Barker (1984), 25n18.
11. Barker (1984), no. 10, 28; *Odyssey* 8.40–end.
12. *Iliad* 22.405–end.

Achilles, who has retained Hector's body, addressing each man by his name while he rolls in the dung near the city gate, and the Trojan men wail after he has finished, as a response. Subsequently, Hecuba leads off (*exerche*) the lament on behalf of the Trojan women, and the word used here is the same as that used for the two tumblers in the *Iliad.* Finally, Hector's wife Andromache hears the lamentation and comes to the wall of Troy, fainting when she sees the body of Hector out on the plain. When she recovers she wails and addresses the Trojan women, and at the close of her grim anticipation of the future that awaits her son Astyanax the women wail in response.

120

The laments of Priam and Andromache are articulate, whereas only sounds are attributed to the groups of men and women. But Hecuba is portrayed as an *exarchon,* and the wail from the groups is made in response to a leader in all three cases. The corpse of Hector is still remote from the mourners, and when it is returned to Troy at the close of the twenty-fourth and final book it is spotted first by Cassandra and then met by Hecuba and Andromache, who tear their hair and touch Hector's head. They are surrounded by a wailing crowd. The corpse is subsequently brought through to the palace and laid on a bier:

> And they set alongside it *aoídoi*
> as leaders of the laments, who in the wailing song
> had the role of singing the laments, and the women wailed back.
> For them white-armed Andromache led the cry of grief.
> (*Iliad* 24.720–23)[13]

The verbal formula for the completion of her lament is the same as before, and Andromache is replaced by Hecuba as *exarchon* and, then, by Helen. At the conclusion, the people as a whole (literally the "limitless people" or *demos*) wailed in response. So there is singing, not movement, and a pattern that suggests itself as ritualistic, although minimal elements of ritual are indicated. Within the confines of the palace, the *aoídoi* are given the privilege of singing the laments, but the narrative almost cancels this priority by advancing the women relatives and allowing them a full and articulate voice. It might be attractive to construct a "real-time" sequence here; but once again one detects the subordination of other phenomena to the privileges of the *aoídos.* It is this preeminence of the *aoídos* in the Homeric poems that probably accounts for the impression gained by Anderson, the prominent musi-

13. Barker (1984), no. 3, 20; *Iliad* 24.719–76, in excerpts.

cal historian of ancient Greece, apparent in his observation that, in what are loosely termed the "dark ages," "choruses had a subordinate place."[14]

In contrast to the Homeric poems, the mainland poet Hesiod provides us with a theology of the Muses, one that resonates throughout antiquity and has profound implications for song and dance and for *choroí.* The opening of his *Theogony,* like the Homeric poems, begins the song with the Muse(s), who are here the Muses of Mount Helikon in Boeotia, who dance around the spring and the altar of Zeus.[15] These Muses first wash in sacred water and then "make their *choroí* on highest Helikon." They dance at night, veiled in mist, "releasing a most lovely voice, hymning Zeus . . . and Hera" and other gods and immortals. They taught Hesiod "fine song" (*kalen . . . aoiden*), and it seems that "hymn" is not to be distinguished sharply here from *aoidé:* so, in *Works and Days,* Hesiod claims that "the Muses taught me to sing (*aeidein*) awesome song (*hymnon*)" (662). Hesiod explicitly provides the art of the *aoidos* with a divine essence. The Muses, when they address him on Helicon, claim to know how to speak lies like the truth, as well as the truth, and they instruct him to "give fame to what will be and what has been" and to "hymn" the immortals, always singing of the Muses at the beginning and end of a song. So the art of the *aoidos* here embraces that of "hymning" the gods, according to the precedent set by the Muses. It is interesting that the Muses themselves are conceived as a *choros,* even though they initiate Hesiod as an *aoidos,* a solo singer. It is also interesting that there is no mention of an instrument, for either the Muses or Hesiod, for whom they provide a rod (*skeptron*) that they pluck from a bay tree.[16]

With this account of his inspiration completed, Hesiod "begins" again from the Muses,

> who with their hymns
> please the great thought of father Zeus on Olympus,
> telling of what is, what will be, and what has been,
> in vocal accord. An untiring, sweet sound flows
> from their mouths.
> (*Theogony* 36–40)

and they sing of Earth and Heaven and their offspring, then of Zeus as they begin and end their song, and of the "race of men" (*anthropon . . . genos*) and of

14. Anderson 1994, 20.
15. Barker (1984), no. 16, 34–36; *Theogony* 1–104.
16. *Skeptron* is the same word as is used for the rod of kings, heralds, and priests—figures of authority who may invoke the gods.

giants. The nine Muses are the daughters of Zeus and of Memory, and *aoíde* is their care. They occupy a place a little way down from the peak of Mount Olympus, and there are their "shining dancing-places" (*choroí*) and their homes, and the Graces and Desire live alongside them. "They sing of the laws of all and make famous the noble ways of the immortals" (66–67); "sing" here is the verbal form of *molpe*.

> They went then to Olympos, delighting in their beautiful voice,
> with an immortal song. The dark earth resounded about them
> and their hymns, and a lovely sound arose from under their feet
> as they approached their father.
> (*Theogony* 68–71)

Here again "song" is *molpe,* and Barker indicates that he believes that it must signify both song and dance because plainly dance is implied in the following lines.[17] The Muses, according to Hesiod, are responsible for the good judgment of kings, and while *aoídoi* and *kitharistaí* come from Apollo and the Muses, kings come from Zeus. The associations here are interesting, tactfully and carefully placing *aoídoi* alongside those kings who are inspired by the Muses to give sound judgments, and who are accordingly greeted like a god in public places. It would be surprising, and presumably disappointing to Hesiod, if such kings were not patrons of *aoídoi.*

Hesiod establishes a complex and satisfying theology of song, and his poem *Theogony* proceeds to repeat for mortals the themes of the archetypal song/hymn of the Muses on Olympus. The "hymnic" qualities also find expression in the so-called *Homeric Hymns,* addressed to particular gods, of which the most interesting for our purposes and the earliest is the first *Hymn to Apollo,* which addresses itself to Apollo of Delos.[18] The Aegean island of Delos was the cult center of the Ionian Greeks, reputed as the birthplace of Apollo; the other part of the *Hymn to Apollo,* apparently a later composition, is addressed to Apollo at/of Delphi. The composer/singer of the Delian hymn finds it difficult to hymn Apollo, because Apollo has the whole range of *aoíde* in his care, whether on the mainland or on the islands (19–21). But at the

17. Barker 1984, 35n11.

18. The general consensus is that the form adopted by these *Hymns* is that of a prelude, perhaps originally sung as part of a larger program; this view receives support from the description of the *Hymn to Apollo* as a "prelude" (*prooímion*) by the fifth-century historian Thucydides. But see the comments by Barker (1984, 38–39), who provides an excellent introduction.

conclusion of the hymn, he turns his attention to the people of Delos, "whenever they set up their gathering" (*agona*), when the Ionians come together in numbers (150–52). The Ionians are complimented on being wealthy (155), and these occasions delight Apollo most, "when they turn their minds to boxing and dancing and song" (149). In particular, the composer admires the "Delian girls, servants of Far-shooting" (Apollo the archer),

> who when first they have hymned Apollo,
> and also Leto and Artemis shooter of arrows,
> turning their thoughts to men and women of old
> sing a hymn, and enchant the tribes of men.
> (*Hymn to Delian Apollo* 158–61)[19]

In *Theogony* the past, present, and future are envisaged as part of the subject matter of *aoide*, but it is not made clear what these events might be. What is suggested of the Delian girls' *choros* here is that it begins with a hymn to the gods of the festival and, then, proceeds to what we should call myth, heroic or human. In this respect it picks up the idea of *klea andron* in the *Iliad* and sets this as the format for a *choros*, or a choral song. There is no explicit mention of dancing as well for the Delian girls, but we have no reason to assume that this *choros* did not dance.[20] The composer is interested, clearly enough, in their voices, and he goes on to ask the girls to mention him as the best singer, if requested; he will reciprocate and carry their fame with him to the cities of men across the earth.

The Delian *Hymn* offers us a substantial festival for an area of Greece, supported by a wide community, founded in honor of specific gods, one of whom is strongly associated with song, with a *choros* of young girls that is an institutional rather than an occasional event, as it seems, and which might expect (like the festival) to be renowned throughout Greece. There is no good reason to believe that this event in the island of Delos is a fantasy, unlike the Homeric visions. What is appropriate to a *choros* is certified here, and it receives an impressive validation in Hesiod's *Theogony*, in what I termed a theology of the *choros*. There are many paths that open up from this point

---

19. Barker no. 18, 39–40. They are complimented further by the fascinating comment that they know how to "mimic the voices of men," and their song is so well-fitted to them that each person would say that he himself was giving voice (162–64).

20. Calame (1997) has written a specialist study of *choroi* of young women in ancient Greece, and he comments on this *choros* at 104–10; I review his approach below. Euripides, in his tragedy *Heracles*, envisages the Delian girls as "whirling" (*Heracles* 687).

and from what is found or suggested in Homer, Hesiod, and the *Hymns*. I shall give closest attention in what follows to the relationship of composers to *choroí,* as it emerges from this time forward.

The earliest surviving texts of songs for *choroí* are by the composers Eumelus and Alcman, from the former a tiny fragment and from the latter substantial parts of one song and part of another.[21] Eumelus dates from approximately the time of Hesiod, around 700 BCE, and Alcman from the middle to the end of the seventh century, something under a hundred years later. Eumelus may even date from the later eighth century, which would place him at the same time as the Homeric epics were beginning to be settled in the form known to us.[22]

Both Eumelus and Alcman were active in the Peloponnese, which spoke the dialects of Greek known as Doric, settled as it was by Dorian tribes. Although only two lines of the song by Eumelus are preserved by a later writer, their context is provided.[23] The song was a processional composition for a *choros* sent by the Messenians to Delos, and this undoubtedly indicates those festivals of Apollo mentioned in the Homeric *Hymn.*[24] Messenia had the misfortune to be geographically located next to the Spartans, who set about annexing its territory in a series of wars during the times of Eumelus and Alcman. What is particularly interesting here is that Eumelus was a Corinthian, and a member of its ruling family or clan, the Bacchiads. He was also an *aoidos,* or at least a composer who brought together in epic form myths relating to Corinth, and may have composed other epic poems.[25] The choral composition may have had a political quality, since the lines that are preserved refer to the enjoyment previously gained by the Messenian Apollo (of the Messenian citadel, Ithome) from the Muse's song and dance of freedom.

21. For text and translation of the songs of Alcman, see Campbell (1988); there is a translation by Lattimore of Alcman's best preserved song (1960, 33–35). West (1993) provides a comprehensive collection of translations of ancient Greek songs but in the barest possible format, without any commentary.

22. On the date of Eumelus, see Janko (1982, 231–33); West questions this early date (1992, 15n8).

23. Text, translation, and brief discussion in Huxley (1969, 62); text and translation in Campbell (1988, 290–91).

24. How far "processional" defines a kind of song is difficult to say; Käppel (1992, 82) questions the weight of the term, and Rutherford (2001, 459) believes that Eumelus's song may have been a *paian,* dedicated to Apollo of Delos.

25. Huxley (1969) gives considerable space to Eumelus as an epic poet, in his chap. 5, 60–79.

The songs of Alcman have drawn extensive commentary ever since the substantial fragment now called the Louvre *partheneion* was discovered on papyrus in 1855. Alcman composed repeatedly for *choroi* of girls at Sparta, and although the classification *partheneion* comes from later antiquity, this is the term adopted by modern scholars for *choroi* of this kind. What is striking about his best preserved song is the open self-reference from the singers, the indications of the number of girls in such *choroi* (ten or eleven), and the praise given to named, contemporary Spartan girls. In the papyrus, this fascinating section follows an unfortunately mutilated opening to the song, which is mythological.

Calame has made a special study of this kind of *choros,* maintaining a focus on this song by Alcman and considering structural features of organization and the ritual context in which such *choroi* might be placed. His work has had a significant impact, and the first volume has been translated into English.[26] What has impressed others is Calame's emphasis on the value of such *choroi* to those involved in them and to the society that institutes them. Calame is insistent on the idea of function, something that connects firmly for him to a characterization of such *choroi* as ritual activities, with the ritual in this case tied to an educational purpose. There is much in Calame's study of the *choroi* of young women that is helpful to the appreciation of the tragic *choroi* of Athens. His structuralist approach alerts us to the components and the social setting of a *choros,* and since many of these aspects are rather better known in relation to tragedy and the festivals of Dionysus at Athens than they are in the case of archaic Sparta, his insights may sharpen our critical sense of the nature of tragic *choroi.*

My own reservations are mainly on the larger scale of theory and critical assumptions, but I should also note minor doubts, since they matter. Calame devotes a great deal of attention, in his morphology of the personnel of the *choros,* to the figure of the *choregos.* But despite a sophisticated, sociolinguistic investigation of the multiple terms for the "leader" or "setter-up" of *choroi,* we are still left, truthfully, with little more than speculation on the precise function of the *choregos* in any given case. The same problem is apparent in the crucial issue of the distinction between the respective contributions of the *choregos* and the composer, which the study cannot resolve.[27] Calame also uses tragedy for the purposes of heightened comparison, and here we need to be wary. For example, he contrasts what he believes to be the prevalence of circular *choroi* with "the tragic chorus grouped in a rectangle," the conven-

26. Calame 1997, x.
27. Calame 1997, 230.

tional vision dependent on commentators from the Roman and Byzantine periods.[28] Yet at the conclusion of the section, Calame adds a severe qualification to this picture: "The tragic chorus would therefore originate in a lyric form, and the dichotomy between tragic chorus characterized by 'rectangle' and lyric chorus characterized by 'circularity' is probably not as marked as my remarks at the beginning of the paragraph would suggest."[29] Calame's specific point is that there is actually a third "category of disposition in rows" available to *choroi* from the "lyric" or archaic period, and so the tragic chorus can by that means be linked to rather than divided from the lyric. But this qualification is presented in a way that reinforces the questionable notion of the rectangular tragic (and indeed comic) *choros*.

The first of my larger reservations concerns the passing allusion Calame makes to the literary dithyramb, or to "the literary form it assumed in the classical period, notably at Athens," which is contrasted to its "ritual form in the Archaic period."[30] Now this is a very strange idea, granted that we are categorically certain of the performance of dithyrambs in tribal contests at Athens in the city festival of Dionysus throughout the fifth century. In addition, I am worried by the implications of this relatively casual comment for Calame's methodology. The emphasis on ritual is an exciting and relatively conventional anthropological approach to what one might term "performative phenomena," and Calame exploits it to good effect as a vision of Spartan society. Of course, the farther back in time and in (a decreasing) availability of evidence that we go, the more attractive such an interpretation of phenomena might seem. Presumably, according to this thinking, early societies have rituals, while later societies "end up with" literature or art.[31] But are these categories, or critical assumptions, valid, and if so for whom are they valid? In relation to Calame's hesitation about the role of Alcman, the com-

28. Calame 1997, 34. Statements that the tragic, comic, and satiric *choroi* danced in a rectangular formation come from late Greek commentary of the Byzantine era. They all depend, plainly, on the pun created between *trag/oidía* and *te/trag/onon* (rectangular): indeed, this is explicitly advanced as one of a list of etymologies explaining the word *tragoidía* by the *Etymologicum Magnum* (764, under *Tragoedia*). The correlation is totally spurious, since the word for "rectangular" is a compound of *tetra* (four) and *gonion* (angled), and so the apparent *trag* element is a purely fortuitous result of the compound. There can be little doubt that this speculation also took inspiration from the knowledge that the dithyrambic *choros* was invariably defined as "circular."

29. Calame 1997, 38.

30. Calame 1997, 79.

31. This was very much the broad assumption in Victor Turner's influential distinction between "liminal" and "liminoid" phenomena; for a detailed critique of Turner's anthropological theorizing, see Ley (1999), sec. 4.1, 141–74.

poser of the song, are we to see that role as purely ritual? Did Alcman con-
ceive of it in that way? Did Sophocles later? And how did the *choros* of ten or
eleven young women at Sparta view their involvement? Is the *aoidos* of epic,
who sees himself in some respects as a mouthpiece of the Muse, nonetheless
to be understood as a secular figure in comparison with the composer of
choroí? Are all *choroí* ritualistic?

My second reservation concerns education. Calame's widest conclusion
is that *choroí* of this sort performed an educative function within the society,
offering a kind of "rite of passage" or transition rite for those involved. This,
again, is a sound and established anthropological classification and interpretation of ritual activity, which the work of van Gennep has done a great deal
to popularize.[32] But it is also a Platonic idea, or assertion, advanced in direct
connection with an idiosyncratic conception of *choroí* in Plato's *Laws*. I shall
be looking more closely at Plato's theories later in this chapter, in relation to
dancing. But I note here that Calame, without explanation, associates his
proposed educative function directly with mimesis, in a Platonic vision of
music and dance: "If music seems to be the essence of the education Spartan
girls received in the chorus, we must remember that neither music nor dance
were ends in themselves in Greece: they are the means of communicating by
performance and assimilating by *mímesis* a precise set of contents."[33] In fact,
Calame experiences obvious difficulties in giving an outline of this education in relation to Alcman's songs. His conclusion is fair-minded, but hardly
lends weight to his thesis:

> But how about the girls? What were they taught in Sparta of the seventh cen-
> tury during the choral dances at the festivals described above? If their instruc-
> tion aimed at making adult women of adolescent girls, what was the status of
> the adult free woman for which the girls were prepared? What was the social
> role to which they were destined?
>
> ... Besides procreation and the care of the child, it is difficult to imagine
> what else the wives of these warriors did.[34]

With the exception of physical exercises, Calame has little to add.

Calame's hesitation over the precise role of the composer in relation to
choroí, which actually betrays a larger uncertainty about composition as such,

32. The work of Van Gennep (1960) formed the basis for Turner's theories of the liminal
and liminoid.
33. Calame 1997, 231.
34. Calame 1997, 234–35.

should not obscure the fact that in Eumelus and Alcman (taking them as a continuity) we have something remarkable. This can be appreciated if we contrast what we find in these two composers with the notion of *choroi* received from the Homeric poems. Both Eumelus and Alcman are applying the skills of composition to a *choros,* skills that we perceive through words but that are realized in song and dancing. We cannot know if either figure was responsible for the choreography, but we can probably be sure that each was responsible for the music and for the form taken by the accompaniment, whether playing an instrument personally (probably, in that case, a lyre) or passing the melody across to an *auletes.* Furthermore, we are dealing in both cases with something like a commission, which in the case of Alcman was a repeated event, as is clear from the other fragments, a status of some kind in itself. The speculation, which dates from antiquity, that Alcman was not a Spartan may well be unfounded. But Eumelus was an aristocratic Corinthian, a composer of an epic that promoted the fame of his own city, who was also willing to compose a *choros* to be performed by Messenians. So in the seventh century, and possibly by its beginning, composition for *choroi* became established, and the commission issued from a community or from those who were accepted as representing it. This structure is long lasting and is found embedded in the range of *choroi* at Athens.

So the Homeric picture is confronted by a completely different social and artistic formation, and one that emerges into view at a similar time to the final period of composition for the epics. In the epics, the subordination of *choroi* to the prominent role of the *aoidos,* who is envisaged in close relation to the *aoidos* or composer of the epic itself, presents us with a fundamental separation of artistry and composition from the spontaneous or traditional activities of song and dance. We might classify even the Homeric *ekphrasis* of the shield of Achilles as a "folk" picture of *choroi,* provided that we accepted that this representation was only a more exaggerated and formalized version of the relationship between *aoidos* and *choros* found in other passages, notably in the *Odyssey.* The realization that at some point around 700 BCE a completely different formation of some kinds of *choroi* existed, and that we do not know whether it had a previous history, should complicate our reception of the Homeric presentation. Categorically, we must accept that the Homeric "evidence" is already artistic. But the invitation is still there to believe that there were two kinds of *choroi*: those that were not specifically composed for an occasion and that may have relied on traditional formulas of song and dance, which Homer chooses to see accompanied or supplemented in some manner by his model of the *aoidos,* and those that were "composed," in a sophisticated and presumably quite formal structure of commission.

We might indeed be bewildered by the eventual variety of Greek *choroí,* and the variety of occasions on which *choroí* were formed. The collections of authored songs made in the Hellenistic period are responsible for our categories of what, in the modern era, has been called "lyric" poetry. They offer to us, in surviving poems and in other fragments or quotations attributed to named composers, a number of "genres," which include the *partheneion,* the *epithalamion* (a wedding song), the *threnos* or lament, the *epinikion* or victory song for success in the athletic games, the *prosodion* or processional *choros,* the *paian* addressed to Apollo, the dithyramb associated with Dionysus, and hymns. How reliable these categories are is open to question, and that issue was helpfully explored by Harvey.[35] More recently assumptions about a clear distinction between choral lyric and monody, or songs sung by a solo performer to the lyre, have been radically questioned. This renders our grasp of the songs we have, and of the environment in and for which they were composed, even more tenuous than the patchy nature of the survival of texts would guarantee. But what obviously confronts us in these texts, and in the anecdotes or circumstantial evidence that may accompany them, is the fact of composition, and when the compositions are for *choroí* they are undoubtedly commissions. In many cases we can also determine that the composers were "professional," if we mean by that that they repeatedly composed over a lifetime and became renowned for doing so.[36]

So it would seem that the establishment of festivals, whether civic or open to other Greeks, from the later eighth century BCE onward provided occasions for *choroí* and for other forms of singing that tend to be classified under the single term "monody" (solo singing). These environments might be competitive, as they certainly were at Athens in the fifth century BCE. The religious orientation of many occasions might be a more reliable and embracing idea than that of ritual because we cannot necessarily be sure of the place that a song or a *choros* might occupy in a ritual structure or of how the song or *choros* was understood to contribute to a specific rite. Greek festivals were religious, but in important respects this was also true of another set of occasions that might, in contrast, be regarded as secular. Songs occasioned by an individual or individuals, such as those relating to weddings or funerals, or to victory personally or by proxy (chariot racing) in the pan-Hellenic games are religious by implication, even if the commission itself proceeds from a prominent individual or a family. The games, for example,

35. Harvey 1955.
36. Clearly, we need to detach both terms, commission and professional, from any close associations we are likely to bring to them from the modern era and allow them to reform themselves as the ancient evidence permits.

that paradigm of human physical effort and skill, are held at a sanctuary of a god or a hero, or both (Zeus and Heracles at Olympia). In this kind of cultural context, the notion of personal poetry, which is so dear and so essential to the modern tradition, may have difficulty in finding a place. Questions have been raised about almost all the varieties of composition that confront us, and there is a growing tendency to regard composition as an inherently public activity, no matter what the style of performance.[37]

The place of commissioned songs alongside other kinds of song, and of commissioned *choroi* alongside other forms of singing and dancing groups, is almost impossible to determine. As Calame notes, weddings might occasion singing (and dancing) at different moments of what might be a lengthy procedure. We know that Greeks used cries in given circumstances, whether these were a form of words or a particular sound, and the abundant evidence is that a particular group would (gather to) give voice to them. So *io paian* is the simplest form of the *paian,* understood to be addressed to Apollo, while *ololuge* is a cry raised to a god by women.[38] Between these and the commissioned song or *choros* may be countless other forms of singing and movement or dancing, acquired through what we should now most probably call a popular tradition. What is certain, in contrast, is that commissioned songs proceed from some recognized authority or in relation to the status of an individual. A composed *choros,* to take the grouping in which we are most interested, is never going to be a casual or spontaneous event.

Unfortunately, all too little is known about the performance conditions of most of the composed texts that have come down to us, even when we might be confident that a particular text represents a commission. The *paian* (plural, *paianes*) offers a good example here. Those who have studied the *paian,* such as most recently Rutherford, are confident from contextual and social evidence that the *paian* became a composed *choros* as well as retaining its more spontaneous form of a cry to the god Apollo as a healer or helper, a cry that might be an appeal or a celebration.[39] But in relation to one of the major composers of *paianes,* Pindar, direct evidence about the nature of such a *choros* of singers/dancers arising in the fragmentary texts themselves is desperately limited. In fact, we have just the one reference incidentally addressed to

130

---

37. Despite her use of the term "poetry" in the title of her chapter, the survey "Poetry, Memory and Performance" by Thomas (1992, 113–27), in the context of her study of orality in Greek culture, provides an excellent introduction to the situation in general.
38. There is a good short discussion on this subject by Calame (1997, 76–79).
39. For a short introduction to the *paian,* in a discussion of its relation to tragedy, see Rutherford (1995).

"young men" in one of these songs, which might guide us to the conclusion that Pindar's composed *paianes* were performed by a *choros* of young men.[40]

Even if one shares Rutherford's confidence that the performances of *paianes,* by groups of men and particularly young men, represented "the organization and exhibition of the collective strength of adult males," and that the *paian* accordingly offers a "precise analogy to the initiatory function of the partheneion," it is very hard indeed to translate this into any convictions about the performance itself.[41] Rutherford is clearly influenced in his analysis of the form by the conclusions of Calame on Alcman and on *choroi* of young women, but it has to be said that Alcman's compositions permit these conclusions more readily than the compositions of Pindar. We should undoubtedly expect *paianes* to be a major part of the worship of Apollo at Delos, and the *choroi* of Delos and those sent to Delos were famous. But, in this connection, we appear to have only Pindar's *Paian* 4 and a badly mutilated fragment from Simonides, which a commentator notes was a *paian* written for the Athenians at Delos, with neither offering us anything substantial on performance.[42]

The fifth-century composer Pindar is, indeed, a case in point for this general issue of performance. His poems were classified, much as Harvey has indicated, by later Greek scholars into genres that many believed were those of *choroi,* including those mentioned above: the *epinikion,* the *paian,* the dithyramb, *threnoi,* and *partheneia.* But anxiety, notably from Lefkowitz, was forcefully expressed about the composer's use of the first person, the poetic "I," in the large collection of songs celebrating victory in the games, and it has proved extremely difficult to extract from the extensive collection sufficiently unequivocal evidence of reference to *choroi.*[43] Pindar indeed uses the word *komos*

40. Race (1997) provides texts and translations of the surviving *paianes.* Pindar *Paian* 6, 122, is apparently an invitation for the young men to call out "the measures [*metra*] of *paianes.*" A possible reference to "I shall celebrate Artemis . . . in a *choros*" (*choreusomai*) in Pindar's *Paian* 4, 1–2, is only a conjectural restoration, albeit a plausible one.
41. Rutherford 1995, 115.
42. For the fragmentary *paian* by Simonides, see Campbell (1991), Simonides no. 519, frag. 35, 390–91. Plutarch, in his *Life of Nikias* 2, gives an interesting account of the *choros* sent to Delos on behalf of the Athenians in 426 BCE, which would appear to envisage the *choros* as a *prosodion,* or processional song. The context for *choroi* of this sort is helpfully traced by Rutherford (2004, 67–90, esp. 82–86), but it is difficult to determine how far it can help us in picturing performances of *paianes.*
43. The modern bibliography of this dispute is too lengthy to include in its totality: Lefkowitz (1991) has advanced her doubts, the dispute is addressed by Carey (1991), with contributions by others, and more recently there is the exchange between d'Alessio (1994) and Lefkowitz (1995).

to describe groups of young men who will be singing in connection with the particular victory being celebrated, but the compositions fail to make explicit their own conditions of performance. So it is that scholarship, exercised strenuously on both sides of a debate, has been unable to resolve this anxiety or doubt in relation to the large collection of Pindar's *epiníkia*, or songs celebrating victors at the athletic festivals of Greece. Although this is frustrating it should warn us that, whatever the truth of the issue, we are likely to gain very little insight into the performances of *choroí* from the composed texts themselves.

132

This is a caution that probably extends very far indeed and, unfortunately, applies perhaps as firmly to tragic *choroí*, generically and in any given instance, as to any others. Oddly enough, one of the more revealing aspects of Pindar's activity comes in a composition classed as a *partheneíon*, in which the much-debated first person is expressed in the feminine, and where the names of some of the leading players in the conduct (organization and performance) of the *choros* are given. But, once again, those details that we have about the nature of this *choros*, and the occasion for which the composition was commissioned, are contextual rather than integral, supplied by an outside source and not in the words of the song itself.[44] The strong temptation might be to conclude that if the compositions classed as *partheneía* were *choroí* for performance by young girls, and dithyrambs at Athens were categorically *choroí* for performance, as we know, then we should have no real need to doubt the contextual evidence that *paíanes* too were compositions for *choroí*. That consolidated argument would position Pindar as an established composer for *choroí* and make it quite plausible that the *epiníkia* belong to that expertise, as has regularly been believed.

MUSIC: METER OR MEASURE, MELODY, AND MODE

At this point we need to turn to the subject of music and dancing in relation to the *choros*, and it is probably right to consider music first. Ancient Greek musical culture operated primarily with two classes of instruments, what I have termed the lyre group, capable of being held and plucked or strummed, and the *aulos* or *auloí*, pipes that were blown.[45]

44. The most recent discussion of this song comes from Stehle (1997, 93–100); but see also Lefkowitz (1991, 15–17). Text, sources, and translation can be found in Race (1997, 322–30).
45. Detailed accounts of the instruments, with illustrations, can be found in West (1992), Anderson (1994), and Landels (1999).

Some examples of *auloí* have survived, and it is plain that they were made from a variety of materials, some extremely and perhaps coincidentally durable. The *aulos* has often been described, in the singular form, as a flute, which is unfortunate and misleading, since it operated with a reed, and a reed that was itself held in the mouth.[46] So the tendency now, in the search for a working analogy, is to look toward the oboe rather than the clarinet or to settle for the word "pipes." Furthermore, the standard form of the instrument was double, with the player using separate hands to play each pipe.[47] Illustrations of the *auloí* are clear and unmistakable, and regularly the pipe player (*auletes*) is shown with a band round his cheeks, a *phorbeía,* which was intended to support the cheeks during the strain of blowing. Unlike the lyre group, which underwent considerable variations in design and in the number of strings, starting most prominently (as in the Homeric poems) with the *phormínx,* the *auloí* appear consistently from archaic through classical times. Two features are of particular importance: first, this was an instrument that had to accompany the voice of another or others, unlike the lyre, and second its sound was, for want of a better, general term, piercing. So it is that we read of its use by soldiers marching, and to accompany the beat of oars in warships, and one of the most evocative vase paintings of early Greek culture we have shows an aulete with hoplites, or heavily armed Greek foot-soldiers.[48] There is sufficient evidence from literature and vase paintings to suggest that a lyre-group instrument and *auloí* together might accompany singing and dancing, but the *auloí* are particularly prominent in connection with *choroí.* This is absolutely true of the theatrical *choroí* at Athens, and rules were established for the allocation and payment of the *auletes.*[49] There were other, relatively familiar instruments, but their use in performative and public contexts was limited in comparison.[50]

The principal role of both of these instruments was as an accompaniment

46. An exploded diagram is given by Landels (1999, 27), fig.2a.3.
47. I have adopted the later Greek use of *auloí,* the plural, alongside *aulos* simply as a reminder that there were double pipes.
48. This is on the so-called Chigi vase, dating from about 640–30 BCE. Anderson calls this "the earliest significant depiction of the double aulos" (1994, 18).
49. Csapo and Slater (1994), sec. 3, no. 84, 144, dithyramb in the fourth century BCE; Pickard-Cambridge (1988, 75–76), dithyramb, and (1988, 88), comedy and tragedy. Wilson (1999, 2002) has closely examined the cultural significance of the *aulos* and the *auletaí* at Athens. For the role of instruments from what I have called the lyre group in public performances at Athens, notably from the later fifth century BCE, see the complementary essay by Wilson (2004), who traces the ideological implications of stringed instruments in Athenian *mousike.*
50. See West (1992, 70 ff., 109 ff.) and Landels (1999, 69 ff.) for other instruments.

to the activities of singing and/or dancing, and although instrumental music was not unknown, music would be understood throughout Greek antiquity as an emphatic and delightful manifestation of the rhythms of words or physical movement. There is now reasonable doubt whether any purely spoken poetry existed in the archaic and classical periods, and sufficient evidence to support the view that prose forms—recitations of historical writing, the public art of rhetoric—would have made use of a similar sense of rhythm in the human voice, albeit without instrumental accompaniment. This is a difficult aspect of a culture to capture, and detailed descriptions of standard cultural practice are notorious absentees in historical records, for the obvious reason that vital and almost intuitive assumptions rarely occasion comment.

In Hesiod, the Muses already affect the public judgments and presumably the diction of a responsible king, and the concept of *mousike* embraces far more than anything we might find in our own term "music." The range implied by *mousike,* for any given period in ancient Greece, cannot strictly be determined, and we might do worse than to translate it as "culture," a word with a similarly debatable and variable set of connotations at any given social moment. But prominent in *mousike* are the notions of sound and language, often of rhythm, and its connection with another term *paideia* are profound. *Paideia* is more limited, because its derivation indicates its close relation to the "upbringing" of children or adolescents.[51] But since "upbringing" conjoins the child's sensibility with visions of adult values, then we may expect to find adult culture (*mousike,* in this instance) often envisaged in "paedeutic" or educational terms. We find this particular tendency marked in Aristophanes and in Plato, and present in a far more relaxed form in Aristotle, and it is a tendency in Greek thought that we need to acknowledge.

The lyre group seems to have occupied a prominent place in *mousike* because it comprised instruments that could accompany the player's own voice, and that is the definitive role these instruments have in the Homeric poems, notably the *Odyssey.* I am not aware of anything written directly on this topic, but I suspect that it was the instrument used by composers even in such cases as the preliminary composition of danced songs for *choroi.* There is little that we can take as convincing evidence here, but the practicalities would make an interesting argument. To compose in coordination with an *auletes* would involve a process of intricate difficulties; to compose on or with the lyre would seem far more plausible. I should be reluctant to take Aristophanes as

---

51. The great study of *paideia* was made by Jaeger (1939), who allowed the term to assume the broadest of its connotations. There is a good summary of the relationship between the two terms, *mousike* and *paideia,* in the introduction by the editors to an important collection of essays on the culture of *mousike* in Athens: Murray and Wilson (2004, 1–8).

direct and simple "evidence" for anything, but the tragic playwright Agathon is apparently shown composing with or to a *barbitos* (a lyre-group instrument) and a lyre in *Women at the Thesmophoria* (136–37). Anecdotes of the life of Sophocles tell of him playing the lyre in one of his own tragedies, *Thamyras,* the myth of a lyre player who provoked the anger of Apollo, the divine lyre player, and also of how he led the celebratory song for the victory of Salamis playing on the lyre. That composers learned *mousíke* on and with the lyre seems to be implicit in everything we know or assume about composition in the fifth century BCE. The corollary to this is that the *lyra* was without doubt the instrument of *paideía,* in the repetition by adolescents of known songs or melodies. As such, it was surely in addition the instrument of the amateur, and no doubt many aspiring dramatic composers fell into that category. Even successful dramatic composers at Athens were "professional" only in the sense of repeated and skillful activity by men of independent means; but one shudders to think what an amateur might produce on the *aulos,* whose leading practitioners were indeed renowned professionals.

135

In mentioning the difficulty of communicating a melody to an *auletes* at the time of composition, I have been thinking of composing uniquely by the ear. There was, it seems, no widespread system of written notation during the periods that concern us, although the written alphabet was reintroduced into Greece toward the close of the eighth century BCE, at about the time when the poems of Hesiod were composed.[52] The role of writing in the verbal composition of songs is a fraught issue, on which there is hardly any truly reliable evidence. But there seems little doubt that songs were composed and transmitted orally and aurally and that textuality played a marginal and only gradually significant part in transmission. There was a trade in manuscripts by the end of the fifth century BCE, which included play texts. The exact origin of our own texts of the plays is unknown, although an official collection of scripts was made later, toward the end of the fourth century, a kind of authorized edition.[53] So it can be reasonably assumed that the Athenian dramatic *choroí* in the fifth century were taught by ear, not from "the book," and it is almost certain that the standard practice was that the composer was the *didaskalos* (teacher/trainer) of his *choros,* since he remained the producer of the play.[54] It is equally clear that, at least in the early part of the

52. On notation, see Landels (1999, 206–7) and West (1992, 254 ff.).
53. Csapo and Slater 1994, sec. IA, 1–38.
54. There are apparent exceptions in the case of Aristophanes: Pickard-Cambridge (1988, 84–85) on the composer as producer and (1988, 90–91) on the introduction of the specialist *chorodidaskalos* to tragedy, possibly dating from the fourth century BCE. Compare Csapo and Slater (1994), sec. 4, 352–53.

fifth century, the tragic *choros* was taught the dance as well as the song by the composer, and there is no particular reason to believe that this role was dropped by either Sophocles or Euripides.[55] The performance of the tragic *choroi* incorporates singing, accompaniment from the *aulos,* dancing, and the central fact of rhythmic verbal composition, and the skills of the composer himself must have embraced the means to realize all of these. What remains to us is the verbal composition, in the scripts or texts of the songs in the plays. The two standard forms of modern analysis of the scripts are rhythmic and critical: analysis of the meter or measure in which the words are composed and analysis of the thematic and evocative qualities of the songs, and of their place within the tragedy. Studies of tragic music and dancing are almost inevitably placed within wider studies of ancient Greek music and of ancient Greek dance, creating a division between these two components of *choreía.*

This is apparent in two examples of diligent scholarship intended for a relatively wide readership, Webster's *The Greek Chorus* and West's *Ancient Greek Music.* West is certainly not concerned with the *choros* to any pronounced extent, but his constructive and highly informed approach to music carries virtually no references to dance. For his part Webster appears to be mostly concerned with dancing in the first section of his book, which is devoted to illustrative archaeological material. In the second section, devoted to literary sources, Webster relies largely on metrical analyses of songs, but it is not clear whether he believes he is concentrating on singing or on dancing; there is, in fact, very little reference to anything to do with music. So, to an extent, as we progress farther down either line of inquiry we are led farther away from the unity we are expecting, if (tragic) *choreía* is our principal interest.

It would be useful if unity was emphasized before the problems of division were faced, and a short book by Georgiades addresses itself with limited success to this issue.[56] Georgiades is not very strong on dancing, and the prominence accorded to the round dance in his thinking—for the Homeric vision of *aoidos* and dancers, for classical *choreía,* and in modern Greek folk dance—seems relatively simplistic. But he does advance successfully the contention that the implicit, syllabic rhythm of ancient Greek is essential to

55. Further textual and pictorial evidence on the institution of the Athenian dramatic *choroi* has been assembled ably by Pickard-Cambridge and his later editors (1988) and by Csapo and Slater (1994), and I shall not review it redundantly here. There is now even a book-length study of the role of the *choregoi,* the wealthy Athenians who provided the money for the productions of dramatic *choroi,* which enhances the available information on the organization of the festivals at Athens (Wilson 2000).
56. Georgiades 1973.

both music and dance, distinguishing ancient "meter" from European meters after antiquity. Ancient Greek is already musical, measured as it is purely
by the short or long of the syllable, and not subject to variable or discretional
stress (which he terms accent) as in modern meters. The rhythm is inherent
in the words: "The syllables themselves are the rhythmic matter from which
a rhythm originates."[57] In modern meters, the rhythm is a predetermined,
"abstract" entity to which the words are fitted, and emphasis plays a great
role. These qualities will permit, even demand, the application of an independent musical rhythm as an accompaniment. In ancient Greek, once the
pattern of short and long syllables is established in and through the words
themselves, an independent musical rhythm cannot be joined to it, "for an
independent rhythmic musical composition would necessitate some manner of alteration of the verse . . . and that is not possible."[58] The composition
of the words to a rhythm, their disposition with a view to a patterning of
their short and long syllables, establishes the measure for both accompaniment and dance.

　　This principle is of the greatest importance, and we might add to it the
vital distinction between an inflected language (such as ancient Greek) and
the emphatic stress placed on part of the word that is found in many modern languages, including English. Inflection has to do with pitch, not emphatic stress. It is marked by diacritics placed over Greek words on the page,
commonly (and rather confusingly) known as "accents," and the notation of
these pitch accents stems from the Alexandrian period. In his discussion
of inflection, Anderson notes that the Alexandrian terms for the three accents were "high-pitched" (oxeía), "low-pitched" (bareía), and "turned around"
(perispomenos). These adjectives modified an understood noun, prosoidía, which
in this context means "singing . . . in accompaniment" to words. As Anderson observes, "the terminology, therefore, is musical," and so even the spoken language of ancient Greece would be inherently musical. Unfortunately,
the intervals for these pitches are unknown, as is the degree of insistence
with which these inflections may have been sounded in all circumstances.[59]
The existence of inflection may have had some effect on the patterns
achieved by rhythm, particularly in relation to the conclusions we might be
tempted to draw about melody in the songs of choroí, and I shall return to this
briefly in a later section of this chapter.

57. Georgiades 1973, 55.
58. Georgiades 1973, 64.
59. Anderson 1994, 45.

Meter

I have mentioned meter (or measure) and melody, and with mode we have three major aspects of Greek music and song; it may be helpful to pursue these separately. The evidence for meter is the fullest, for the meter is apparent, or may be determined with more or less confidence, within the words of the songs, and the texts are the only secure survival from ancient Greek *choreía*. There are several good introductions to meter for students of ancient Greek, but for those primarily interested in music and *choreía* the natural and essential question is whether the determination of meter implicitly reveals any musical qualities.[60] If meter is in fact measure, and to that extent controls both musicality and dance, can we track anything of the qualities of these from an analysis of the meters of a song?

The answer to this is, unfortunately, largely in the negative. The only method available to metrists, working from what is after all the skeleton or the fossil of *choreía,* is to exercise a wide, comparative survey of the contextuality of distinctive meters, notably in tragedy. The method is bound to be crude, and the yardstick will almost inevitably be the detection of different kinds or degrees of emotion evinced in the language and situation of the song or, in cases where the meter varies distinctly within an extended song, in its different sections. Perhaps the most accessible essay on this subject comes from Dale, who performed a complete analysis of the meters of Greek tragedy and addressed this problem in "Expressive Rhythm in Greek Drama." Her general conclusion offers a summary with which few other metrists would disagree: "When all this is said, much the greater part of the *rhythmike* of the lyrics of Greek drama remains . . . not susceptible, at least with the knowledge at our disposal, of any definite analysis in terms of emotional suggestion. In general, one and the same meter can in different contexts and with different words be used to convey the most diverse effects."[61] The exceptions that Dale identified are obviously of considerable interest, although in the light of this general conclusion it is hard to assess their real value. The first is the highly variable meter called "dochmiac," which falls in extreme forms into a run of short syllables. Like many other metrists, editors, and textual critics Dale believed that this meter indicated or was plainly associated with passionate feeling; others might call it excited, disturbed, animated. I shall return to this quality of tragic *choreía* later in this chapter. Her second exception is

60. West 1982.
61. Dale 1969, 257.

the meter known as Ionic, which is found, in exemplary fashion, in the first
choral song of Aeschylus's *Persians* and in Euripides' *Bacchae,* at the beginning
and the end of our series of surviving tragic scripts from the fifth century
BCE. Dale tentatively links the Ionic meter to the worship of Kybele and of
Dionysus, both associated firmly with Asia in Euripides' tragedy, and risks
the following comments: "Perhaps this rhythm, which some of the audience
might actually have seen and heard performed by leaping priests to the clash
of cymbals, conveyed here indirectly a suggestion of Oriental *habrotes.*"[62] The
Greek word *habrotes* indicates softness, and what Dale points to here is not
exactly "emotional suggestion," but ethnic characterization. Yet it would be
perverse to ascribe to either *Persians* or *Bacchae* notions of "Oriental softness."

If the dochmiac meter is to be associated with emotional or passionate
disturbance, then why should it be an outstanding case in an artform such as
tragedy? Our best guess would have to be that dochmiac also entailed the
expression of disturbed emotion in disturbed movement or dance. In other
words, there was a clearly marked difference between the varieties of expression (musically and in dance) between most tragic *choreia* and that involving dochmiacs. When a playwright composed in dochmiacs, he was envisaging a kind of dancing that was continuously disturbed, and when he
composed in other meters he was not setting a program for that effect to be
realized consistently.

An ambitious approach to the use of meter as an indication of musical design has been adopted by Scott, who has written two books on that subject
surveying the plays of Aeschylus and those of Sophocles.[63] Scott has a particularly strong conviction about metrical signification and association in
the musical design of Aeschylus's *Oresteia,* and he combines this analytical
approach with more traditional formal and thematic criticism, or appreciation, of the choral songs in the plays. Scott shows little interest in dance as
an integral feature of *choreia* and writes little about music (either melody or
mode) throughout his study. So the impression gained is that the phrase
"musical design" is an enhanced version of formal criticism and that "music"
as such assumes an almost abstract status in his thinking. Scott is consider-
ate in providing a chapter titled "Introduction for Readers in Translation,"
with a list of the meters, and he prefaces each discussion of a song with a
metrical analysis, although it will inevitably be difficult for those reliant on
translation to gain more than an overall impression from these formulas.

62. Dale 1969, 256–57.
63. Scott 1984, 1996.

Scott's close argument about Aeschylus's *Oresteia* is founded on a primary contention about the qualities of the choral metric in *Agamemnon,* the first play of the trilogy, established in the first song from the elders, the *parodos.* His contention is that the *parodos* demonstrates that two metrical forms, the lyric iambic and a meter known as the lecythion, carry distinctive, thematic connotations: "The two thematic meters of the trilogy have been clearly defined and established, each within a context: lecythion for humanity's progress under the just kingship of Zeus, and iambic for the infatuation that leads men to sin and requires punishment."[64] But Scott also sees characteristics in other meters. Dactyls are the meter of epic, and Scott readily associates the dactyls of the *parodos* of *Agamemnon* with "oracular pronouncement" and notes that in listening to them "the spectators would recall the mass of folklore and saga surrounding the Trojan expedition."[65] He also subscribes to the general consensus about dochmiacs, noting their prominent use in the *parodos* of Aeschylus's *Seven against Thebes* and describing them as "heavily emotional," of such strength that "they virtually avoid the themes of the play."[66] In the *Oresteia,* however, he tentatively ascribes a different, thematic value to dochmiacs, which overrides or extends their role "as the appropriate meter in which to express extreme happiness or wretchedness." So, by the climax of *Libation Bearers,* the second play in the trilogy, his analysis has led him to consider that "it is also possible that in this trilogy the dochmiac assumes a thematic function as the meter that accompanies murders."[67]

The contribution of the characterization of meters to what I have termed a largely formal criticism (Scott's "musical design") is most apparent at the reappearance of the lecythion in the last play of the trilogy, in the song of the Furies at lines 490–565. The lecythion, according to Scott's thesis, represents "the just working of Zeus," and in this song in *Eumenides* the Furies "dwell more on their role as protectors of world order," presenting themselves "as divinities of justice."[68] Similarly, in the final singing of the trilogy, at lines 916–1020, "the lecythion grows stronger and more insistent as the Eumenides sing of endless blessings that they will shower upon Athens in cooperation with Zeus and Athena."[69] The conclusion of this song also returns to dactyls, and so the ending recalls the beginning in the *parodos* of *Agamemnon.*

64. Scott 1984, 38.
65. Scott 1984, 35.
66. Scott 1984, 39.
67. Scott 1984, 106.
68. Scott 1984, 47, 125, respectively.
69. Scott 1984, 130.

One difficulty in Scott's analysis is explicitly acknowledged by him, which is that the *choros* is at times "singing the wrong song," an idea that he introduces early in the study.[70] What Scott means is that a meter that he has identified as carrying certain thematic characteristics appears again in the trilogy devoid of those characteristics or that the thematic characteristics appear without that particular meter. Scott develops this into a sophisticated idea of wrong thinking on the part of a *choros*, a discrepancy between music and words that the audience will identify and that will accordingly carry meaning.[71] Such an interpretation of the phenomenon is subtle, but the problem more obviously undermines the idea of the thematic meter.

141

Other plays by Aeschylus make life even more difficult for Scott's thesis. Admittedly, these plays survive as single tragedies, unlike the *Oresteia*, and so the broader context is hidden from us. But the results of analysis are frustrating. With regard to *Persians*, although "it is difficult to assert strongly that there is a developing scheme in the progression of meters," Scott believes that iambics seem to be associated with laments and dactyls with "political concerns."[72] Despite Scott's appeasing comments, these are not really the associations he has asserted for the *Oresteia*. The results with *Suppliants* and *Seven against Thebes* are more disappointing: the latter "does not seem to develop its themes through an association with specific meters," while in the former "musical form does not seem to develop in any organic way throughout the play."[73]

The other major difficulty that must be acknowledged is surely the identification of themes. There is clearly a danger here of substantiating critical preconceptions about a tragedy and, perhaps, even simplifying them to create the associations between meter and theme. Scott's major leitmotifs for the *Oresteia*, found in iambic and lecythion, might be debated as interpretations of the substance and import of the trilogy, and we might hesitate to conclude that an Athenian audience would seize on just these themes through some kind of musical intuition. When they are expressed as a summary of the experience of watching the trilogy, it is questionable whether Scott's themes are adequate to the task that has been asked of them: "The musical design of the trilogy adds evidence to the debate about a static or an evolving Zeus by focusing attention on the necessary reconciliation of the two basic themes at the trilogy's conclusion: Zeus's justice must embrace proper

70. Scott 1984, 17–19.
71. A good example comes at Scott (1984), 47–48, and another at 98.
72. Scott 1984, 155, 156, respectively.
73. Scott 1984, 160, 166, respectively.

punishment for a crime."[74] There is something dangerously circular about this formulation, and we should remember that the debate that Scott mentions is a modern one, and one that is now less highly regarded by critics than it might once have been.

142

Scott's work on Sophocles follows a similar approach and format, but since these are all single tragedies, isolated from the plays that accompanied them in their original productions by Sophocles, there is an incentive to look for a different conclusion. Scott draws attention to the distribution of corresponding parts of a song in the structure of a play and of the audience's musical experience of it. So it is that in *Philoctetes* one part of a song that may sound initially as if it is free standing (at lines 391–402) is actually balanced later by a corresponding part (at lines 507–18). Scott calls this phenomenon a "hyperform," since its "form" is not immediately expressed but only later perceived as an entity, one that embraces a part of the developing action of the tragedy. He is particularly attracted by the finale of *Antigone,* noting that here the chorus engages with Creon in spoken iambic, while Creon sings in lyric, and that the balancing form of Creon's song is revealed gradually. What might seem formless is actually not so, and the corresponding parts of the song work metrically in the pattern A, A (repeated), departing to a new metrical design B, and then another C, but finally answered by a repeat of B and then of C. Scott's conclusions, once again, relate his notion of musical design to that of divine design, as in his interpretative formula for Aeschylus's *Oresteia:* "The laws of Zeus provide a powerful ordering force that drives *Antigone* from start to finish," and that force is revealed to the audience through the "hyperform" and metrical/musical design, even when the chaos of suffering seems paramount.[75] The composer, Sophocles, has felt "the need to introduce an unseen force on stage" in the hyperform, a concept that presumably corresponds to the enigmatic and unseen "ordering force" of the "laws of Zeus" in Scott's earlier formula.[76] Here art, through its formal methods of operation, is firmly in the service of a principle that might well be that of "justifying the ways of god to man," and the theology has a resoundingly monotheistic tone.

Scott's merit is to subject an intuition about the possible signification of individual meters to a thorough investigation. He has taken pains to open his discussion to those who do not have Greek, insofar as that is likely to be successful with such an intimate linguistic phenomenon as Greek metric. His

74. Scott 1984, 144.
75. Scott 1996, 206.
76. Scott 1996, 209.

two related studies raise interesting questions about the nature of audience response and lead us to examine our own preconceptions about the thematic characteristics of choral song. After reading his work, we should be left in doubt whether looking for or expecting only emotional qualities in tragic choral songs is sufficiently sensitive to the variety of implications that might be found in tragic *choreia*. The equation of lyricism with emotionalism is one that is deeply related to our own cultural history, and our "lyricism" has, in any case, little to do with tragic *choroí* accompanied by an *aulos*. In reminding us that it must be the audience's response that permits and completes the composition of *choreía*, that it is their competence and not just that of the skilled composer that is at issue, he provides us with a sense of *mousíke* that is at once both public and cultural.

Melody and Modes

Greek verbal texts have survived in some quantity of original compositions dating from about 700 BCE downward, but Greek music has not survived in anything except the sparsest fragments. The explanation for this must be in the lack of notation for the early periods and, presumably, in the lack of a motive to provide notation. In this respect, speculation on the reperformance of the specific melodies originally given to compositions, or on the alternative of a relatively carefree discarding and replacing of melodies, is desperately hampered by silence. One strong possibility must be that songs were remembered with (and as) their melodies, but the situation may have varied greatly, from song to song, according to its popularity.

The tiny fragments of the notation of tragedy are chance discoveries, dating from periods far later than the works themselves, and severe doubt has been expressed that these can possibly be remnants or survivals of the original melodies. In his "Appendix C: Musical Examples," Anderson reviews the fragmentary notations from the early and late third century BCE (respectively) of some few lines from Euripides' *Iphigenía at Aulís* and from Euripides' *Orestes*. He notes of the former that "the possibility that we have here a portion of the original setting of Euripides' tragedy . . . must be called remote" and of the latter that "nothing can justify the assumption that it has preserved the melodizing of Euripides."[77] His conviction is that these are resettings by professional performers from later periods. In contrast, West is inclined to accept the fragmentary notation of *Orestes* as genuine, part of Euripides'

77. Anderson 1994, 214, 222, respectively; discussions of the fragments from 210–22.

melodic composition for the tragedy, although he notes that "lyric and dramatic texts were normally copied without music" and that the earliest musical theorist, Aristoxenus, paid scant attention to notation.[78] It is fair to say here that when the experts disagree so radically, the rest of us have no way forward. Transcriptions are provided, and recordings of modern reconstructions are available, not only of these fragments but of the other texts that have notation, which belong to later periods and which are not for the theater.[79]

144

The sound we wish to hear would have been composed, in ancient Greece, of what we might term melody and mode. If melody is all but vanished, then mode might seem to offer a means to realize—at least imaginatively—some impression of the kind of music involved. Unfortunately, the difficulties with mode are extreme, although the written evidence lays claim, in various ways, to be authoritative. Anderson's position here is the most skeptical: "To ask what was the nature of fifth-century modality is to pose the most difficult question of all about a period that holds far too many difficulties."[80] The *harmoniai* or modes carried titles apparently relating to ethnic divisions of the Greek world, but also to ethnic divisions of the Near Eastern peoples (the western part of modern Turkey, on the coast of the Aegean Sea) with whom the Greeks had close relations in the period from the time of Homer. So we hear, from different sources, of the Dorian, Aeolian, Ionian (Greek ethnic divisions) but also of the Lydian and Phrygian and of the Mixolydian. But the first systematic treatise on harmonic theory was written toward the end of the fourth century BCE, and the status of later theories is extremely difficult to validate.

The early evidence, of apparent internal references by composers within their own songs, is often preserved in short quotations in presentations on the theme of music by later writers, and it has to be treated with great caution. So we hear of "raising a sweet shout of a hymn / in the deep-sounding Aeolian *harmonia*" in a fragment of a hymn to Demeter and Persephone by the composer Lasus, active in the later part of the sixth century BCE.[81] In the same context, the composer Pratinas from the fifth century BCE is quoted briefly, apparently placing the Aeolian *harmonia* as a middle way between a "tense" *harmonia* and the "slack" Iastian (or Ionian). Anderson is inclined to interpret this brief fragment as having sexual connotations and to read

78. West 1992, 270. Landels (1999, 221) follows West, but his preliminary comments on a "library of scores" held at Alexandria (220) are highly speculative.
79. Anderson (1994) provides a discography of modern recordings.
80. Anderson 1994, 139.
81. Text, translation, and surrounding context (from an author of the Roman period) in Campbell (1991, 306–7).

Aeolian in close relation to the verb *aiolízein*, also present in the fragment, with the sense of "shifting about."[82] This interpretation is by no means as arbitrary as it may seem in my account here, because Anderson rightly draws attention to the explicitly sexual connotations of one major (fragmentary) comic "discussion" of music from the fifth century BCE.[83] Anderson also provides a good review of the passages from Pindar that are believed to refer to modes, concluding that only one, in the victory song *Nemean 4* (at line 45) to the Lydian *harmonía*, can be taken to be explicit.[84]

The search for early sources for the titles or names of *harmoniai* is fundamentally prompted by the concerns that Plato, in his *Republic*, expresses through the character of Socrates. These look as though they may be revealing and offer us—in the absence of melody—some means of appreciating something about Greek music. In *Republic*, Plato presents a brief typology of the modes, which suggests their firm association with kinds of occasion and states of feeling, in a general context that advances the thesis that different kinds of story or of music may have an adverse (or an admirable) affect on the soul. So Plato's character of Socrates dismisses the Mixolydian mode as "mournful" and as unsuited even for respectable women, let alone for men, while the Iastian and the Lydian *harmoniai* are suitable only for the *symposion*, or drinking party. He then chooses to associate the Dorian *harmonia* with manliness, notably in war, and the Phrygian with peaceful activities characterized by restraint and proper conduct.[85]

These last two modes alone are those that Plato's Socrates finds acceptable, in the belief that since they are associated with warlike manliness and peaceful self-restraint and conduct, performances that adopt them will induce such ethical qualities in the host society and culture. This he regards as simplicity, a healthy state of the soul that can be contrasted favorably with the licentiousness of diversity and *panharmonion*, a use of the full range of modes in the composition of melodies and songs.[86] Aristotle largely follows Plato in accepting and confirming an ethical scheme of *mousike* in principle, although he disagrees with Plato in one important particular. In his *Politics*,

145

---

82. Anderson 1994, 89, 92.

83. This is a fragment from the comic dramatist Pherecrates, which is discussed by Anderson (1994, 127–34) and translated with notes by Barker (1984, 236–37); see also the essay by Dobrov and Urios-Aparisi (1995).

84. Anderson 1994, 96–100.

85. Csapo and Slater (1994), sec. 4, no. 282, 344–45; see in addition the translation and notes in Barker (1984), no. 149, 130–32.

86. Repeated exposure to "the sweet and soft and mournful *harmoniai*" will, inevitably, undermine the Platonic manly soul (Barker [1984], no. 151, 137–38, translating from a little later in *Republic*). For *panharmonion*, see Barker's summary at the close of no. 150, 136.

Aristotle contrastingly associates the Phrygian *harmonia* with the *aulos* and Dionysian celebration and dancing and, also, with the dithyramb, although he accepts the general contention that music has ethical qualities.[87]

This relative consensus, which combines the ethnic titles of the modes with a severe, predominantly ethical view of their effects in performance, finds its curious partner in later periods in a pseudohistorical scheme of the degeneration of Greek music. So Athenaeus in the Roman period imagines a musical world that licentiously defied the emphasis Plato would place on self-restraint: "It was the case that in antiquity the Greeks were music lovers. But later with the onset of disorder all the ancient practices became moribund, this principle lost its hold, and debased kinds of music were revealed, and all who used them substituted softness for gentleness, and licence and corruption for self-restraint."[88] Athenaeus concludes with the observation that, amazingly, the situation will get even worse unless the *patrios mousike* ("the ancestral *mousike*," or, literally, "the *mousike* of our fathers") is restored. Athenaeus is undoubtedly influenced here by the satire on composers of the later fifth century BCE advanced in the comedies of Aristophanes and other fragments.[89] Strictly speaking, this is a separate body of "evidence" from Plato's austere theorizing, and it is directed primarily at composers of the dithyramb and for the lyre, or kitharodes. Barker provides a survey of the relevant passages, which testify at least to the amusing tensions and comic possibilities available in the collocation of forms of theatrical composition at Athens.[90] One of comedy's major satirical resources is sexuality, and allegations of effeminacy and sexual innuendo are a staple. So it is that the tragic composer Agathon is identified with his own music in Aristophanes' *Women at the Thesmophoria,* with both understood to be effeminate.

But passages in comedy may give rise to deeply sober interpretations from commentators, which can then contribute to the picture drawn by Athenaeus and to convictions about the supposed ethical qualities of the *harmoniai.*[91] In Aristophanes' *Knights,* the dominant political figure of Cleon is satirized as the Paphlagonian throughout the comedy, and in one song there

87. Csapo and Slater (1994), sec. 4, no. 283, 345; Barker (1984), no. 161, 180–81.
88. Athenaeus *Philosophers at the Dinner Table* (*Deipnosophistai*) 14.633: this text, with translation, can be found in Gulick (1950), a volume that contains the musical sections of the fourteenth book of Athenaeus's strange work, written late in the second century CE.
89. Apparent to us, significantly, in the fragment of the comic dramatist Pherecrates noted above.
90. Barker (1984), chap. 8, 99–116, on Aristophanes. Both Csapo (2004) and Wilson (2004) discuss aspects of the broad ideology of opposition to the "new music" in two essays from an important collection on *mousike* in Athens (Murray and Wilson, 2004).
91. See, in general, Anderson's earlier study of this subject (1966).

is a reference to his unwillingness, as a boy, to tune his lyre to anything but the Dorian (*harmonia*). This is the feed line for a joke, which is that the lyre master was angry at this and claimed that the only *harmonia* Cleon knew how to take in was *dorodokisti*, which Barker translates uncontentiously as "bribery-style." But in his notes on this passage, Barker leads off with the statement that "the Dorian *harmonia* was associated with manly and straight-forward music," citing Plato and Aristotle, and only then allows for the pun between "Dorian" and *dorodokisti*.[92] Now allegations of taking bribes were leveled almost automatically at leading Athenian figures, and this is plainly the point of the rather feeble joke, which supposes (if we take it logically) that Cleon was already taking bribes at school. Quite why we should believe that Aristophanes would associate Cleon, of all figures, with "manliness" I cannot imagine, and if those connotations were definitely attached to the Dorian mode by Aristophanes and his audience, then the punning abuse of Cleon would have been registered at the expense of a compliment. We should also note that the joke does depend on the assumption that children were supposed to learn more than one mode, which makes Plato's vision of the simplicity of an "ideal" education remote from that actually practiced in the fifth century. This is indeed rather what one might expect of a radical and contentious reform, proposed by a philosopher to a limited circle of readers and listeners.

The sad fact is that we know very little of the music for tragedy and the tragic *choros,* and very little indeed about the use made of modes by tragic composers. There are occasional references in later writers, but these suggest variety, and Plato's proposed restriction of the modes must take place against the background of their relatively widespread use, perhaps not least in the theatrical *choroi*.[93] But the ideology of the Dorian mode has established itself firmly in accounts of Greek music, partly because the later theoretical scheme for scales seems to have been devised on the basis of the Dorian.[94]

147

92. Barker (1984), no. 133, 102n13. Wilson (2004, 302–3) places more emphasis on the pun but, in citing Barker's note, is still inclined to believe that the passage connects with the "normally positive ethical evaluation of the Dorian mode."

93. West (1992) reports comments, mostly to be ascribed to Aristoxenus in the later fourth century BCE, on the fifth-century tragic use of the Phrygian, Lydian, and Mixolydian (180–82). But how reliable any specific comments from later periods on fifth-century practice are must remain uncertain.

94. Most commentators would agree that there is a division, after the fourth century BCE, between a theoretical system of scales (*tonoi*) and the earlier range of *harmoniai*, used in the practice of music. *Harmonia,* as a term, seems primarily to point to "tuning." See the discussions by Barker (1984, 163–68) and by Anderson (1994) in app. B, "Scale Systems and Notation."

Similarly, the musical proposals for the older *harmoniai,* offered in the same theoretical treatise by Aristides Quintilianus and discussed by modern commentators, are claimed by Aristides to be those known by Plato, a claim that it is impossible to verify but that reveals just how significant Plato was in the formation of later Greek musical theory. Crucially, we should resist the temptation to believe that there was an automatic set of associations of an ethical kind implied by the use of any mode, a kind of reductive reading of performance that regarded deviations from "manliness" as an indication of weakness, indulgence, or even degeneracy of some sort.

The political implications of this approach to the variety of music are not only apparent in Plato but are also part of the aristocratic culture of late fifth-century Athens into which he was born. The final defeat of Athens by Sparta seemed to confirm, to aristocrats such as Plato, that democracy and its major features (the cultivation of public speaking and the theater, in particular) were deeply flawed and that the traditionalism of Dorian societies, especially Sparta, was to be highly valued. A restricted form of government had become the objective of a significant part of the wealthy class at Athens in the late fifth century, and a short-lived counterrevolution in 411 BCE had played nominally with the idea that only five thousand citizens should have voting power, while actually restricting power to four hundred. Later, with the defeat of Athens in 404 BCE, the Spartans installed a regime of thirty, who became known as the tyrants and who conducted a regime of murder and confiscation before they were ejected by the democrats. Both the Spartans, and the Four Hundred before them, made use of the ideological term *patrios politeia,* the ancestral constitution, and that phrase accompanied a reactionary vision of the early political reforms of Cleisthenes and of Solon before him.[95]

The politics of the era of Aristophanes and of Plato's childhood and youth are of importance in relation to the ideology of the modes. Not only do we see an echo of the term *patrios politeia* in the *patrios mousike* of Athenaeus, but we are also faced by a similar scheme of cultural degeneration as was obviously advanced in support of an overtly reactionary, antidemocratic politics in the later fifth century itself. This may seem surprising, if we are not inclined to associate music with politics or to assume any theoretical connection between them. But both jazz and rock and roll have been subject, in their time, to ethical judgments that are also ethnic and arguably racist judgments, and propositions about the degeneration of culture were by no means

95. Aristotle *Constitution of the Athenians* 29.3, 34.3.

absent from the twentieth century.[96] In this respect, it is interesting that Plato seems to have been influenced by a figure called Damon, who was an intellectual and theorist in the middle to later fifth century.

Much has been written about Damon, to whom Plato himself refers as an authority, but it has to be reliant on very little that can be ascribed to the man himself.[97] In opposing innovation in and changes to established music, Plato alleges in *Republic* that Damon stated that music cannot suffer such changes without there being accompanying changes in the greatest laws of the *polis*, and the basis here for a scheme of degeneration is obvious.[98] We also read, in Athenaeus, that those "around Damon" believed that songs and dances were produced by a motion of the soul, and so that there was an intimate connection between "free and fine" souls and the music and dance produced by them.[99] How far Damon advanced or developed a precisely ethical theory of modes is almost impossible to say, but the political implications of his theorizing are explicit, and it is tempting to believe that Plato's view of *harmoniai* is at least adapted from this source. Damon would appear to have been determining a class-based view of music and dance, since the terms "free" and "fine" (*kalos*) together indicate not just that which is appropriate to citizens but to the best of the citizens, regularly known as the *kaloi kagathoi,* the "fine" (or simply "beautiful," "handsome") and the "good." Damon must also have postulated an "unchanged" kind of music and must have suggested that either the laws of Athens (in particular) were threatened by change or that they had been changed. There is, indeed, no reason why the ideology of the coup d'état of 411 BCE, which viewed the developed democracy as a degenerate "change" from the original constitution of Solon and Cleisthenes, might not have been developing at the same time as the views of Damon. One strange piece of information is that Damon delivered a speech to the council of the Areopagus, a body of past Athenian magistrates that had been finally stripped of its political powers in the democratic reforms of Ephialtes in the late 460s BCE but that had in earlier times been the governing aris-

149

96. West (1992) notes a prejudice against jazz in his discussion of musical ethos (247n79). It was preceded by a similar demonization of ragtime.

97. Csapo and Slater (1994), sec. 4, no. 281, 343–44, translate the ancient sources on Damon. See the discussions in Barker (1984, 168–69), chap. 10, app. B; West (1992, 246–47); Anderson (1966); Anderson (1955), who argues for a degree of "creative independence" from Damon in Plato's writings; and Wallace (2004), who places Damon firmly alongside the leading Athenian politician, Pericles.

98. Csapo and Slater (1994), sec. 4, no. 281D, 344, is rather too brief a quotation from Plato; Barker (1984), no. 152, 139–40, provides a fuller context from Plato's *Republic*.

99. Csapo and Slater 1994, sec. 4, no. 281B, 343.

tocratic council of Athens. As a symbolic entity, it might have been taken to be a highly appropriate body to which to address the kind of political concerns about music that are ascribed to Damon.

150   So the problem of the modes of Greek music presents itself to us already highly charged with various forms of political and cultural ideology, although we have little or no evidence about what the fifth-century audience, or fifth-century tragic composers, associated with the various *harmoniai*. There can, however, be little doubt that Damon's proposals were controversial or new, for the simple reason that he gained a name for advancing them, and Plato himself is inclined to be a controversialist, with arguments in *Republic* and elsewhere presenting themselves as contradictory of the commonplace. But by the early fourth century BCE there was clearly a tendency toward harmonic theorizing, since it is heavily criticized in a fragmentary argument that is most plausibly dated to that time, just before Plato founded the Academy.[100] The writer of this fragment scathingly refers to *harmonikoi*, people who do not concern themselves with the practice of music but consider themselves experts in theory and who claim that melodies have an effect on the audience, making them brave or cowardly, self-restrained or otherwise. Although he terms such people *harmonikoi*, the writer does not discuss their views with explicit reference to the *harmoniai*. But he does appear to be dismissing a position that is analogous to those held by Damon and Plato and, possibly, somewhere between them in the development of a broad ethical theory of music and its reception. It is a fascinating objection from within the period itself and indicates at the very least how skeptical we should be in accepting the application of such theorizing to the creation and reception of Greek music during the earlier century of tragic composition.[101]

DANCING

"The Greek dance" has a weight to it as a phrase or a concept that places it on a level with "the Greek chorus," and we might be well advised to recognize in this a considerable admixture of our own cultural values. Something

100. The document is known as the Hibeh papyrus: Csapo and Slater (1994), sec. 4, no. 284, 345–46; Barker (1984), no. 162, with introduction and notes, 183–85; more briefly, West (1992, 247–48).

101. Csapo writes, in his incisive account of the politics of *mousikē* at Athens in this period, assertively of the "historical fiction" of a "timeless musical tradition" and warns scholars "to be more sceptical" of the aristocratic critical view of *mousikē* stemming from Plato and Damon (2004, 230, 237, respectively).

similar applies to both ideas, since Greek dancing and Greek *choroi* are clearly multiple and probably diverse, while the single concept suggests uniformity and solidity and may remove our sense of the span of time involved.

"The Greek dance" has also something of the syllabus of the dancing school about it, in suggesting an ethnic and geographical category that might be learned alongside others as part of a repertoire, and this should indeed serve as a warning. Conceptions of antiquity have played a massive ideological role in the formation of modern European culture, and in relation to dance "modern" applies every bit as much to the twentieth century as to the whole post-Renaissance period. In fact, "modern dance" as a radical break from the classical traditions of ballet cohabits in the earlier part of the century quite comfortably with a revisionist and revivalist sense of ancient Greek dance. Most readers will be aware of Isadora Duncan, but few may know of the Association of Teachers of the Revived Greek Dance or of the publication by Ginner with the title *The Revived Greek Dance.*

Ginner places this revival firmly in the context of "health and beauty," in which "we may learn much from many of the Greek ideals," and one thinks here additionally of Jaques-Dalcroze and eurhythmics, of the modern Olympian ideal, and ultimately of less attractive fixations.[102] According to Ginner's racial theory, the Hellenic race was produced from the combination of an indigenous people—"short, dark-haired ... passionate, superstitious, imaginative"—with Northern invaders, who were "blue-eyed, tall, and fair, of a magnificent physique, essentially warlike," and in addition "brave, chaste, self-controlled, and law-abiding."[103] Despite these rather disturbing pronouncements, Ginner's exposition of the approach she adopted in her school, which she considered indebted to Duncan and analogous to that of other schools, is serious and earnest in its desire to draw on the sources.[104]

So the Greek dance has its modern history, and scholars such as Lawler draw attention to it, looking back behind its role as a companion to modernity toward scholarly interest from the Renaissance forward. But it was even possible, in the period before 1945, to consider the whole history of classical ballet as a tradition founded in Greek antiquity. A popular survey of ballet, published in 1938, outlines this prestigious charter in relation to specialist dancing that belongs to the stage and is intended for a public: "Such dancing

102. Ginner 1933, v.

103. Ginner 1933, 1, 3.

104. The association was founded in 1923; Ginner's book was first published in 1933 and went through four editions, the last being published in 1947. She outlines the history and principles of the movement at 11–17, with schools mentioned 12–13.

existed in the heyday of Greek culture, was known to the Roman emperors and practiced by them, journeyed from Italy to France, and was, so to speak, codified by the logical French mind to become the art we know today."[105] Ginner's assertions of "the beautiful simplicity of Greek art," her Platonic quotations, and her vision of the social value of the cult of the Greek dance in modern times create a unified impression, but her discussion takes into account the diversity within this whole. Similarly Haskell, in the charter outlined above, implies an awareness of other kinds of Greek dancing, but both writers play overtly with a conceptual abstraction that has ideological value in the present. According to these writers, the Greek dance is something that we need, and it will embody principles, constituting a particular essence, perhaps even a Platonic ideal. That which is lost is perhaps always prey to this kind of conceptual construction, and we should be duly warned not to deduce too rapidly or with too much credulity from what evidence there is, perhaps especially where that evidence is presented in a conceptual form.

One of the largest cautions emerges conveniently in Haskell's apparently casual (and tendentious) summary above. The wording of his proposed continuity reveals that he must be thinking, primarily, of the dancing of the Greek *pantomimos* of the Roman period, about which we know a very great deal. This solo figure danced in a mask with a closed mouth, while others sang extracts from the myth, and the dancing was expressive and emotive in the extreme. Most later Greek sources, from the Roman era, discuss Greek dance in the light of their perceptions of this immensely popular form, which itself has a history of derivation from aspects of the earlier Greek mime.[106] But the dancing of the solo *pantomimos* has little or nothing to do with the dancing of a *choros* in the theater of Dionysus some five hundred years earlier, and constructions that overtly or covertly associate the two should be regarded with the greatest suspicion.

From the later eighth century BCE to the Roman era of the later second century CE is a period of just under a thousand years, and Greek culture encompasses a great diversity of original practice and even of relatively established or local traditions. Those who have written on Greek dancing have adopted extremely diverse approaches to it, and in general scholars have rarely risked presenting a summary or overview. I shall be looking here at studies that have emerged in the second half of the twentieth century,

105. Haskell 1938, 18.
106. The treatise by Loukianos (Lucian), *On Dancing*, from the second century CE is almost exclusively devoted to this kind of dancing. Csapo and Slater (1994), sec. 5, 369–89, is devoted to "mime and pantomime," and they provide a short introduction.

specifically for their insights into or commentary on the tragic *choros.* I have already mentioned Lawler, and I shall also discuss Webster and Prudhommeau, with attention to their distinctive methodologies rather than the chronology of scholarship, because the writers do not form part of a consistent tradition.[107]

Webster's approach to the *choros* is closely related, in large part, to the study of the meters used in composition, but his principal subject does seem to be dancing. His book carries a title, *The Greek Chorus,* that would place it in the forefront of any reading list, but it is fair to say that reactions to it are generally of disappointment. Webster does not, as one might have imagined, preface his detailed analysis with any discussion of music or of dancing, nor does he sketch the outlines of a cultural history of *choroi* in Greece. *The Greek Chorus* is divided into two sections, the first a survey titled "The Archaeological Material," and another (and far longer) titled "Literary Sources." The first section reflects Webster's interest in artifacts and monuments that might "illustrate" performance. The second section aims to use the meters in which songs are composed as a means to a limited impression of performance. So Webster describes his book in the introduction as "an attempt to trace the history of the dance of the chorus rather than its words, in so far as we can apprehend it from the meter, which controlled the feet of the dancers as well as organizing the words of the song, and in so far as we can see it on Greek vases and reliefs."[108] He also is dismissive here of the later Greek writers on dancing, noting that they are "probably much more influenced by the solo dances of the Hellenistic and Roman pantomimos than by the tradition of archaic and classical choral dance." In the introduction to the first section he explains his periodization and introduces his categories of *choroi,* which are those that "grew fairly naturally out of the [archaeological] material" and so do not really correspond to genres of composed *choroi* as found in texts but, instead (for example), have a marked emphasis on maenad and satyr dances.[109] He also introduces at this point a classification of foot movements and, to a limited extent, of arm movements.[110] The volume is sparsely illustrated and offers no line drawings.

The introduction is promising, but the absence of illustration or drawings soon begins to be felt, while the attention to foot or hand movements

107. In addition to these figures, there is a short and sober overview compiled from the lecture notes of Fitton (1973).
108. Webster 1970, xi.
109. Webster 1970, 2.
110. Webster 1970, 3–4.

remains insistently descriptive rather than more broadly interpretative. Webster's claim for the monuments (artifacts) in the introduction that "we can learn from them what different kinds of chorus looked like" is not really substantiated in his presentations, unless we take the artistic portrayal of a posture, and its possible correlation to similar postures elsewhere, as an adequate image. Like Green in more recent times, Webster is adamant that we must not see vase paintings as photographs or films but must appreciate the "prevailing conventions" of the art.[111] Although this advice is comprehensible as a criticism of Prudhommeau and the French school of reconstruction, as we shall see, it hardly proves helpful in Webster's own short descriptions.[112]

For tragedy in the classical period (450–25 BCE in Webster's periodization) there are very few examples, and what emerges from them is a quite basic descriptive method. Several figures are, reasonably, described by Webster as "running" while another "strides," and another "dances" because she is raising her knee. In one instance, of a vase taken to illustrate Sophocles' lost tragedy *Nausíkaa,* the two "running" figures justify the conclusion that there was "an agitated dance" from the *choros* at a particular moment of the action.[113] In fact, Webster's major terms of analysis, despite the complex classifications of the introduction, prove to be categories of this kind, which he introduces quietly but retains and deploys repetitively to indicate different kinds of dancing. "It is not always easy to distinguish between walking and striding; but when one or both heels are raised, I have called the movement striding, and it must be recognized as a quicker dance movement than walking."[114] Later, in a particular discussion of a vase painting, Webster writes of "striding" and then of "two other tempi, walking and running," that are found in his early classical period, and we are left without help to deduce that Webster will treat these three as fundamental categories of dancing.[115] There are other observations, as one would expect, namely, that some groups have linked hands, and much incidental attention to posture or gesture, but for the kinds of dance these categories remain paramount throughout his study.

The first part ("Down to the Time of Homer") of the second, long section, "Literary Sources," draws these categories together into a theory, which Webster never really elaborates later in the book but on which he draws re-

111. Green 1991.
112. Webster 1970, xii.
113. Webster 1970, 29. Sophocles' *Nausíkaa* dramatized and developed the story of Nausikaa in Homer's *Odyssey.* It may have been a tragedy or a satyr play.
114. Webster 1970, 6.
115. Webster 1970, 25, last paragraph.

peatedly. "For singing choruses I would suggest tentatively as a theory to be tested when the evidence becomes fuller that a chorus 'walks' when it has a long line to sing before it can pause in song and dance, that when a chorus 'strides' it is singing a shorter line, and that when it does kicks it sings a shorter line still."[116] His immediate example is that of the hexameter, famil-iar from epic, which if and when it is choral will be a verse line for a walking dance. Similar interpretations of different meters or measures are offered through the sustained metrical analyses of songs in the subsequent parts of this second section, although the same meter cast into different units, longer or shorter, may respectively prompt suggestions of dancing or walking, as in Webster's analysis of Alcman's major poem.[117]

Placing the "pauses" in this theory will be decisive in the interpretation of the kind of dancing, but Webster never chooses to examine his criteria in public view, although he is often diffident about the proposals he makes. Oc-casionally, he drifts into a wider cultural discussion of *choroi,* as he does con-structively on the subject of marriage songs; but one feels then that this is largely because he has insufficient texts to analyze metrically or to assign to the various potential categories of song.[118] Even in this situation, the presid-ing terms for the discussion of movement of *choroi* are those of "walking" and "running," with the third, "dancing," continuing to represent an awkward contribution in the circumstances of a general study of dancing, although some postponed clarification finally emerges in the conclusion. There Web-ster writes of "three tempi," "walking or stately time, striding or dance time, and excited time," the last of which is presumably equivalent to "running."[119]

For tragedy, the proposals in "Literary Sources," the second part of Web-ster's book, do not differ in their terms from those made for other *choroi.* Aeschylus's *Persians* begins the analyses of tragic choral song, with Webster at his most clipped and the conclusions lacking any particular insight into tragic *choroi.* Of the opening song, Webster comments that "the whole is probably walking tempo rather than dancing tempo," relying on the presence of "one or more long lines" throughout the parts of the song. Of the ex-change between the herald and the chorus in the same tragedy, he comments that "everything is in dancing tempo, if not excited dancing tempo," pre-sumably because the metrical lines are short. The subsequent "wild lament" from the *choros* is given a detailed metrical exposition by Webster, but one

---

116. Webster 1970, 54.
117. Webster 1970, 57–58.
118. Webster 1970, 73–76.
119. Webster 1970, 200.

that leaves it in conclusion only as "a wild lament that becomes calmer and slower towards the end."[120] Dochmiacs in Aeschylus's *Seven against Thebes* signal "excited dancing," but of two vitally important and fascinating songs in Aeschylus's *Oresteia,* the graveside invocation in *Libation Bearers* and the entry of the Furies in *Eumenides,* Webster has virtually nothing to say, which is profoundly disappointing.[121] Instead, he offers the concluding summary for the trilogy that "dochmiacs are used for agitated choruses, and dactyls for stately choruses," without explicit observations on other regular meters.[122]

The subsequent analyses of tragedies by Sophocles and Euripides do not set out anything more trenchant than this, and indeed in what he terms the "Free Period" of 425–370 BCE he seems almost to lose sight of dancing for tragedy, as commentary on comedy attracts his attention. Webster's ideal would undoubtedly be to match the images of dancing on vases or other artifacts with composed texts in some manner. His compromise position in the absence of this ideal is to settle for simple descriptions of the movements on the monuments that might arguably be applied to certain kinds of metrical line or measure. There are many incidental observations of some interest on the postures in vase paintings. But the intensity of the analyses and argument, and their curiously concise urgency, do not truly result in an enhanced vision of *choroi* or a better understanding of their performances.

By far the most impressive figure in the modern study of ancient Greek dancing is Lawler, whose approach to writing about the dance is altogether different and owes very little indeed to the use of metric as a means to an end. Her two books, *The Dance in Ancient Greece* and *The Dance of the Ancient Greek Theatre,* are written in an accessible style and provided with detailed references, the first placing dramatic dance in a wide context, and the second being a more restricted study. But both books are reliant on an extraordinary series of shorter studies of specific aspects of Greek dancing and the terminology associated with it, reflecting research stretching back over two decades. The chapter "The Dance and the Drama" in *The Dance in Ancient Greece* is a brief survey with little technical detail, but unfortunately this is the work to which most references are given by other writers, and it seems to be more widely available, perhaps as a result of the considerations I addressed at the beginning of this section. The presentation in *The Dance of the Ancient Greek Theatre* is, inevitably, of greater relevance to the subject here but is still not an effective substitute for some of Lawler's specialist essays. These are

156

120. Webster 1970, 113–15.
121. Webster on *Seven against Thebes, Libation Bearers,* and *Eumenides* (1970), 120, 127, 128, respectively.
122. Webster 1970, 129.

meticulous in examining the sources for terms and aspects of Greek dancing, but they also contain, in varying degrees, considerable speculation.

I shall review here merely a selection of the significant terms that may
affect our view of the tragic *choros* in the light of the discussions presented by
Lawler, who pronounces herself wary of the reconstruction of ancient dances.
As she maintains, "the exact appearance of those dances eludes us," and in
general she does not attempt to draw many conclusions from visual material,
confining herself to a few illustrations.[123] But this kind of caution also sits
uneasily, in *The Dance in Ancient Greece,* with some unexamined assumptions
about the tragic *choros.* So we read of the entrance of the chorus "in a solid rectangular alignment" without any review of the dubious and late sources for
this contention, and of how subsequently "the members of the chorus may
have turned their backs upon the audience, to face the actor who now entered," in a sketch that sounds authoritative but that calls for greater care.[124]

The comments about the appropriate qualities for modern productions of
tragedy are also ill-advised: "Also, in devising dances for the plays, the present-
day choreographer should in general use dignified, restrained, and beautiful
postures and movements, shunning those that are contorted and violent—
which the Greeks regarded as 'ignoble' and at variance with the essential
character of the dance of tragedy."[125] The note attached to this prescription
refers to Plato's proposals for the dignity of *choroi* in the *Laws* and dependent
valuations from the Roman period, which effectively conceals the point that
Plato categorically did not regard existing tragic performances as "dignified
and restrained."[126] On the previous page Lawler herself has written of the
binding song of the Furies in Aeschylus's *Eumenides* that "the weird dance . . .
must have carried with it a breath of savagery" and has earlier referred to extreme expressions of grief in tragic songs and to "wild running, shouting,
tossing of hair" in Euripides' *Bacchae.*[127] Yet, when it comes to a summary and
to issuing guidance for the reproduction of the Greek dance, Lawler pres-

123. Lawler 1964a, 85.

124. Lawler 1964a, 82. Lawler also introduces the rectangle in *The Dance of the Ancient Greek
Theatre,* referring there (1964b, 26) to the *Etymologicum magnum,* which advances the spurious correlation between *tragoidía* and *tetragonon* that I noted earlier. The account of the
movements of theatrical *choroi* in Pickard-Cambridge (1988, 239 ff.) is similarly domi-
nated and introduced (239) by this late tradition of speculation and cannot be considered
reliable.

125. Lawler 1964a, 85.

126. Lawler 1964a, 151n17.

127. Lawler 1964a, 83–84. In *The Dance of the Ancient Greek Theatre,* despite her reference to the
"rectangular" speculation, Lawler observes that "there must have been a great deal of freedom for the choreographer within the framework of the play, and striking dances of many
sorts seem to have been introduced, if they fitted naturally into the plot" (1964b, 26).

ents a conservative and conventional view of classicism, one that she does not subject to investigation but that may still continue to be influential.

In later sources from the Roman period "the tragic dance" is characterized by the term *emmeleia,* in a contrast with the typifying comic dance *kordax,* while the dance of the satiric drama is identified as *sikinnis.* This formulation has prompted many modern speculations, particularly since Plato in the *Laws* divides dance into two categories, the peaceful *emmeleia* and the warlike pyrrhic.[128] Plato is plainly creating an artificial scheme here, but the combination of sources has often led scholars, including Lawler herself, to claim that the tragic dance was stately or dignified. In the book from which that quotation is taken, *The Dance in Ancient Greece,* Lawler has little to say of *emmeleia,* reporting merely that opinion varies between applying it solely to the entry of the *choros* in tragedy and applying it to the whole of tragic dance.[129] In *The Dance of the Ancient Greek Theatre,* Lawler is more trenchant: "Unfortunately, we have from antiquity no clear definition of the *emmeleia,* nor have we in Greek art, so far as we can determine, any representation of the *emmeleia.*"[130] For "definition," we might substitute "description" to some purpose, because what we are dealing with in the later sources, and indeed in Plato, is a schematic system that has no real interest in the substance of actual dances: in that respect, *emmeleia* as it is formulated in this tradition is undescribed and indescribable. Lawler goes on to draw attention to the fact that the *kordax* was clearly a specific dance in comedy, not *the* dance of comedy, and concludes similarly about the *sikinnis* of the satyr play: "Just as in comedy not all the dancing represents the *kordax,* so in the satyr play there must have been dances of types other than the *sikinnis.*"[131]

We are left, or should be, with very little impression of the *emmeleia,* whatever it may have been in the fifth century BCE. Two slight references can be added, one from Aristophanes' *Wasps* where the threat of a "knuckle *emmeleia*" is directed at a comical vision of a tragic (solo) dancer (*Wasps* 1503). The second reference also dates from the fifth century, although it is applied to an earlier period and comes from the historian Herodotus. In a remarkable anecdote about a member of a prestigious Athenian family, which is almost certainly derived from the oral traditions of the Athenian aristocracy, Herodotus uses both the term *emmeleia* and the verbal form of *cheironomia,* another term that later commentaries on dancing deploy. The anecdote concerns the lav-

128. Plato *Laws* 816b, from bk. 7.
129. Lawler 1964a, 83.
130. Lawler 1964b, 59.
131. Lawler 1964b, 110.

ish arrangements made by the tyrant of Sicyon in the sixth century BCE for the marriage of his daughter. Suitors arrived from around the Greek world, and trials were made of them. On the final day, the tyrant Cleisthenes laid on a banquet, and at its conclusion the suitors continued to compete with each other in speaking and in *mousike,* which presumably suggests singing to the lyre as an accomplishment. As the drinking advanced, the young Athenian aristocrat Hippocleides ordered the *auletes* to play *emmeleia* and performed a solo dance. At this, Herodotus says, the tyrant began to be dissatisfied, but Hippocleides called for a table and jumping onto it first danced some Spartan figures (*schematia*), then some from Attica, and finally placed his head on the table and performed *cheironomia* with his legs. Herodotus uses the word *orchesis* throughout for dancing, and the outcome (as indeed the whole amusing story) is best read in full.[132]

Plainly, we do not need to spend time doubting that this is what Hippocleides did, if only because our faith in the historical reality of this incident is not at issue. What is obvious is that Herodotus, in writing this story, is using terms that he feels will be comprehensible to his fifth-century audience and readership, notably fifth-century Athenians. The evidence of the *aulos* in combination with solo dancing could well point to a tragic model in his mind for this *emmeleia,* although it has to be said that the Spartan figures are unlikely to be tragic. In other words, Herodotus seems to understand *emmeleia* here as a form of music accompanying solo dance (*orchesis*), and he is writing in the second half of the fifth century, contemporaneously with Sophocles and Euripides. Herodotus does not suggest how Hippocleides came to know these dances, and anachronism is vigorously at play in the story if tragic dances are being suggested, since tragedy was not established at Athens until the later sixth century, a generation after the time of this event.

So the picture, although amusing, is extremely confusing to us, but it hardly provides support for the *emmeleia* in relation to the tragic *choros,* nor is the context explicitly "stately" or "dignified." The passage also offers us our best glance at *cheironomia* as a fifth-century writer and his audience might understand the term, which appears to be generally descriptive of the movements of the hands (and arms) in dancing, only remarkable here because Hippocleides substitutes his feet and legs. In the later sources from the Roman period it gains far more prominence, but once again one might expect that to be true of a period strongly affected by the *pantomimos* as a form of solo *orchesis.* Our early evidence on *cheironomia,* such as it is, is for solo dancing,

---

132. Herodotus *Histories* 6.126–30.

since that is also the context for a brief reference (a mime performance) in Xenophon's *Symposion*.[133] But this does not prevent *cheironomia* featuring as a certainty in modern accounts of the dancing of Greek *choros*.

160

Lawler, by contrast, has little to say on *cheironomia* in her accounts of tragic dancing, but this is probably because she goes behind the general term to offer detailed commentaries on other ancient terms applied to dancing. Her essay "*Phora, Schema, Deixis* in the Greek Dance" subjects three terms found in Plutarch to close examination.[134] Plutarch is writing in the Roman period, probably toward the end of the first century CE, and Lawler believes that he is likely to have the pantomime rather firmly in view, even though one of the speakers castigates pantomime at the close of piece. In this imagined exposition by one Ammonius, a "philosopher," *deixis* is an indication by the dancer of actual physical objects, and a *phora* would be expressive of an action or capacity/ability, suggesting on the one hand a predominantly gestural use of the hands or arms, and on the other an indicative movement or movements of the body. Lawler pays closest attention to the definition given to *schema*, which is said by the character of Ammonius in Plutarch's narrative to be the static pose that is held in place at the end of a movement.

Lawler questions this definition, since it seems to conflict with the more regular associations of the word *schema* when applied to dancing. The *schematia* of Hippocleides in Herodotus do not appear to be poses but essential, defining figures of the dance, and in Xenophon's *Symposion* of the early fourth century BCE the character of Socrates contrasts *schemata* with a state of rest. The scene in this dialogue is largely occupied with the entertainments introduced by a Syracusan dancing master to an Athenian drinking party (*symposion*) at which Socrates is present, which are provided by an *aulos* player (female), a boy who dances and plays the lyre, and a girl dancer/acrobat. The word *schemata* is used repeatedly, and Socrates responds to the boy's dance by saying that, even though the boy is attractive in himself, "he seems even more attractive with the *schemata* than when he stands still."[135] He also observes that the boy's "neck, legs, hands were exercised at the same time," and that dancing is clearly a good exercise for the whole body.[136] This would seem to justify Lawler's comment in her essay that *cheironomia* embraces some varieties

---

133. Xenophon *Symposion* 2.19, in Marchant and Todd (1923). There is also a translation by Tredennick (1970).

134. Lawler 1954.

135. Xenophon *Symposion* 2.15, in Marchant and Todd (1923).

136. These technical issues do not, unfortunately, feature in Wohl's extended discussion of the idea of dancing in Xenophon's *Symposion* (2004, 337–63).

of *schemata,* and she is surely right to conclude that the word *schemata* is broadly used "to denote many features of the dance."[137]

Many of Lawler's essays are devoted to examinations of the possible interpretation of the names for individual *schemata* that are provided by the sources, and they make a fascinating series of investigations that combines the scholarly with the speculative. But she also groups the *schemata* in two principal discussions, in the second part of the essay introduced in the paragraph above, and in *The Dance of the Ancient Greek Theatre,* where she attempts to make some links with the texts of Greek tragedies. In the earlier discussion from the essay she provides a categorization of the *schemata* "into what we should call gestures," those that indicate a pose, others that "denote a characteristic movement or action," and those that suggest "a sustained motion or figure."[138] The names of the *schemata* come from later sources, but some of them are fixed in quotations from earlier texts. So we are not dealing just with a late or theoretical compilation, but with a composite list, which reflects early names and possibly includes those that may have been still current in the Roman period and, perhaps, might be associated with the pantomime.

Examples are interesting: from Lawler's first category ("what we should call gestures") there are "the seizing of a club," the "sword-thrust," the "snub hand," and the "hand flat-down," while from her third category ("a characteristic movement or action") there are "fire tongs, two foot, elbows out, spin-turn, whirl, slinky walk . . . split, high kick, rotating the hips, mortar, kneading trough, itch, raising the armpit, snort."[139] It is likely that many of the latter have obscene connotations, and in another essay Lawler comments on that aspect, in relation to the apparently martial and mimetic "sword-thrust." She observes here that we should envisage "a gesture of the hand, a strong extension, in the manner of a sword thrust, often with the hand held under a cloak" and that the gesture is a characteristic of the comic *kordax* "and seems to be obscene in implication, rather than military." She also suggests links with "rotating the hips," which was an obscene feature of the *kordax.*[140] Yet much later, in *The Dance of the Ancient Greek Theatre,* Lawler is drawn into suggesting that this figure "originally was a mimetic sword thrust with the hand, used in tragedy by either actors or chorus," and she offers possible contexts from a number of tragedies. Despite her previous association of the gesture directly with the *kordax,* a dance of old comedy in the fifth century BCE, she

---

137. Lawler 1954, 156, 154, respectively.
138. Lawler 1954, 152–53.
139. Lawler 1954, 153.
140. Lawler 1945, 69.

proposes here "that in later times the gesture of the thrust of the hand, especially under the cloak, acquired an obscene significance."[141]

One might wonder, at this moment, what the *kordax* did for its obscene gestures before it had corrupted those of tragedy. So, in this same discussion devoted to embodying tragedy, "taking hold of the wood" is described as a gesture useful for *choroi* carrying staves, which pictures with difficulty an artificial gesture elaborating a physical reality, at the same time as it suppresses an obvious connection with a convincing repertoire of suggestive obscenity. The confusion that emerges here, in what seems to be an almost explicit contradiction in interpretations by Lawler of the same gesture, is undoubtedly occasioned by preconceptions about the need to discover mimesis in Greek dancing as in tragedy as a whole, a problem to which I shall return below in a discussion of Plato's *Laws*. Yet Lawler does not argue strongly for a mimetic understanding of dancing at any point, largely because her researches in detail do not primarily suggest such a conclusion.

Lawler's attitude toward images on vases in principle is guarded: she comments toward the close of *The Dance of the Ancient Greek Theatre* that "despite innumerable conjectures, we have in art no sure portrayal of any dance of the ancient theatre."[142] But earlier in the same work she is prepared to draft a list of ten kinds of significance that a study of vase paintings reveals in relation to dancing.[143] Her judgment here avoids exciting possibility in favor of reliable indications and components, and the list, granted its originator, may well be of considerable value. It comprises muscular tension, rapidity of motion, worship or deference, surprise, marked admiration, pointing, mimetic carrying of an imaginary object, abandon, deterrence, caution, or stealth. As Lawler observes, members of tragic (or dramatic?) *choroi* might well be found using these reactions to startling events or messenger speeches, which extends consideration of the *choros* beyond the activity of dancing.

One of Lawler's passing but weighty comments in another essay is that "any attempt to parallel ancient and modern dances is necessarily fraught with hazard."[144] This severe reservation is undoubtedly leveled against the work of Emmanuel, which was extended and developed by Prudhommeau. This approach set about the reconstruction of Greek dancing working from two premises, summarized neatly by Naerebout: "that the movements portrayed in antique works of art are identical to the movements of contempo-

141. Lawler 1964b, 39.
142. Lawler 1964b, 121.
143. Lawler 1964b, 36–37.
144. Lawler 1939, 486.

rary French ballet . . . [and] that the classical material can be combined into analytical series, comparable to the results obtained with modern chrono-photography."[145] In the first premise we see shades of the interest in the Greek dance in the early part of the twentieth century that I sketched at the beginning of this chapter. In the second premise we see the effect of moder-nity, the application of techniques gained from photography and the filmic image, which would permit the display of separate moments in an otherwise uninterrupted movement. This analogy then encourages the reconstitution of whole movements from separate images on vase paintings. Clearly, this will always be a highly contentious attempt at reconstruction, and criticism will debate not merely a suspect method but also the nature of the images on vases. So Naerebout argues that what we see on the vases are not pictures of movements in progress (or "medial moments" of a dance): "These so-called medial moments cannot be part of *movement* at all, but must be an initial or final moment or a sustained pose."[146] What are regularly called the "conven-tions" of vase painting are actually open to debate, and it is significant that Webster in his introduction, in referring to the approach of Prudhommeau, has a different view of what we see in the paintings.[147] But the consensus of disapproval for reconstitution by this method is very strong indeed, and Naerebout is savage in his condemnation of Prudhommeau, under this and other headings.[148]

In fact, there is a third principle at work in Prudhommeau's method, which is the allocation of dance steps, once determined, to particular meters and measures, and Webster's severe disapproval of this may well account for his own preference for a relatively open system of interpretation, using only walking, striding, and dancing.[149] The culmination of Prudhommeau's study is a set of proposals for dancing sections of *choroi* from Greek tragedies, which she groups under old men (Aeschylus's *Agamemnon* 1448–54), adult males in "full vigour" (Euripides' *Alkestis* 435–45), soldiers (Sophocles' *Ajax* 909–14), and women (rather curiously the Furies in Aeschylus's *Eumenides* 255–69).[150] The categorization by gender and by physical and social type accepts stan-dard types of the characterization of tragic *choroi* and carries some simple as-sumptions about appropriate movements: soldiers might jump, old men will

145. Naerebout 1997, 61–62.
146. Naerebout 1997, 236.
147. Webster 1970, xii.
148. Naerebout 1997, 86–88.
149. Webster 1970, xi–xii.
150. Prudhommeau 1965, 497–524.

not; women will perform turns but not jumping turns. In general, Prudhommeau's commentary assumes naturalistic gestures and the presence of
mimesis for the expression of character and sentiment, although she admits
that our knowledge of the variety or conventions of this kind of expression
is desperately limited. Her reconstruction of the dancing aims to clarify the
sense of each word or phrase, but significantly Prudhommeau makes no attempt to incorporate or really acknowledge either the idea of *schemata* or
any known examples of *schemata*. The steps for each metrical element are
painstakingly outlined in each analysis, according to the premises and principles given above.

Prudhommeau's metrical grasp and her combination of sources of all
kinds from all periods, without adequate critical or chronological assessment, into a composite vision of "the Greek dance" have been heavily criticized. For my own part, I am struck by the fact that Prudhommeau engaged
in practical exploration of her methods, which she describes in sober terms
in connection with her analysis of the short section of Aeschylus's *Eumenides*.[151] Here she writes of using a "style analogue à celui des Anciens, avec
des danses qui pouvaient être exécutées par eux" (a style analogous to that of
the ancient [Greeks], with dances that could have been executed by them),
and I find that formulation both acceptable and defensible. We should note
that a figure such as Barba, from contemporary performance studies, has spent
considerable time and energy investigating what he believes to be common
principles underlying the physical work of the performer across cultures. Although I would be critical of many of Barba's premises and conclusions, and
of some of the tendencies of his theoretical writing, he suggests a context in
which the second part of Prudhommeau's proposition might well be accepted.[152] We could certainly say that Prudhommeau has provided a means
by which a choreography of an ancient Greek tragedy might be elaborated
and realized by dancers trained in ballet. If we were to see her work from this
angle, as a methodical if flawed attempt to accommodate ancient tragic
scripts to one of the major resources of our own dancing tradition, in order
that they may be danced again, then we might choose to be less scathing
about her research than many have been. We might also ask ourselves one
very simple question, to which there is no answer: if ancient *choreia* (and *orchesis* in general) did not put established and so executable steps to the meter and measure of a given composition, then how did it work?

151. Prudhommeau 1965, 512–13.
152. Barba and Savarese 1991. I have given a critique of Barba's theorizing in Ley (1999),
sec. 4.3, 210–48.

Naerebout, whom I have quoted briefly, provides a study of the Greek dance in three parts, the first two of which are a fascinating inventory of criticism and enquiry since the renaissance and a scrutiny of textual and pictorial sources, with the final section offering a theoretical model for study. The theoretical model is substantially a recommendation for the pursuit of a social and religious approach to the dance, a kind of anthropology of its performance.[153] Naerebout is critical of the exclusion of dance and of *mousike* in general from much research, and his own work yields some important precepts rather than a particular vision. I find his comments here on mimesis and the dance exacting and extremely helpful, and they provide some of the context for my own discussion of this topic: "We have only got evidence that shows *some* dances to have been mimetic, no evidence to enable us to say that the Greek dance tradition was so in its totality."[154] His conclusion there is that "the burden of proof rests with those who want to show the mimetic element to have been characteristic of all Greek dancing."

Modern suppositions about the mimetic quality of ancient Greek dancing are substantially derived from Plato in his dialogue *Laws* and depend on his general assertion that all *mousike* is mimetic. For Plato, it is self-evident that *mousike* should be subject to ethical principles, notably imitating or representing good people, and in *Laws* the participants in the dialogue are asked to determine what a "good" physical movement (*schema*, in dancing) and a "good" melody are, the suggestion being that these phrases should mean to sing and to dance what is good (*Laws* 654b–c). The leading participant in the dialogue, known simply as the Athenian, proposes that the movements and vocal sounds of a manly or brave soul and those of a coward would be different when undergoing the same troubles, and the conclusion is clear: all those of the brave man would be called "good," and all those of the coward the opposite (*Laws* 655b).

Plato's ethical theory of *choreia* would seem to include representations of good and bad (free and adult) men, women, and slaves, and possibly non-Greeks who are not slaves (*Laws* 669c–d), and to acknowledge defining characteristics of these categories such as bravery or "manliness" (*andreia*) and cowardice or evil nature (*kakia*). What good or bad might be in relation to women, slaves, or non-Greeks, whom Greek thought would not regard as free men in the manner that a member of a Greek *polis* is a "free man," is not made apparent in *Laws*: it is quite possible that Plato regarded all mime-

---

153. This approach had been developed by Lonsdale, who stated that his aim was "to recover a wide range of meanings that dancing had for the ancient Greeks" (1994, 2) but excluded performance and theatricality from consideration
154. Naerebout 1997, 109.

sis of these other social categories as undesirable. What Plato then allows is that these fundamental categories of character are shown exposed to "all kinds of actions and chances" (*Laws* 655d) and that the *schemata* of dancing and the melody and *harmonia* should track and express the ethos correctly and appropriately.

166

How far should we be inclined to accept this proposal about *choreia*? With regard to the tragic *choros,* we can acknowledge that the discernible definition of *choroi* (by gender and status) in the surviving plays is according to categories that can be closely related to those of Plato, although age is also a consistently relevant issue in the plays. According to Plato's proposal, the mimesis of any identifiable category (such as older, free men) should be fundamentally the same in any tragedy in which it occurs and should produce reactions that are recognizably part of a consistent range of behavior related to that ethos, even if the "troubles," the "actions or chances," vary immeasurably. We might find it difficult to conclude that the old men of Aeschylus's *Agamemnon,* of Euripides' *Children of Heracles,* and of Sophocles' *Oedipus at Colonus* were of a uniform ethos simply to justify Plato's ethical theory of *choreia.* Furthermore, would the evidence that confronts us in the variety of danced songs in tragedy justify the assertion that these songs are primarily and constantly intended as expressions of the ethos of the *choros* concerned?

Plato never examines what the relationship of a dance step or figure is to movement in everyday life, and yet he assumes an almost limitless range of appropriate and demonstrative *schemata* for each ethos, to accommodate the reactions to "all kinds of actions and chances." We might do best to question his proposal in relation to a specific example, which might seem susceptible of a mimetic approach to dancing and song. In the final section of a short danced song in Sophocles' *Women of Trachis,* the *choros* of young girls sings as follows:

> And then, the clash of fists
> and arrows,
> mixed in with the horns of the bull,
> the ladder climb of wrestlers, vicious
> blows from the forehead
> and straining groans from both.
> The girl sat on a distant bank,
> delicate and beautiful,
> waiting for her husband.
> I tell the story like a mere spectator.

> The bride looks pitiful as she is
> fought for and waits for the end.
> Then suddenly she is gone, taken from her mother,
> like a heifer out on her own.
> (*Women of Trachis* 517–30)

According to Plato's ethical theory of mimesis in *choreia,* the dance movements and melody (subject to the *harmonia*) should be expressive of the ethos of the *choros,* who are unmarried young women. This section of the song describes the fight between Heracles and the river god Achelous for Deianira. What we would have to suppose is that there would be *schemata* and a melody for each verbal part of this section that would, presumably, express the appropriate physical reaction and vocal sound (accompanied by the *aulos*), but would also unequivocally and constantly confirm the ethos of the young girls. It may be helpful to turn the theoretical proposition into specific questions. What kind of *schema* would express, appropriately and unequivocally, the ethos of young girls in relation to the "blows from the forehead / and straining groans" of two monstrous male wrestlers? What kind of *schema* would then express the reaction of the *choros* to another girl sitting on a bank watching this wrestling and contemplating possession by one of these males at the same time? What kind of *schema* would then express the reaction of the *choros* to telling a story like a spectator?

It is absolutely essential to remember that the Plato's theory is ethical, relating dancing and song to the ethos or character of the *choros,* and it provides no justification for any modern "mimetic" interpretations of Greek dancing. Let me illustrate this by reference, once again, to the example of Sophocles' danced song above. Any proposal that the *choros* first imitated the wrestlers in a *schema,* then imitated Deianira sitting on a bank, and finally imitated a heifer can find no basis whatsoever in the Platonic theory of mimesis in *choreia* but is a modern invention. Platonic ethical mimesis is not a broadranging semiotic theory of matching or symbolic signs conveyed through the *schemata* of dancing but a strictly controlled and probably impractical proposal for an ideal *choreia.*

STROPHE, ANTISTROPHE, AND *CHOREIA*

If the victory songs of Pindar, which are numerous, were composed for *choroi,* then they might provide a comparison with the danced songs of tragedy. Of those who subscribe to the vision of Pindar's *epinikia* or victory songs as *choroi,*

Mullen has chosen to elaborate a theory of their performance.[155] His study is highly readable as an interpretation of the artistry of the texts, but his insights into performance are largely based on a standard contention about the structure of the songs. Generically, the *epiníkia* are composed in what is known as a triadic form, which proceeds by one section of the song being followed by a section corresponding to it in terms of meter or measure, with that pair then followed by a further section without responsion. These sections are known, respectively, as strophe, antistrophe, and epode, and the pattern may be repeated twice or to a much greater extent, with the measure varied between each triad but remaining related.

In an appendix to his study, Mullen lists the passages from later Greek commentators that assert that for the strophe the *choros* turned in one direction (to the right) and for the antistrophe it turned in the reverse direction. This contention then allows him to provide interpretations that understand the composed text to be working its impressions on the spectators and auditors largely through these means. His understanding of the epode in this context is that it is a coda to the dance, requiring the *choros* to rest between its movements: he calls this effect "epodic arrest," and much of his interpretation of the songs relies on applying this theoretical scheme to them.[156] The testimonies on which Mullen draws not only are very much later than the period of composition but also include components that Mullen chooses to reject or doubt, since their vision seems to be that of a circular *choros* dancing round a central altar, something that Mullen finds unsuitable for the predominantly secular *epiníkia*.

The triadic structure of composition is a form that Pindar used regularly outside the *epiníkia*, as far as the surviving fragments allow us to judge, but not exclusively. He also composed in responding strophe and antistrophe without an epode, and tragic *choroí*—which were contemporary with Pindar— make constant use of these responsive forms of composition.[157] It is, however, by no means clear how we should interpret the terms "strophe" and "antistrophe." There is a little evidence that the idea of "twisting" or "turning" implicit in strophe may have been applied to the composition of songs in the fifth century, but in a musical or metrical sense, rather than in relation to dance. So Agathon is said to be "bending his *strophaí* into shape" with the help of the warmth of the sun in Aristophanes' comedy *Women at the Thes-*

168

---

155. Mullen 1982.
156. Mullen (1982, 129), and the analyses in his chap. 3.
157. I have elsewhere given a brief outline of this form in tragic song (1991b, 48–52).

mophoria (68), a joke that Wiles would relate to the "difficulty of writing paired verses."[158] The problems of applying the terms to dance are considerable. Without a coherent or convincing vision of any part of the dance, it will be fruitless to imagine an inversion or repetition of it. An inversion of a dance is, in any case, a remarkably difficult concept, which is almost indecipherable in relation to practice.

Correspondence between strophe and antistrophe is an apparent fact of meter, but opinion is tentative when it comes to translating that metrical responsion into melodic responsion. The reason for this is the inflected nature of the Greek language, to which I referred earlier in this chapter, in the section on music and melody. Put simply, composing two corresponding systems of metric (strophe and antistrophe) based on the short and long syllables in words is one thing; but doing so in a manner that also has the accentual inflections in the words corresponding consistently is a matter of extreme difficulty. Since inflection is a matter of pitch, and the patterns of inflection will vary between strophe and antistrophe, then the problems for melody become unavoidable. Landels has an excellent, illustrative survey of this aspect of "responsion," and he offers the following list of possibilities:

(a) The *antistrophe* had its own different musical setting.
(b) Its words were sung to the same notes as the *strophe,* with rises and falls of pitch in the "wrong" places.
(c) Some compromise was made, by delaying or advancing rises and falls of pitch in the *antistrophe,* so that essentially the same melodic outline was adapted to the different words.[159]

He illustrates the problem with an analysis of a choral song from Sophocles' *Antigone* (lines 332 ff.), on which he marks both meter and inflection over a transliteration of the Greek words, providing a translation beforehand.[160] Landels finds a certain degree of correspondence between pitch patterns in strophe and antistrophe but declines to favor one solution over another. Anderson has also offered an analysis of the same problem, with the opening lines from strophe and antistrophe in a song of Pindar as an example, and he concludes that the pitch patterns do not match. But he is, nonetheless, inclined to accept "the possibility of a compromise," speculating that

158. Wiles 1997, 96.
159. Landels 1999, 124.
160. Landels 1999, 124–29.

the composer "fitted the melody of a given work to the word accents."[161] Implicit in the analyses of both scholars is the belief that the formal correspondence of words in this widespread system must have been accompanied by some kind of parallelism in performance, which they approach in the musical aspect.

170

The existence of response has also prompted a semiotician and structuralist such as Wiles to offer detailed proposals about a number of tragic songs, principally in the aspect of dancing or choreography. The same passages from ancient commentators that support Mullen in his approach are also adopted by Wiles, although the problem of a reversal or inversion of a dance sequence is even more awkward than the adjustment of melody to inflection, which involves a relatively simple principle of repetition.[162] The antithesis (to the right, to the left) is bound to be attractive to a structuralist, and Wiles subtly combines an idea of choreographic "symmetry" (perhaps conscious of a pun on "combined measure" that the Greek etymology of the word contains) with that of "oppositions."[163] These he detects in and through the words of each corresponding strophe and antistrophe that he analyzes. His resultant principle is firmly stated—"the metrical identity of strophe and antistrophe means choreographic identity"—and accordingly "the same visual image receives two meanings."[164] In this kind of scheme "the epode restores the chorus to a fixed central position," and this observation makes it clear that fundamentally Wiles is adopting Mullen's approach.[165] The presiding perception is that of the semiotic vision of the audience member, and the means of realization are apparently gestures and significant movements, which have the capacity to carry two corresponding but distinct meanings.

Wiles, in his challenging discussion, seems to combine two major ideas. The first is that a corresponding "measure" (in strophe and antistrophe) must entail a corresponding dance; and the second is that such a dance must be semiotically charged, carrying a symbolic, visual "meaning" that in some way can be detected through the existing words of the song. His analysis is predominantly theoretical, and there is little attempt to provide any account

161. Anderson 1994, 95–96.
162. Wiles (1997, 93–94), who adduces Plato's cosmology to support "the symbolic importance" of "rotation and counter-rotation"
163. "Left and Right, East and West," "Inside/Outside," and "The Vertical Axis" are titles of later chapters in Wiles (1997).
164. Wiles 1997, 103, 104, respectively.
165. Wiles 1997, 109.

of the kinds of dance or gesture that might be involved. But it is clear that this vision is in some way related to the idea of a mimetic *choreía*.[166]

Wiles also acknowledges his debt to Aylen, who made related proposals in an earlier study. In some prefatory comments on music, Aylen expresses confidence that "we know a very great deal about the music of the Greek plays," despite the absence of melody. This confidence seems to be built on the assertion that "we know the emotional connotations of the main tempi," of the rhythms of the verse.[167] But his account offers the standard observations about the dochmiac rhythm and about the Ionic (respectively, "excited" and with "Oriental connotations"), with the comment that "a number of metres . . . are not very specific as to mood." This leaves many important meters without settled characteristics and is little more than a résumé of the limited conclusions of Dale, expressed in an ebullient rather than a qualified manner. Similarly, Aylen states that "certain modes had very obvious emotional connotations," relying presumably on Plato's typology, but he leaves these largely unexamined.[168]

Aylen's central chapter, "Dance Drama," aims to substantiate his proper assertion that dance was "not just an element in the staging of the fifth-century plays" but an integral part of the culture, as of the performance. Once again he insists on the "emotional"—the choruses "provided an emotional medium for everyone in the audience"—and he relies confidently on Webster's association of particular movements with particular meters.[169] But the centerpiece of his chapter is a textual analysis based on the metrical correspondence between strophe and antistrophe and on his acceptance of the assertions by the late commentators on movement in alternate directions, with the chorus working "more directly to the front" in the epode. He also assumes, for his thesis, that dance was potentially mimetic, despite a short summary of the *schemata* that hardly establishes that conclusion, and insists that "we can often see the necessity for one dancer to emerge from the crowd as a temporary soloist," a belief that in fact depends on his own interpretation of the texts.[170] After briefly reviewing some possibilities in the

---

166. The title of the relevant chap. 3 is "The Mimetic Action of the Chorus" (Wiles 1997, 87–113). There is a short, preliminary reference to *Laws* at 88. In his introductory book on Greek theatrical performance, Wiles unfortunately takes Plato's mimetic propositions in *Laws* as a sure guide to the nature of theatrical choreography (2000, 136–37).

167. Aylen 1985, 104.

168. Aylen 1985, 109.

169. Aylen 1985, 115.

170. Aylen 1985, 121; his discussion of the *schemata* comes at 117–18.

plays of Aristophanes and Aeschylus, he considers a song from Sophocles' *Antigone* (lines 332–75) in some detail. One of his major contentions is that a sense break in the words of the song will afford a breathing space or a pause for the *choros*, and in this song such a break occurs roughly in the middle of each strophe and antistrophe.

The analysis depends on two major methods: the first detects links between ideas and images in strophe and antistrophe, and the second envisages movements and groupings in the *choros*. One of the most vivid links that Aylen makes is between threatening "rain, sleet and hail" in his translation of the second strophe of the song from *Antigone* and the "awe of God's natural law" in the antistrophe, which is how he translates *dike*, more generally rendered as "justice." He suggests for the strophe that the *choros* "must put their hands above their heads to form some roof beneath which they can cower safely," a vision that is clearly mimetic, and then pursues this into the antistrophe, which he accepts might have been assigned other forms of choreography without this prior indication. As it is, Aylen maintains that his reconstruction offers "an important insight into Sophocles' theology": "*Dike* is something that we would like to get away from—like hailstones. We cannot. But we can protect ourselves from it, if we take care."[171] Perhaps. But, there again, we might doubt that the text justifies Aylen's vision of the choreography or that his vision of the choreography does much to illuminate the text.[172] There are too many assumptions here to justify much conviction, and the example is not exceptional. Earlier, Aylen has suggested, in relation to Aeschylus's *Seven against Thebes*, that "the similarity of the sex act and a breaking wave in choreographic terms need hardly be stressed."[173] There is nothing necessarily ridiculous in this idea, but there is nothing inherently plausible in it either.

What is most curious about the analyses presented by Aylen and Wiles is that neither explores the problems associated with the reversal of choreography that they appear to accept, as an explanation of strophe and antistrophe, from the late and questionable sources. How would a combination of movement and gesture (*cheironomia*) of the indicative or semiotic kind they propose be set in reverse, rather than simply repeated? What exactly is the relation between movement and gesture in Greek dance? Is there any dis-

171. Aylen 1985, 130.
172. This kind of problem had been identified in a short essay by Kitto (1955), who was commenting on the second strophe and antistrophe of the first danced song (the *parodos*) of *Antigone*: "How can the same dance-figure, if it has a sharply defined character, fit two passages so different in mood?" (39).
173. Aylen 1985, 124.

tinction to be made between combined movement and gesture in Greek terms and our own modern sense of choreographic design? We might also expect an explanation of what mimesis might mean in relation to dancing and choreography, something that is hardly self-evident. If a *choros* is envisaged holding its hands above its head to protect itself from sleet and rain, is this mimetic? Of a tree? Of a roof? And can we assume that such a literalist, objectifying version or vision of mimesis will also accommodate a metaphorical meaning such as a shelter or sheltering from justice or natural law? A semiotics of the city, such as Wiles develops, cannot be allowed to constrain the theater unless it is accompanied by a semiotics of mimesis, if mimesis is assumed to be the means of communication, and unless a case for the meaning of that term and for its presence in the theater is argued convincingly.

173

DITHYRAMBS

I indicated earlier in this book the importance of the dithyramb to our understanding of the theater of Dionysus at Athens and to the festivals of Dionysus at Athens. The dithyramb became, through the reorganization of the *polis* under the influence of Cleisthenes, the defining *choros* of the democracy, since its performance at the City Dionysia encompassed and represented the new tribal structure of Athens.[174] The dithyramb also has the aura of the authentically Dionysian attached to it, because we can be sure that it has a history stretching back beyond tragedy. Aristotle's observation that tragedy developed from those who "led off" the dithyramb (from the *exarchon* of the dithyramb) at least acknowledges this precedence, although we cannot tell if Aristotle was promoting a theory or had available to him oral or other information.[175]

But this observation connects forcefully with one small fragment from the composer Archilochus, whose work dates from the middle of the seventh century, a generation or more after Eumelus. Archilochus uses the verbal form of *exarchon* in making a claim that he knows how "to lead off" or "to begin" (*exarxai*) a dithyramb, a fine song of lord Dionysus, when his mind has been struck by the lightning of wine, and speculation on the state and form of

174. For the dithyramb at the City Dionysia, readers need to combine passages from secs. 3.Ai and 3.Aii in Csapo and Slater (1994); on the establishment of dithyrambic contests, see Herington (1985, 87–97) and Wilson (2000, 12–21); on their organization, see Pickard-Cambridge (1988, 74–79), and on aspects of performance, Pickard-Cambridge (1962, 31–38).
175. Aristotle *Poetics* 1449a, chap. 4; Csapo and Slater (1994), sec. 2, no. 11, 99–100.

the dithyramb can proceed from there.[176] By the fifth century the dithyramb was a composed *choros,* and we know from the example of Eumelus that composed *choroi* were a distinct possibility at the time of Archilochus.[177] Since in another fragment Archilochus refers to himself "leading off" or "beginning" a *paian* to the *aulos,* we may at least suppose that a *choros* of some sort was involved, even if we can conclude nothing about its performance.[178]

174

A generation after Archilochus we have the second case of a composer associated with the dithyramb, and in this case the composer, Arion, is stated to have been "the first man of those of whom we have knowledge to compose, name, and teach [produce] a dithyramb in Corinth."[179] The statement comes from the historian Herodotus, and we should add to that the information that Arion was a native not of Corinth but of Lesbos. His patron was the tyrant of Corinth, Periandros, whose father had seized power from the Bacchiads earlier in the seventh century. It is impossible to say what Herodotus thought he meant by "name" here, but the situation he presents is of the organization of dithyrambic *choroi* at Corinth, quite probably where there had been none before.[180] Tyrants won power by suppressing the power of the established aristocracy in favor of autocracy supported by populism. They are repeatedly found, in the seventh and sixth centuries, in mainland Greece and the Aegean islands and, in the fifth and fourth centuries, in the Greek cities of Sicily, exercising patronage over composers in connection with performances that they establish or develop, notably at festivals.

So these examples prove the antiquity of composed dithyrambs, almost certainly associated with festivals of the god Dionysus, and (at least in the case of Arion) representing commissions to a composer for a *choros.*[181] Sig-

---

176. Archilochus frag. 77, translated by Csapo and Slater (1994), sec. 2, no. 1, 95; for a discussion, see Pickard-Cambridge (1962, 1 ff.).

177. Privitera (1988) believes that Archilochus was both composer and *didaskalos* of the *choros* for his dithyramb, as well as its *exarchon,* commenting that "it was not improvised, but composed in advance and taught to a chorus" (125).

178. The one-line fragment translates as "I myself leading off a *paian* to [the accompaniment of] the Lesbian *aulos.*"

179. Herodotus *Histories* 1.23 ff.; sources on Arion are collected usefully in Campbell (1991, 16–25).

180. Giving songs specific titles is one possibility, favored by Pickard-Cambridge (1962, 12). Zimmermann (1992, 24–25) would see Arion adopting an old name—the dithyramb—for his work, and/or filling an old form with new substance, since Archilochus had already composed dithyrambs.

181. Privitera (1988) provides this estimate of Arion's activity and achievement: "With his invention Arion aligned the song for Dionysos with the other principal choral songs composed and executed on the occasion of religious festivals" (127).

nificantly, we have a history here—in bare outlines—that predates the reference to the earliest appearance of a tragic *choros,* which once again comes from the fifth-century historian Herodotus. It arises in relation to Cleisthenes of Sicyon, whose entertainment of suitors for his daughter led to the performance of Hippocleides discussed above in my section on dancing. Cleisthenes' daughter Agariste was in the event married to Megacles, an Athenian of the Alkmaionid family or clan, and the son of that marriage was the Athenian reformer Cleisthenes, who laid the foundations of the democracy and whose reforms led to the remarkable development of the festival of Dionysus in Athens.

Herodotus believed that the reforms of the Athenian Cleisthenes were indebted to those of his maternal grandfather and namesake, who reorganized and renamed the tribal groupings at Sicyon in the first quarter of the sixth century BCE. These reforms asserted the independence of Sicyon from its powerful neighbor, Argos, and included in them was a change in cult at Sicyon. The Argive hero Adrastos was honored in Sicyon with a shrine, rites, and *choroí,* which Herodotus calls *tragikoí,* noting that the "sufferings" of Adrastos were celebrated in them and that the Sicyonians accordingly honored Adrastos, not Dionysus. Cleisthenes acted drastically, importing a substitute hero from Thebes and transferring the sacrificial rites from Adrastos to him, but he allocated the *choroí* to the worship of Dionysus.[182]

Once again, it is relatively clear that Herodotus is describing something in terms that would be familiar to his fifth-century audience, but his account provokes major issues. We appear to have *choroí* devoted to the local cult of Adrastos, and Herodotus makes a direct connection between the "sufferings" of the hero that they celebrate and the idea of the later, Athenian model of Dionysian tragedy. Herodotus is well aware of the existence of the dithyramb as a form in the generations preceding Cleisthenes, and Arion's activity at Corinth is as close to Sicyon (in the northern Peloponnese) as it might be. The firmest conclusion is simple, which is that the cult of Dionysus, and the establishment of *choroí* in his honor, was developing strongly in this part of Greece (at least) in this period. Beyond that, someone or something has suggested to Herodotus that the closest analogy to the traditional *choroí* in honor of Adrastos at Sicyon was the tragic *choros.* There is also the implication that this model for *choroí* continued with those instituted to honor Dionysus at Sicyon, about which we know nothing more. It is just possible that they may, if they still existed in the fifth century, have resembled tragedy

182. Herodotus *Histories* 5.67.

rather than dithyramb and that Herodotus is projecting that resemblance back on to the traditional *choroi* that they replaced.

Cleisthenes of Sicyon was another of these political figures classed as tyrants, and his displacement of the traditional aristocratic governance of Sicyon is apparent in his dissolution of the tribal structure that undoubtedly supported aristocratic rule. Peisistratus of Athens, and his sons Hippias and Hipparchus, had also come to power by displacing the aristocracy of Athens and Attica, and their rule was only terminated by Cleisthenes leading a popular revolt that began to emancipate the Athenians by introducing democratic forms. His reorganization of the Athenians from four into ten new tribes grouped portions of Attica together, demographically, into each of the tribes, so local power bases for aristocratic influence were no longer viable to the same degree. The dithyrambic contests at Athens, from the last decade of the sixth century BCE, were an overt confirmation of this new governance, with fifty members of each tribe in separate *choroi,* of men and also of boys, in a display that occupied the first day of performances at the grand festival of Dionysus, known as the City Dionysia.[183] These were composed *choroi,* and the composers were not necessarily Athenians, a ruling that may have originally allowed the finest composers to be brought into the festival from outside. Dithyrambs were also performed at other Athenian festivals, but this occasion was central to the ideology as well as the religious life of Athens.

It is perfectly possible that Herodotus sees the development of *choroi* in honor of Dionysus, and the role of this development in the context of a major demographic and ideological revolution, as a significant part of the debt of the Athenian Cleisthenes to his grandfather.[184] Dithyrambs may well have been performed at Athens under the Peisistratids, who were certainly responsible for major cultural initiatives, including the development of the festival of the Panathenaia.[185] Similarly, the tradition was that the legendary founder of tragedy, Thespis, operated under the Peisistratids.[186] The categorical distinction between tragic *choroi* and the dithyrambic *choroi* is the emergence of a separate performer, from whom the actors of tragedy (and drama)

183. The cultural history of the Peisistratids and the reforms of Cleisthenes are well described by Herington (1985, 82–97).
184. A good discussion comes from Lonsdale (1994, 254–55).
185. On the Panathenaia and the Peisistratids, and on the introduction of the dithyramb, see Herington (1985, 84–87, 93–94, respectively) and Wilson (2000, 15–16).
186. The name of Thespis was the object of much highly dubious conjecture in late antiquity, and I shall not be discussing that material; it is reviewed at length in Pickard-Cambridge (1962, 69–89). The studies by Connor (1989) and West (1989), mentioned at 5n12 in this book, both encourage skepticism.

are developed. Aristotle theorized this with his observation that tragedy developed from those who "led off" (the *exarchontes*) the dithyramb, and if this
theory is to be entertained we might look for signs, certainly at Athens, of such
exarchontes in the dithyramb.[187] So the evidence for the Athenian dithyramb is
important, in attempting to determine the particular qualities of the tragic   177
and the dithyrambic *choroi,* juxtaposed as they were in the same festival for
the same audience.

Of the dithyrambs of two of the most significant names from the early
period at Athens nothing is known. Both Lasus (of Hermione, in the northern Peloponnese) and Simonides (of the Aegean island of Keos) were at
Athens in the later years of the Peisistratids and almost certainly composed
dithyrambs in those years, and Simonides at least was prolific in this kind of
composition, continuing to compose under the democracy. Pindar also composed dithyrambs, and although the fragments of these are meager, some of
them were for Athens; in addition, there are the songs known as dithyrambs
in a major collection of compositions by Bacchylides discovered on papyrus.
Both composers belong to the fifth century.

What kind of *choros* was the dithyramb? Zimmermann reviews the fragments of Pindar and Bacchylides' dithyrambs individually, and his concluding summaries are both helpful and interesting.[188] It is relatively clear, even
from the fragments, that Pindar used the triadic form of strophe, antistrophe, and epode and also followed a format analogous to that of his victory
songs, with an introduction followed by a myth. As the introduction orien-
tated the song to the city for which it was composed, so the myth may reasonably be assumed to have had connections with that city. Furthermore,
Pindar seems to have paid particular attention to the occasion of the festival
and, prominently, to the god Dionysus. In contrast, Bacchylides displays less
overt concern with what I have called the "commission," although he too
uses the triadic or the responsive (strophe and "responding" antistrophe)
form for his songs.

Nonetheless, Zimmermann employs a degree of finesse in teasing out the
possibilities of the occasion from Bacchylides' songs, presenting ultimately a
convincing case for their interpretation as dithyrambs.[189] The "Heracles,"

---

187. Aristotle *Poetics* 1449a, translated by Csapo and Slater (1994), sec. 2, no. 11, 99.
188. Zimmermann 1992. His "Summary: Typical Elements of the Pindaric Dithyramb"
and "Summary" for Bacchylides are at 61–63 and 113–16, respectively. For Pindar's
dithyrambs, see also Van der Weiden (1991); and for Bacchylides, Burnett (1985).
189. Text and translations of the songs of Bacchylides are in Campbell (1992) and in Burnett (1985).

sixteenth in the collection from papyrus, is explicitly destined for Delphi, and the offering of dithyrambs to Dionysus in the winter months when Apollo was believed to be absent from the shrine provides a sufficient occasion. The fragmentary twentieth, "Idas," was for the Spartans, and the remaining four (15, 17, 18, 19) Zimmermann connects firmly with Athens, even noticing an Athenian presence in the subtle mediations of the myth in the seventeenth, explicitly an offering for the Keians at Delos. The prominence of Theseus in this song, and the identification of the young girls and men traveling with him as Ionians, undoubtedly encourage an interpretation of it within the terms of the leadership of Athens over the Ionians immediately after the Persian wars, when the center for the confederacy was located at the sanctuary of Apollo on Delos.[190]

In terms of performance, this kind of discussion brings with it some interesting possibilities. For the seventeenth, for the Keians, and the eighteenth, for the Athenians, in both of which the figure of Theseus is of paramount importance, Zimmermann proposes connections of the kind Calame had emphasized for the *choroí* of Alcman, suggesting that the songs engage with the roles of the young on the threshold of maturity.[191] Since the myth of the seventeenth involves youths of both genders, Zimmermann is willing to support the contention that this was sung by a mixed *choros* of Keian youths, who number fourteen in the mythical narrative of the song. Since this song is not destined for the festival of Dionysus at Athens, then fourteen (or sixteen, if we include the protagonists of the narrative, Theseus and Minos) is a feasible number for a *choros*. But in performance terms Zimmermann is less interested in the number of the *choros* he proposes than in the substantial proportion of the song given to direct speech, in the mouths of Theseus and Minos. He is inclined to see the extent of this exchange as a premonition of the completely spoken exchanges that characterize the remarkable eighteenth song, in which, in two pairs of strophe and antistrophe, Aegeus the father of Theseus answers the concerns of an unidentified speaker or speakers.[192]

190. In contrast, Maehler (2004, 173–75) links the song closely to the iconography of Theseus, specifically but not exclusively in vase painting, suggesting a date before the Persian Wars. In that case, it might readily be associated with Athenian support for the revolt of the Ionian Greeks from Persia.
    Note that the "Persian Wars" is a historical term that generally refers to the period between 490 and 479 BCE; similarly, the "Peloponnesian War," between Athens and a confederation led by Sparta, refers to the period between 431 and 404 BCE.
191. Translations of both of these songs were also provided by Lattimore in his *Greek Lyrics* (1960), with the eighteenth as no. 1, and the seventeenth as no. 2.
192. Zimmermann (1992), 95–96, and earlier comments at 80.

Zimmermann accords with many others in reading the strong influence of tragedy in the eighteenth song, not solely through its explicit form of a direct exchange between what is probably a group (of Athenians) and its king but also in the dramatic qualities of the composition. The group addresses Aegeus (strophe 1) because it has heard the blare of a trumpet and has "come" in fear and apprehension to seek reassurance from the king, seeing him as being able to command an impressive force of young soldiers. Aegeus responds (antistrophe 1) that a messenger has arrived, reporting the remarkable feats of strength of a stranger; the group (strophe 2) wonders, and asks for any more information the king may have; the king responds (antistrophe 2) with a flattering description of a young man, who is heading toward Athens. Theseus—for it is he!—is never mentioned by name, and the play on the audience's awareness has a distinctly dramatic quality to it. Zimmermann debates the possibilities but is finally inclined to assign this song to a boys' *choros* at the Panathenaia.[193]

I shall return to characteristics of this song later in this section. But for the moment it seems important to pick up on Zimmermann's strange idea that there is something significant in the relationship between the seventeenth and eighteenth songs in terms of the development of what we might be inclined to call "direct speech" but which is obviously "direct song." In the eighteenth, the group and Aegeus are respectively allocated the complete strophe and antistrophe in both of the pairs that compose the song. In the seventeenth the exchanges between Theseus and Minos do not fall into this formal pattern, with Theseus overlapping from strophe 1 into antistrophe 2 and Minos included within (but not occupying all of) epode 1. The *choreía,* as a song and dance, must also be different in each case, because the seventeenth is triadic (strophe, antistrophe, and epode) while the eighteenth has only responding strophe and antistrophe. So, if Zimmermann is inclined to divide the *choros* for the performance of the eighteenth between two distinctly characterized half-choruses, this strong feature cannot obviously be foreshadowed in the seventeenth.[194] Furthermore, the presence of quotation from a figure from the myth is a relatively familiar feature of other kinds of song and is included even in those of Bacchylides that we have, such as numbers three and five from the victory songs. So there is no particular reason why we should see the curious conception of the eighteenth as a direct development from the arts of composition found in the seventeenth.

193. Others have in the past, as he notes, opted for other festivals (Zimmermann 1992, 99nn21–24).
194. Zimmermann (1992, 96, 96n5), in favor of the half-choruses and against the possibility of a soloist taking the role of Aegeus.

180 If the eighteenth is indeed a dithyramb, and even if it is not for performance at the City Dionysia by fifty singers, we still might reasonably doubt whether an Athenian dithyramb was ever anything but a circular *choros*.[195] If that is the case, then it is difficult to envisage how the semichoruses might have performed. Dithyrambic *choroi* were not masked, and a circular *choros* offered no possibilities for the disposition of parts of itself in the performing or playing space, unless it were to break its circularity. The song might have been easy to teach to two parts of a *choros;* but its dramatic (or, strictly speaking, tragic, if we accept a limited definition here of "tragic") qualities will have emerged as a choric performance only with great restrictions in comparison to the possibilities available to tragedy. So what we can envisage, if we accept the classification of the song, is a strange kind of compliment to the Athenians, one that allows their dithyramb—as a kind of *choros*—to be assimilated to another prominent and highly characteristic artform.[196] The absence of any explicit reference to the occasion of the song, to elements of the commission, is also striking and indicates—as Zimmermann notices—a marked contrast with Pindar.

We need to consider this carefully when we are drawn toward determining the extent of the Dionysian element in Athenian performances. Bacchylides is unquestionably sensitive to Athens in this composition, but he is not overtly sensitive to the Dionysian in it, except perhaps (and significantly) in what I have called the compliment to tragedy. Of course, we cannot regard this as typical, even of Bacchylides' dithyrambs for Athens. The nineteenth, which Zimmermann assigns to the City Dionysia, though short is explicitly directed to the praise of Athens and the honor of Dionysus, to whom its short myth leads. Zimmermann amusingly selects performance at the City Dionysia for this cursory composition precisely because of the large number of dithyrambs that were presented in one day at that festival. If the fifteenth was also composed for Athens, as Zimmermann and others believe, the absence of an explicit commission might be explained by its performance at a non-Dionysian festival.[197]

195. References to this designation of the dithyrambic *choros* in the comedies of Aristophanes (*Clouds* 333, *Frogs* 366, *Birds* 918) make it very likely that this was the traditional formation.
196. Maehler (2004, 193) suggests a specific influence from Aeschylus's *Agamemnon,* but I would suspect the allusion to tragic form to be more generic.
197. The variety of festivals at Athens for which dithyrambs might be composed, not all of which were devoted to Dionysus, is outlined in Pickard-Cambridge (1962, 35–38); for descriptions of the individual festivals see Parke (1977). Maehler (2004, 157–58) plausibly relates the fifteenth song of Bacchylides to the Panathenaia and so, more distinctly, to the cult of Athena, reflected in the Trojan priestess Theano in the song.

THE THEATRICAL *CHOROI*: DEFINITIONS
AND DISTINCTIONS

In his summary on the dithyrambs of Pindar, Zimmermann uses the phrase
"typical elements," and it is tempting to feel that a similar kind of concept is
required in tackling the immense problem of the tragic *choros*. For this purpose we are, in many respects, overwhelmed by detail. Calame in his study of
the *partheneion,* Zimmermann in his of the dithyramb, and others in similarly
excellent studies of kinds of *choroi* have the advantage of restricted material.
The relative diversity of tragedy, despite an extremely patchy survival, combined with its relatively precise chronology and our knowledge of Athenian
history and society, make specific appreciation and interpretation attractive.
Of course, formal or generic considerations may be applied, notably in connection with the intriguing puzzle of the origin of tragedy or in attempted
determinations of its pattern of development.[198]

In this connection, the eighteenth song of Bacchylides has inevitably attracted attention, largely in relation to Aristotle's observation that tragedy
developed from those who "led off" (the *exarchontes*) the dithyramb. A theoretical scheme might readily construe a progression from ritual origin to
the artform of tragedy, and there are sufficient indications in Homer and
Archilochus to paint an early picture of the *exarchon* and *choros*. So Bacchylides'
eighteenth song, composed for Athens, might be read as a late reflection of,
or an allusion to, this emergence of one kind of *choros* from another. The
problem with all these speculations is that our first complete tragedy (or
Greek drama of any kind) dates from 472 BCE, and it seems most likely that
Bacchylides' song was composed at a similar time, after the Persian wars.[199]
This is a generation after the reforms of Cleisthenes and the reorganization
of the festival of the City Dionysia, which comes twenty to thirty years after
the traditional date for the introduction of tragedy to Athens, under Peisis-
tratid rule. Athens may have been relatively late in the welcome it extended
to Dionysian *choroi*. But the first name associated with the dithyramb at
Athens is that of a highly sophisticated composer, Lasus, who came from the
northern Peloponnese, an area in which the composed dithyramb (and possibly composed *choroi* for Dionysus) had been established.

The origins of the *choroi* performed in the theater of Dionysus may be intriguing, but the fact remains that we must study them as comparative forms,
much as the Athenians watched them. In this final section of the chapter I

198. The most influential study of the formal qualities of tragic song was by Kranz (1933).
199. Zimmermann (1992, 99n27) records a convincing view.

should like to introduce some defining features of the three *choroi* from satyr play, comedy, and tragedy, features that distinguish them principally from each other. These features must ultimately be related to reception, but they may also be helpfully outlined in relation to the question of what it means to have such a reduplication of *choroi* in honor of one god at one festival.[200] I am, of course, largely concerned with the *choros* in these forms, and most of these features may be inspected, readily enough, by the reader with a script in hand, either in the original language or in translation.

The satyr drama, like the dithyramb, in some respects suffers from the restrictions of the available material, but it has in similar fashion been the subject of some impressive study. Seaford offers a fine account in English, and like many others is inclined to see the origin of the satyr play in the proverb "nothing to do with Dionysus."[201] Some late speculations from antiquity in connection with this proverb do not precisely accord but suggest that satyr plays were introduced to retain or reintroduce the satyric element in the theatrical festival. According to this scheme, either tragedy or dithyramb began to desert Dionysian themes, and this prompted the reaction and the creation of a new kind of *choros*.[202] But plainly the satyr play has other origins, not least in the celebrations that are presumed to account for the many early images of satyrs or *silenoi* on vases, which Webster painstakingly details in *The Greek Chorus* and to which Seaford refers. Seaford also believes that the satyr play was not originally attached to a tragic trilogy, which is a persuasive deduction from the evidence. It may, in other words, originally have been composed by specialists before it became adopted by those who composed for tragic *choroi*. We cannot tell when this happened, but the system of three tragedies followed by a satyr play by the same composer was at least in place by 472 BCE.

The "satyric" is a far more difficult concept to trace, but it informs Aristotle's second suggestion about the origin of tragedy, which was that tragedy underwent a (slow) "change from the satyric," discarding a longer verse line or measure that had been more suitable for dancing along with limited plots and ridiculous language.[203] Aristotle's observations may, of course, have in-

---

200. For the general problem, see the essay by Osborne (1993).
201. Seaford's stimulating introduction to his edition of Euripides' *Cyclops* (1984) discusses the genre as well as the play succinctly; Sutton's more exhaustive treatment (1980) is also valuable. Seidenstucker (2003) concentrates on the iconography of satyrs, in a manner that recalls the approach of Webster, in his review of the *choros* in satyr drama.
202. Seaford (1984, 11–12); see also Pickard-Cambridge (1962, 124–26).
203. Aristotle *Poetics* 1449a.19–25; Csapo and Slater (1994), sec. 2, no. 11, 99–100.

fluenced the later speculations on the meaning of the proverb. But if tragedy as a composed song for a festival, from the time of the Peisitratids, was indeed designed to be ridiculous, then the contrast with its earliest visible form in the fragments of Aeschylus is remarkable.[204] If the scheme is accepted, the removal of laughter from tragedy would then account not just for the satyr play but also for the introduction of composed comedy to the festival of Dionysus in 486 BCE.

The problem with Aristotle's scheme of tragedy finding its true nature or achieving its full development is that it is tied to an assertion that both tragedy and comedy arose from "an improvisational beginning/origin." The question that arises is whether an improvisational form would have been introduced to a festival. The introduction of comedy to the City Dionysia is recorded for the 486 BCE, with the name of the composer, Chionides.[205] That the dithyramb at Athens was a composed *choros,* even under the Peisistratids with Lasus, cannot be doubted. The suggestions about the introduction of the satyr play do not envisage an improvisational form, but a composed play introduced to an existing festival. The same source that gives Hypodicus of Chalcis as the victor (composer/trainer, significantly a non-Athenian) of the first dithyrambic contest in 509 or 508 BCE—perhaps the first under the new regime—also supplies an approximate date for Thespis, between 536 and 534 BCE.[206] We have no means of knowing whether Thespis competed at a festival in the city at this time or precisely when tragic *choroi* were introduced to the City Dionysia. But it is as unlikely that we should associate the first occurrence of tragedy at a festival organized under the Peisistratids or the early democracy with improvisation as that we should

183

204. Some, at least, of the fragments of Aeschylus must be assumed to date before the *Persians,* and we can detect nothing ridiculous in them beyond the fragments that are thought to be from satyr plays.

205. For the evidence on Chionides and the introduction of comedy, see Pickard-Cambridge (1962, 189–90); Csapo and Slater (1994), sec. 3, no. 46, 120–21. The text of one of the most important fragmentary inscriptions relating to the festival of Dionysus actually begins with the comic composer Magnes, whose victory is recorded for 472 BCE, in the same year as Aeschylus's *Persians.* Magnes is the earliest of his predecessors mentioned by Aristophanes in *Knights,* 520–21, where he is portrayed as winning many times against rival *choroi.* For the inscriptional record on Magnes, see Pickard-Cambridge (1962, 190n2; 1988, 82, 112), where the probabilities are discussed in relation to another, chronological list of comic composers at the Dionysia.

206. On Hypodicus, see Pickard-Cambridge (1962, 15); for the inscription mentioning both Thespis and Hypodicus, see Csapo and Slater (1994), sec. 3, no. 45, 120. The text of this inscription has been subject to judicious criticism from Connor (1989), who, like West (1989), is skeptical about the traditions on Thespis.

associate Lasus or Hypodicus, Pratinas (for the early satyr play) or Chion-ides with improvised forms.[207] Composed tragedy has an early history that is hidden from us, as much as tragedy or the satyr play may have further ori-gins in improvised or ritual *thiasoi* dedicated to Dionysus or as comedy plainly has in the *komos*.[208]

184

In considering the "function" of the satyr play, and so of the satyr *choros*, Seaford makes a strong case for regarding satyrs as "not of the *polis*" (*ou poli-tikon*): "In an urban culture the preurban *thiasos* acquires a sharper symbolic significance," and the satyrs "represent a community that is antithetical to the *polis*, because representative of more ancient social relations."[209] Seaford bases his view of the satyric and Dionysian *thiasos* largely on activity that may have been established early but that remained in existence alongside the produc-tion of satyr plays, pointing to the Athenian festival of the Anthesteria, which the Athenian fifth-century historian Thucydides calls the "more ancient Dionysia."[210] Yet in his functional analysis there are elements of a relatively standard theory of progression from ritual to drama, since the *choros* is pre-sumed to be "representative of more ancient social relations." Seaford also provides a fascinating summary of what, using Zimmermann's term, might be called "typical elements" of the satyr play, drawing on the longer frag-ments from Aeschylus and Sophocles, the titles of plays, Euripides' *Cyclops*, and other evidence. He identifies "the captivity, servitude and liberation of the satyrs" as one of the major themes, which is fully apparent in *Cyclops*.[211]

Euripides' *Cyclops* is the only complete text of a satyr drama that has come down to us. It may or may not be a typical version of the form, but it does offer us a dynamic impression of what the values of the *thiasos* were felt to be in the theatrical context. Many of these values are impressed on us by their absence or denial in the situation of the drama. The satyrs have been search-ing for Dionysus but have been made slaves of the Cyclops, Polyphemos, constrained to that immediate locale and status and acting as shepherds in-stead of shouting the cry for Dionysus in his dances (Euripides' *Cyclops* 23–26). The desire for union with the god, and for participation in the *thiasos*, is

207. On Pratinas, see Seaford (1977–78).
208. On comedy and the *komos*, see the discussion in Pickard-Cambridge (1962), chap. 3 "The Beginnings of Greek Comedy," sec. I, 'The *Komos*,' 132–62.
209. Seaford 1984, 31, 30, respectively. Sutton (1980, 134–79) shows less interest than Seaford in the Dionysian *thiasos* in his discussion of the nature and function of satyric drama, which offers a more conventional literary and dramatic criticism of the form.
210. Thucydides *History of the Peloponnesian War* 2.15, and Seaford (1984, 5–10); on the An-thesteria, see Pickard-Cambridge (1988, 1–25) and Parke (1977, 107–20).
211. There is a translation of *Cyclops* by Arrowsmith (1956).

defined by this objectionable separation and reduction of status, which incidentally underlines for us how distinct the satyric is from the pastoral. The
epode to the opening *choros* of the satyrs moves from the current activity of
herding, which occupies the strophe and antistrophe, to an expression of
what is missed: "This is not Bromios, these are not his *choroi,* nor maenads   185
carrying the *thyrsos,*" and the epode continues to list what is lacking, including wine, Aphrodite, music, dancing, shouting the ritual cry, ending with the
plaintive "sundered from your love." The term used here is *philía,* which expressed a wide range of commitment and allegiance in Greek society. Yet it
is striking that when Odysseus arrives his reaction on seeing the satyrs is that
he has "come to a city [*polís*] of Dionysus," and the discussion between him
and Silenus that follows of the way of life of the Cyclopes repeats standard
antitheses between the city and the desolate space, bare of human beings.[212]
The Cyclopes live in caves, not houses, they are not gathered into society,
have no political organization, eat strangers, and do not have wine, "since
they live in a land without *choroi.*" In this survey of savagery, it is plain that
the Dionysian, as represented by the satyrs and Silenus, is an essential—
almost a defining—part of the society of the *polís,* which should have all of
these things and so should have (satyric) *choroi.*

Restoration, to some degree, is the task of the rest of the play, and once
the wine is introduced by Odysseus then the desire for a *choros* is the immediate result. Silenus smells it first, then is persuaded to taste, and once he has
done so he shouts "Dionysus is calling me to dance a *choros!*" (156). The next
step is the expression of the desire for freedom from slavery and the awakening of erotic excitement, while the means to deceive the Cyclops is that of
initiation into the Dionysian *thíasos* through wine. What condemns the Cyclops utterly is his abuse of sacrifice and of respect for strangers at his own
hearth and altar: eating people is wrong and an utter dislocation of the organization of civil sacrifice. Seaford argues that the reference to his altar
within the scene building is intended to contrast forcefully with the altar to
Dionysus in the center of the *orchestra.*[213] When Odysseus himself contrasts
Dionysus with the Cyclops, after a gruesome account of the meal in the cave,
he is identifying the satyrs' search for reunion with Dionysus—the *thíasos*—
with the conventional values of the Greek *polís.*

If Athenians and other Greeks gained satisfaction from dressing up as

212. In his note to "city of Dionysus," Seaford suggests that the audience may have seen an
allusion to the satyric quality of their own festival of the Anthesteria (1984, 122, in a commentary on *Cyclops* line 99).
213. Seaford (1984, 170–71), in a commentary on *Cyclops* lines 345–46.

satyrs, as Seaford argues, then this will partly have come from closer identification with the god and with each other in their aspect as celebrants. We may see this function continued for the *choros* members in the satyr play, and the assertion of the values of the *thiasos* is strong enough in Euripides' *Cyclops* for us to have no doubt about its function for the audience in the festival. The myth of the play, in its elaboration as a plot, amply confirms the value of Dionysian celebration in the *polis* and provides a grotesque evocation of the absence of Dionysian *choreia*. The remoteness of the satyric when embodied as a dramatic myth provides a comfortable fantasy for its audience, and its performance would be a pleasurable rather than a fraught activity.

Comedy operates nearer the bone, because it is contemporary in its themes and characters, at least in the form that we have it from Aristophanes, and comedy and the comic *choros* are far more complex phenomena than the satyr play. This is partly a matter, once again, of composition. Satyr plays became attached to the tasks of the tragic composer relatively early, and, as Seaford observes, the surviving fragments display much of the technique deployed in tragedy. Comedies were composed as single dramas by specialists, and their analogies with tragic (or satiric) composition are apparent but limited. Much in comedy is certainly reliant on *rhesis*, or on the elaboration of spoken parts for actors/characters, but the *choros* as we can observe it in Aristophanes has a distinctive character.[214] My observations here are confined to the comic *choros* and to those aspects of it that have some bearing on distinguishing features of the tragic *choros*.

The most distinctive features of the Aristophanic comic *choros* lie in its explicit definition, which is heavily associated with its theatrical appearance (*Wasps, Clouds, Birds,* etc.), and in a core role in the play known as the *parabasis*. Aristophanic comedy appears to continue a tradition, represented in vase paintings earlier than the fifth century BCE, of animal *choroi* in performances about which we know very little.[215] In Aristophanes, these traditional definitions are given a sophisticated metaphorical exploitation, rendering aspects of the life of the *polis* open to satirical treatment, which can then be developed and explored by the actors/characters: Aristophanes *Wasps, Clouds,* and *Birds* all provide examples of this ability of the comic composer. These "animal" *choroi* seem to provide a continuity within comic performance, but in

214. The comedies of Aristophanes are the only complete comedies we have from the fifth century. The fragments from his contemporaries or predecessors do not come near to allowing us to look at, or even guess at, the form of a complete play. There are speculations on significant fragments in Harvey and Wilkins (2000).

215. On animal *choroi*, see Sifakis (1971) and Pickard-Cambridge (1962, 151 ff.).

surviving Aristophanic comedies there are also other kinds of definition, which exploit caricature by defining a human type within the *polis:* such *choroi* may represent Athenian women, defined in a particular aspect or context (*Women at the Thesmophoria, Lysistrata*), or Athenian men (*Knights, Acharnians*), or even the dead. This variety makes it difficult to believe that members of a comic *choros* felt, or were perceived to have, through these definitions alone a distinctly Dionysian identity within the festival, in the way that the *choros* of a satyr play inherently and consistently had.

Nor is the second of the distinctive features, the *parabasis,* explicitly Dionysian. If comedy originated from a *komos* in honor of Dionysus, or from celebrations of that kind, it displays in the *parabasis* a degree of formal organization that is impossible to detach, as it stands in Aristophanes, from the arts of composition.[216] Indeed, modern scholars have been attracted to the *parabasis* precisely because it demonstrates qualities of formal structure, and its gradual deterioration over the time span covered by Aristophanes' surviving plays can be readily tracked.[217] It might be attractive to attribute this deterioration to a gradual diminution of a ritual sense in both composer and audience. But that inclination must be placed alongside an awareness that in 425 BCE, in Aristophanes' earliest surviving comedy *Acharnians,* what confronts us is a traditional form of theatrical presentation, composed by a young Athenian to accord with what he had seen in the theater. We have no evidence that there was, or ever had been, a ritual that took this form. But we do have every reason to suspect that Aristophanes inherited his sense of the form from earlier composers of comedy and felt inclined or obliged to reproduce it, although that sense of obligation faded over time.[218]

216. Aristotle's speculations on the origins of comedy refer indirectly to the *komos* and firmly to "those who led off the phallic [songs]." He also distinguishes carefully between comedy in the festival, with a *choros* formally granted (to a composer) by the appropriate magistrate, and the earlier performances of "volunteers." For translations of the relevant passages from Aristotle's *Poetics,* see Csapo and Slater (1994), sec. 3, no. 133, 174 (in relation to the *komos*), and sec. 2, nos. 11 and 12, 99–100. The *komos* and phallic songs are discussed in Pickard-Cambridge (1962, 132–62).
217. Pickard-Cambridge (1962) gives a classic formal analysis of the *parabasis* and comedy in "Excursus: On the Form of Old Comedy" (194–229); a brief and accessible introduction to its components is provided by Dover (1972, 49–53). A more recent discussion comes from Hubbard (1991).
218. Hubbard (1991) believes that there is no evidence for the *parabasis* as a "cultic remnant," insisting that "many received assumptions about the form's fossilized archaism are mistaken: I believe available evidence to reveal the *parabasis* rather as a very dynamic and flexible form of essentially literary origin" (25, 17, respectively). I would substitute "theatrical" for "literary."

The aspects of the *parabasis* that are most relevant to this discussion lie in its use of extended direct address to the audience by the *choros*, which takes a variety of forms but which as a composed script is never detached from the controlling voice of the composer. In this respect, the *choros* is actually sheltered by the overt presence of the composer, in a manner in which it would not be in any ritual or nontheatrical context. If we were to see a Dionysian license in comic invective (a broad characteristic of the *parabasis*, as of comedy generally), then the status of the composed *choros* of theatrical comedy will be far from any ritual antecedents or parallels, which have no composers to form their words.[219] We must certainly assume that one of the capacities of the Dionysian within Athens was to provide a degree of both license and protection to those engaged in celebration. But the act of theatrical composition affects the identity of the celebrants, by removing the members of a comic *choros* from the unqualified assumption of the Dionysian that they might exercise in a *komos*. Composition is distinct from ritual, and the accent on the contemporary in comedy, which might acknowledge the *choros* members as Athenians, coincides with an alienation of their voice. If in the dithyramb at the festival Athenians compete in *choroi* as themselves, and in the satyr play they indulge themselves in an evocation of the place of the *thiasos* in the *polis*, then comedy sees them constrained and directed to a larger theatrical and dramatic purpose. As Aristophanes was all too aware, the art of comic composition was an art that could fail, something that must have been possible from its beginnings in the festival, when a *choros* was granted to competing composers.[220]

That larger dramatic purpose will, of course, often carry strong characteristics of the Dionysian. Much of what the satyrs desire for the full satis-

219. Aristotle plainly believed that invective was originally the most pronounced characteristic of comedy, one that continued to dominate in compositions for comic *choroi* at the festival until the time of Crates, who was probably active from the middle of the fifth century BCE (Csapo and Slater [1994], sec. 2, no. 12, 100). What Csapo and Slater translate here as the "iambic character" signifies, in Aristotle's terms in this part of *Poetics*, the equation of the iambic measure with invective or lampoon. Aristophanes advances his own, apparently different, view of his predecessors' activity and appeal in the *parabasis* of *Knights* 507 ff., short-listing Magnes, Cratinus, and lastly Crates. It would appear from the opening lines of this passage that Aristophanes believed all three composers included a *parabasis* of some kind in their compositions.

The relationship between old comedy and the invective of those who wrote "iambics" of a nondramatic kind is carefully studied by Rosen (1988), who unfortunately presents Greek without accompanying translations.

220. Apart from the public meditation on success, failure, and audience rejection in *Knights*, the *parabasis* of a revised version of *Clouds* 510 ff., also reveals Aristophanes confronting the disapproval of audiences.

faction of their *thiasos,* at least in fantasy or aspiration, is also apparent in comedy, which in many instances directs itself toward what one might call the restitution of the wholeness of cult. For Aristophanes, the particular circumstances of Athens from the time when he started composing may have determined certain qualities of the comic. During the 420s BCE Athens was regularly deprived of the use and enjoyment of the countryside of Attica by invasions of the Spartan army, and its inhabitants were forced to live within the city walls of Athens and the Piraeus. As a consequence, the political theme of peace could be combined with Dionysian desires, since peace could be seen to bring restoration and full enjoyment of everything of which the Athenians were deprived. In that respect, the rural celebration of the Dionysia by Dicaeopolis in *Acharnians* is symbolic of how the wholeness of cult cannot be separated from the land and a reminder that Dionysus cannot be confined to life within the city walls. It is, in that interesting way, a sign of the limitations of the celebration of Dionysus in the festival of which the comedy is a part, a feature of comedy that shows how radically comic composition can function within the theatrical festival. But the *choros* and the composer may also embrace pan-Hellenic themes, extending the Dionysian valuation of the wholeness of cult to a vision of peace that embraces Hellas as well as Attica, such as we find in *Peace* and, to a more limited extent, in *Lysistrata.* One might regard this as merely logical—peace can hardly be unilateral—but we must also acknowledge the presence of non-Athenians at the City Dionysia and, consequently, the degree to which pan-Hellenic concerns might be relevant to both comedy and tragedy.

It is likely that no interesting descriptive statement that we can make will apply without exception to all eleven of Aristophanes' surviving comedies. For the purposes of this inquiry, I believe we should be interested in one particular aspect of the relationship between the *choros* of comedy and the speaking actors/characters. Aggression and conflict are major constituents of the action and language of Aristophanic comedy, and they appear in many guises. Like the *parabasis,* what is known as the *agon* (here "contest," "dispute") is a regular and recognizable feature of comedy, with a formal structure of conflict through debate, and the expulsions of unwanted intruders that often occupy the later parts of a play allow for displays of individual aggression.[221] Physicality would appear to have no place in dithyrambic performance, and the role of physical violence in tragedy is controlled in various

221. The *agon* is discussed in Pickard-Cambridge (1962), in the "Excursus: On the Form of Old Comedy," 200 ff.

ways. The fragmentary state of satyric drama makes conclusions difficult, but it is noticeable that the extreme violence of *Cyclops* is controlled in a similar manner to tragedy, despite the exuberant physicality of the satyr *choros*. So it might be the case that comedy is exceptional here, and we certainly find this general aspect of comedy extended to the comic *choros*.

Indeed, one of the defining features of the Aristophanic *choros* is regularly its capacity for aggression. This is explicit in *Wasps*, figured in the costume of the *choros,* but it is also generated for comedy in the broad expectation of anger, conflict, and opposition. This suggests a generic element, stretching beyond Aristophanes, because an expectation of this kind clearly belongs in the audience. Furthermore, aggression in the Aristophanic *choros* is often closely geared to a leading figure. *Knights* provides a good illustration of what we might call this "elemental trigger" in comedy, when the appearance of the dread Paphlagonian bully from his house (the *skene*) is immediately answered by the onward rush and appearance of the *choros,* summoned in a kind of class war of aristocratic cavalry against demagogue. Aristophanic comedy has a marked tendency to generate the dynamics of its action from this elemental opposition between a leading character and a *choros* and, often, between the power of speech and argument (*rhesis*) manifested in the character and the power of *choreia.* This opposition will then become part of a *choreia* of aggression, in which the leading characters become the potential victims of massed attack or pursuit and in which the impressive numbers (and costumes or equipage) of the comic *choros* are realized to spectacular effect. In the contrary mode, we also find the *choros* destined, by its initial opposition, to be won over by the leading character, or strongly supportive of the most purposeful of the characters, and potentially opposed to others. As a dynamic factor of performance, the comic *choros* exists in this flux between support and opposition, participating in the generic physicality of comedy and answering to what appears at least to be a regular expectation of aggression.

In estimating, in comparison with dithyramb, satyr play, and comedy, any typical features of the tragic *choros* we are confronted by two complicating factors, those of the more plentiful survival of tragic texts and of chronology. Not all surviving tragedies can be dated, but secure datings of complete plays span a period from 472 BCE to the end of the fifth century. So it might be suspected that as fast as one might attempt to determine essential features within this material, these features would display an alternative tendency to change, adapt, or even disappear over the century. Similarly, the far greater number of surviving tragedies (than comedies) and the spread of composers are bound to reduce the likelihood of apparent, defining characteristics. In many respects, to acknowledge these points is merely to acknowledge the capacities and qualities of original composition, which is itself a defining characteristic of all four theatrical forms. Nonetheless, in relation to this inquiry, it would be helpful to identify and highlight qualities of the tragic *choros* that might be sufficiently prominent to convince us that they were appreciated at the time.[222]

A definition of the tragic *choros* is made apparent in each play, and our substantial selection of tragedies easily confirms a pattern of explicit characterization. Tragic *choroi* may give their name to the play, and we find *choroi* regularly characterized as young girls, women (but not old women), and old men and, rarely, soldiers; the categories of non-Greek and of slave status are also distinctive. The researches of Calame in particular have had a strong influence in drawing attention to the distance of most of these definitions from what is assumed to be the status of those forming the *choros,* generally taken to be young Athenian males, and known certainly to be men. Winkler added much to this perception with his proposal that the tragic *choroi* were formed of Athenian *epheboi,* adolescent males preparing for full citizen status.[223] If this proposal were accepted, an argument might be developed suggesting that performance in tragic *choroi* might be seen as, and perhaps was, a rite of passage in which a temporary identification with an alien status was a significant functional element. It is an attractive if unproven hypothesis, but it really needs to be allied with a more general theoretical approach to representation by males, with the actors included as well as the *choroi.* Such impersonation is a characteristic not only of the masked forms of the Athenian theater but also of other major conventions in the premodern period: one might cite the Japanese *noh* and *kabuki,* and Chinese and Indian theatrical traditions, in addition to the more familiar English Renaissance drama. There are, indeed, critical studies of the Greek theater (as well as of Renaissance drama) that concentrate firmly on this general aspect of interpretation.[224]

222. My own approach to this aspect of the problem of the (tragic) *choros* bears little relation to the contrasts between comedy and tragedy drawn by Taplin (1986) or the criticism of his argument by Wiles (1997, 207 ff.). I would find more points of contact with the tenor of the presentation by Gould (1996), reprinted in Gould (2001).

223. Winkler 1990. Wilson reviews Winkler's proposal skeptically, but fairly, although he blurs a possible distinction between dramatic and dithyrambic *choroi* at the Dionysia (Wilson 2000, 77–79).

224. Foley's introductory essay to her edited collection (1981) is of great value, with her more recent study (2001), and Case (1985) offers theoretical considerations; Jardine (1989) is a leading study of the problematic for English renaissance tragedy, while Zeitlin (1990) in her essay acknowledges the influence of Bamber's (1982) assessment of Shakespeare.

The definitions of *choroí* by status should also lead us to recognize and examine closely the relationship between any tragic *choros* and a leading figure,
or leading figures, in the tragedy. Comic and tragic *choroí* have no generic
leader unlike the *choros* of the satyr play. In the satyr play, the figure of Silenus

192 seems to be a standard component of the presentation, although the evidence is too fragmentary for total confidence, while the god Dionysus is implicitly the constituting figure of the *thíasos* and may make an appearance.[225]
In tragic composition as we find it, the *choros* achieves its definition alongside
that of the setting and of at least one prominent actor/character in the drama.
These relationships are relatively easy to trace in the scripts of the plays, although their ramifications may be considerable, and that subtlety and so-
phistication should confirm to us their intended vitality or dynamism in
performance.[226] If we take Aeschylus's *Persians,* a tragedy composed for *choros*
and two actors, we find an impressive series of relationships to the royal dynasty of Persia realized by the composer through the status of his *choros,* and
realized in a manner that constitutes and completes the tragic action. When
we add to that the fact that the status of the old men who have been left behind vividly—and even more potently for the original audience—conjures
up to our minds the absence of the adult male army, then the culminating
scene of the tragedy may carry its full and supremely contrived effects.

Allegiance and dependence continue to be characteristics of this relationship throughout the body of surviving tragedies. The status of the *choros* may
be measured against the status of the characters of the tragedy and may be
most effectively evaluated in terms of security. A *choros* such as that of Sophocles' *Oedipus at Colonus,* to take a tragedy from the end of the fifth century, typ-
ically belongs to the location in which the action of the tragedy takes place.
They have a sharply local sense of what is holy ground and what is not, but
their enviable quality of belonging, as citizens, is qualified by their reliance
on armed intervention by other citizens against non-Athenians. As old men,
they are as incapable as Oedipus of effective resistance to violence, and their
allegiance to the *daímones* of their sanctuary, to Athens, and to Theseus is subtly accompanied by the development of their sympathy for the blind old
man, which itself is affected by the consideration—the promise—that he
may himself become a *daímon* that will bring benefit to Athens.

225. The position of Silenus between *choros* and actors, an aspect of the presentation that
may have changed over the years, is reviewed by Seaford (1984, 4–5).
226. Most of the features that I mention below will be readily apparent from a reading of
the scripts; I have, in some few instances, included references to line numbers in paren-
theses as a guide.

This concept of security may also be helpfully applied to the many *choroi* of girls and women, although the status of those who have experienced marriage or those who have not is also of significance in a number of instances. So, for example, the *choros* of young unmarried girls in Sophocles' *Women of Trachis* is decisively distanced from the grueling experience and the self-debate that affects Deianira, the wife of Heracles. In Euripides' *Electra,* the minor indications in the text itself that the *choros* is of girls rather than women may be placed alongside the significant ironies of Electra's unconsummated marriage to the Mycenaean farmer. The security of belonging to the *polis* is something that neither Andromache nor Medea has in their name plays, in contrast to the women of the *choros* who are of the locality, while the fact that the *choros* is composed of women slaves has in its simplest aspect a profound effect on our sense of Electra's plight and status in Aeschylus's *Libation Bearers.*[227]

193

Curiously, what is implied by the tragic *choroi* in many of their manifestations is that the full potency of action could only be achieved by what they are not, which is armed adult males. In that respect, tragedy is apparently concealing a profound dilemma of a militaristic culture. The ultimate model of potency that shadows the action of tragedy is drastically ambivalent, since armed men lose as well as win. The categories of tragic *choroi* regularly indicate the absence of the militarily active male and suggest his potency by default, yet tragedy also reveals and explores the consequences of military failure and defeat.

In this respect, it is interesting that the two *choroi* of soldiers in our surviving tragedies from the fifth century are so defined in situations in which their capacity for military action is suspended or irrelevant. In Sophocles' *Ajax,* the allegiance of the *choros* is primarily to a leading warrior whose insanity marks the turning of his aggression against fellow Greeks. As a consequence of his transgression, that primary allegiance becomes distributed, in demanding and difficult ways, between the concubine of Ajax, his son, his brother, and a reluctant acknowledgment of the authority of the military leaders of the Greek force. The self-destruction of their warlord leads the *choros,* in one song (lines 1185–1222), to desire the dissolution of their own status as soldiers. In Sophocles' *Philoctetes,* the use of armed force is in different ways introduced as a possibility but also eliminated, and the allegiance of the *choros* to their young warlord, Neoptolemos, is subject to the fluctuations of that warlord's acceptance of the military authority of Odysseus and the Greek commanders. As in *Oedipus at Colonus,* this pattern of explicit allegiance is accompanied

227. Easterling (1987, 23–26) reviews the motives given for the dramatic presence of *choroi* of women and girls.

by the development of an overt sympathy for one who is outcast. The plight and status of Philoctetes almost achieve a redefinition of the status of the *choros,* drawing them toward an alternative allegiance based on the primary assumptions that they are Greeks and may be *philoí,* regarded as friends.

194   Aggression and pursuit were two characteristics of the comic *choros* to which I drew attention in my discussion of comedy above. Aggression in the tragic *choros* would provoke an interesting link with comedy. It should already be clear, from the observations I have made on status and related considerations, that violence is to a great and significant extent removed from definitions of the tragic *choroí,* but the exceptions are, for those reasons, all the more important. Explicitly Dionysian violence might be of most interest, and we may feel that we can identify it in that most Dionysian of tragedies, Euripides' *Bacchae.* The *choros* of *Bacchae* is subject to threat from the tyrant figure of the tragedy, Pentheus, a situation that results directly from its allegiance to the god, who is present in the form of a leader of the *thíasos.* Yet it is not the Asian *choros* that is actually imprisoned and escapes in *Bacchae* but the women of Thebes itself. These Theban bacchants pursue and inflict the violence on the possessions of Thebes and on Pentheus, initially in self-defense but also as part of the punishment imposed by Dionysus on those who slandered him and resisted his worship. The vicarious anticipation by the *choros* of violent revenge on the transgressor, Pentheus, is openly expressed only when he has finally left the playing space (lines 977–1023), and in that and earlier songs the *choros* draws on the desire for reunion with the god in the *thíasos* and for the celebratory fullness and freedom of Dionysian worship, familiar from the generic qualities of the satyr play. Despite the almost constant, latent threat of repressive or explosive violence in *Bacchae,* there is no explicitly aggressive confrontation, as the tragedy is composed, between tyrant and *choros.*

A similarly significant distance from the aggressive characteristics of the comic *choros* is apparent in Euripides' *Hecuba,* in which the *choros,* as widowed and enslaved Trojan women, is deeply implicated in the violent revenge taken by Hecuba on Polymestor for the murder of her son. When Polymestor tells of the attack made on him in the tent, he speaks graphically of the violence of Hecuba's attendant women (lines 1132–82), yet there is no explicit indication that any members of the *choros* itself had entered the tent beforehand. So violence is associated with, but removed from, the *choros,* and Polymestor's blind, staggering progress toward the *choros* immediately after the event (lines 1056 ff.), full as it is of hatred against women of Troy and attempting to summon armed violence against them, is received merely by two pairs of spoken lines from the *choros* that restrain pity with right thinking (lines

1085–86, and 1107–8). It is as if, here, composition has provided itself with all the elements—of support for one figure, opposition to another, and even the possibilities of choric confrontation—available to the comic *choros,* yet brings them forward only to deflect them significantly from full theatrical expression. The degree of this ambivalent attraction of the tragic *choros* to the qualities of the comic *choros* is marked in another instance in which a direct allusion to comedy is also most unlikely. In *Oedipus at Colonus,* the *choros* appears in pursuit of the transgressing alien, Oedipus, fired with righteous indignation at the profaning of a sacred precinct. But the excited and outraged *choreia* of the first strophe is mitigated by incipient pity for the age and disability of the transgressor in the corresponding antistrophe, with only a short passage of movement intervening (lines 117–69), as we have seen.[228]

Traces of similar features to those of the comic *choros* remain as a latent quality in the tragic *choros* throughout the fifth century, but they appear to be far more pronounced in the few surviving tragedies of Aeschylus.[229] Direct confrontation between the *choros* and more than one leading figure is a striking feature of *Eumenides,* the final tragedy of Aeschylus's *Oresteia,* and its *choros* of nonhuman *daimones* who are quintessentially vindictive makes aggression and violence imposing realities in the action of the tragedy. Neither a god or his sanctuary nor an image of a goddess are able to overawe these Furies, who rage with pre-Olympian intensity throughout the action, which they themselves largely constitute. This is pursuit made into drama, the Greek word for legal prosecution (*diokein,* or "pursue") embodied, hardly parried even by Olympian gods, but finally rendered by persuasion and the threat of force into a symbol of the wholeness of cult in Athens, with the Furies guarantors of well-being for land and people in the most profoundly religious sense.

Dionysian composition, and the powers of the Dionysian festival, are here at their most confident, advancing their capacity to transform a *choros* of the Night into tutelary deities of the *polis.*[230] The concluding irony is that the final song of the tragedy and the trilogy is sung by those who conduct the Eumenides to their restricting abode of enduring benevolence. Aggression is also a strong characteristic of the women slaves in *Libation Bearers,* with the

---

228. Yet later in the tragedy the *choros* is involved in a confrontation with the actor/character of Creon, while in Euripides' *Children of Heracles* and in his *Heracles* there are brief suggestions of confrontation that the composer does not develop into elaborate conflict.
229. Herington (1963) made some proposals about this relationship.
230. In his study of self-referentiality in the tragic *choros,* Heinrichs (1995, 64) seems to interpret the Dionysian in *Eumenides* more narrowly and in direct relation to the Furies, whose frenzy is like that of maenads, as they themselves assert (*Eumenides* 500).

hatred that the *choros* had felt for its enslavers apparently sublimated and redirected into satisfaction at the violence conjured against and inflicted on those who murdered their owner. The three *choroi* of the *Oresteia* are characterized as much by their opposition to leading figures, and by a confrontation with them that is respectively constrained, suppressed, and violently expressed in the successive tragedies of the trilogy, as they are by their allegiance to any leading figures. Such allegiance is at its strongest in the opening play, although it receives little satisfaction; it is diverted through the memory of Agamemnon to his children in the second play, and inverted in *Eumenides,* with only the chiding shadow of Clytemnestra to remind us (and the *choros*) of it.[231]

If pursuit and aggression, conflict and confrontation are features of the *choroi* in the *Oresteia* that might align the tragic *choros* in some part with the comic *choros,* then the qualities of agitation in other tragic *choroi* of Aeschylus do not necessarily do so. The violence of the comic *choros* certainly takes the form of agitation to a far greater extent than it does that of action, and the agitation in the second two plays of the *Oresteia* is unquestionably violent, with the final tragedy threatening violent action quite as much as a comedy might do. But agitation in *Suppliants* and in *Seven against Thebes* takes a far different form, with the *choros* directly under threat, notably in both cases from that which is absent from the generic scope of tragic *choroi,* an armed force of adult males in action. In a more distant sense, this is also true of the aged *choros* of *Persians,* which by evoking its own absent army is also implicitly under threat from the armed forces of the Greeks. What we find in these three *choroi* are modes of apprehension that seek reassurance from divine and human sources, with the human sources embodied in figures of the dramatic action and the divine sources identified firmly with the locale and setting. So, to a large extent, the tragedy is composed from apprehension and the drive for reassurance in the *choros,* with figures either responding to this demand or widening the tragic action by their failure to do so.

In *Persians,* a tragedy that was not, apparently, part of a trilogy, the representative fears of the *choros* virtually summon all four dramatic characters into the action, with the anticipation of lament ultimately realized, offering a kind of closure of defeat and resignation. In *Suppliants,* the allegiance is partly to Danaus, from whom negotiation is expected, but it is most strongly

231. The loss of the "Dionysian" tragedies of Aeschylus, which arguably included trilogies on the myth of Semele and Pentheus and on Lycurgus of Thrace, who also resisted Dionysian worship, is particularly frustrating in this connection. For a general discussion with wider terms of reference than the problem of the *choros,* which includes observations on the lost tragedies of Aeschylus, see Ley (1993).

to the locale of the land of Argos to which the *choros* has come, and the appeal for protection is to the gods of that land, in reliance on the kinship of the suppliant daughters of Danaus with the Argives. Protection is also, subsequently, expected of the Argive king Pelasgus who, unlike the dynasts of *Persians,* is presented as a figure who cannot decide or act autocratically, without the consent of the people. His doubts and hesitations, under pressure from the expectations of the *choros,* almost constitute a refusal by an actor/ character to perform the role that the dynamics of the tragic form demand of these figures, although ultimately the suppliants do gain the protection and hospitality they have sought. In *Seven against Thebes,* the *choros* of terrified girls does not open the play, as the *choros* does in both *Persians* and *Suppliants,* and in this tragedy the appeal to the gods as protectors of the city is not matched, as it is in *Persians* and *Suppliants,* by a related appeal to a leading figure, who would in this case be Eteocles. His rejection of the *choros,* although ultimately qualified (lines 264–86), is also a refusal of a role implicit in the tragic form, and its thematic implications become apparent as the apprehensions of the *choros* turn toward the fear of mutual killing, and consequent pollution, in the dynasty (lines 677 ff.). The drive for reassurance in this play is partly satisfied, and yet also left unresolved and threatened, by the defeat of the besieging army at the expense of the slaughter of brother by brother.

We should also acknowledge that apprehension and the drive for reassurance are strong components of the *choroi* in the *Oresteia,* where the existence of the trilogy allows us to follow their exploitation in a pattern of satisfaction or frustration throughout its full extent. I would propose that apprehension and the drive for reassurance became the defining dynamic of the tragic *choros,* with tragic tension created and supplied through the decisions of actors/characters, who will either satisfy or frustrate this underlying demand. That tragedy was perceived in this way might be substantially confirmed in the meditation on aspects of tragic form apparent in Bacchylides' eighteenth song, whether or not we conclude that that song was a dithyramb. The microstructure of Bacchylides' song cannot reproduce the formal elements of extended tragedy, and we can think of no circumstances in which Bacchylides might be inclined to do so; but it does show a remarkable awareness of the methods and some essential qualities of the impact of tragedy. What is particularly interesting is that these are not dependent on tragic *pathea,* the sufferings of an individual figure, for their effect. The ultimate "tragedy" of Aegeus is undoubtedly implied, since his death is closely associated with a later return of his son from Crete, but that is hardly the subject of engagement in the present time of the song. Bacchylides is offering his audience a recognizable, compressed pattern of tragic feeling, of apprehension from a *choros* that demands reassurance from a leading figure, and that is "dramatic" by virtue of those qualities.

198

Apprehension is also a quality that associates well with the one measure that seems to be outstandingly "tragic," the dochmiac. In a central part of his sensitive study, Herington is willing to argue that the dochmiac was an invention of tragic composers.[232] Dochmiacs are prominent in the opening *choros* of *Seven against Thebes,* and here an extreme agitation that must have been a quality of the vigor of the dance stems from fear and apprehension. Apprehension is an important word in this context because it implies anticipation or "foreboding," and tragedy is essentially dependent on anticipation in a manner that comedy, with its strong sense of the arbitrary and contingent, is not. Agitation, apprehension, and anticipation may require a measure that becomes distinctively tragic, even though the dochmiac cannot be said to characterize tragic *choreia.* So what can all too readily be given the weak description of a meter suited to "emotional excitement" may prove to be a measure capable of revealing a far more profound set of generic qualities in the tragic *choros.*

Apprehension does not entail a resolution, and if the restitution of the wholeness of cult is apparent as a realized objective in the *Oresteia,* it cannot be said with any confidence to have applied generically to trilogies as tragic presentations. Aeschylus's *Seven against Thebes* is a concluding tragedy, and although we sense the salvation of the city of Thebes, and of the *polis* as a cultic center, we are left with much that is threatening to the city. In one other surviving tragedy we can gain a sense of the direction of a trilogy, since Euripides' *Trojan Women* is known to be the final play in a presentation of closely linked tragedies, and here we would seem to have the opposite of a resolution.[233] It appears to be Euripides' objective in *Trojan Women* to demonstrate that the apprehensions of the *choros* are actually insufficient, and its appeals unanswered, as he directs the action toward an ultimate negation of the wholeness of cult in the complete destruction of the *polis,* of the community, and of the locale of worship and celebration.

We cannot conclude anything categorical about the audience reception of tragedy from a generic definition of the tragic *choros.* But one might argue that apprehension passes, in its intensity, from the *choros* to the audience dur-

232. Herington 1985, 114–15.
233. The titles of the lost tragedies that preceded it were *Alexandros* (an alternative name for Paris) and *Palamedes.* The evidence of some fragments and plot summaries makes it clear that these plays dealt with earlier episodes in the history of Troy and of the Greek expedition against it. Reconstructions are offered by Webster (1967) and Scodel (1980).

ing the course of the fifth century BCE. The ways in which Aeschylus expected his audience to be affected by his tragedies are, for the most part, hidden from us, even if we may come to some relatively sound intuitions about his modes of composition. But a comparison of the *choros* of Euripides' *Phoenician Women* with that of Aeschylus's *Seven against Thebes* reveals how diffi- cult it would be for the audience to follow the action of Euripides' late fifth-century tragedy through the forebodings of his *choros*. That *choros* of Phoenician girls, chosen as the spoils of victory to serve Apollo at Delphi but tracing their lineage to Thebes, has some allegiance to the city and its dynasty. But it cannot demand of the characters of the tragedy that they act to remove its fears, because it is conceived in such a way that it can have no hold on any of those characters. The situation of the *choros* might bear analogies with that of a number of Aeschylean *choroi*, including those of *Suppliants* and *Libation Bearers* as well as *Seven against Thebes*.[234] But the characters of Euripides' tragedy act without reference to any demands or aspirations of the *choros*, detached as they are from its marginal allegiance and functioning in an agonized and obsessive interdependence on each other.

This marked divergence suggests to me that by the close of the century tragic composition expected a relatively conventional response in its audience, which would include apprehension for the actions of actors/characters, while in the time of Aeschylus it was still determining (and exploring) what that response might be through the experience of its *choros*. The clear result of this process is that, as the century proceeds, we perceive the actors/characters performing for the audience, rather than for the *choros* in the view of the audience. So it is that a generic definition for the early tragic *choros* of apprehension and a desire for reassurance, which might seem remote from our standard assumptions about tragedy, becomes gradually more recognizable to us as an apprehension on the part of the audience for the actions of actors/characters, which might readily translate into Aristotle's "fear and pity," in his influential doctrine of *katharsis*.[235] The tragic *choros* sows the seeds of its own demise by educating its audience in an art of tragic reception. In that process, ironically, lies the beginning of our own, modern "problem of the chorus."

234. The definition of the Phoenician girls as foreigners arriving in a land to which they can trace their lineage, and their potential reliance on its king, are features that bear comparison with the *choros* of Aeschylus's *Suppliants*. Their status as slaves, who express allegiance to their enslaver, in this case Eteocles, is comparable to that of the *choros* of *Libation Bearers*. They are, of course, placed in the same mythical moment of siege as their counterparts in *Seven against Thebes* and the fear they feel is similar.
235. I shall not be discussing Aristotelian *katharsis* in this book, but it forms part of one of the readings of theatrical theory that I offered in Ley (1999).

Appendix B

This list includes the names of composers, writers, and political figures mentioned in chapter 2 in the text and in notes. It offers no more than an impression of chronology, but it may be helpful for reference.

The activity of these figures obviously stretches over periods, in some cases more than half a century, and my tendency here has been to enter names under the approximate beginnings of activity in such cases.

More precise indications should be sought from a standard reference work, such as the *Oxford Classical Dictionary*. But it must be stated that most biographical dates for Greek antiquity are highly provisional.

Homer (*Iliad, Odyssey*)
Hesiod, composer   700 BCE

Eumelus, composer
Archilochus, composer   650

Alcman, composer
Periander (Corinth), tyrant
Arion, composer
Cleisthenes (Sicyon), tyrant   600
Peisistratus (Athens), tyrant   550

Thespis, tragic composer
Simonides, composer
Lasus, composer

Hypodicus, composer		
Cleisthenes (Athens), politician	500	
Pratinas, composer		
Pindar, composer		
Bacchylides, composer		201
Chionides, comic composer		
Magnes, comic composer		
Ephialtes (Athens), politician		
Pericles (Athens), politician		
Herodotus, historian	450	
Cratinus, comic composer		
Crates, comic composer		
Damon, controversialist		
Socrates, controversialist		
Cleon (Athens), politician		
Pherecrates, comic composer		
Thucydides, historian		
	400	
Plato, philosopher		
Xenophon, writer	350	
Aristotle, philosopher		
Aristoxenus, musical theorist	300	
	200	
	100	
	—	
	50 CE	
Plutarch, writer	100 CE	
Lucian, writer	150 CE	
Athenaeus, writer	200 CE	

Conclusion

I started, in chapter 1, with a consideration of the earliest surviving tragedies by Aeschylus, in which we find two actors playing roles to a *choros* but not predominantly deployed for dialogue between characters. In these plays, the *choros* receives the actors/characters in the playing space, and the situation and state of the *choros,* expressed in song and dance (*choreia*), provides the core of the tragic experience.

We can understand this mode of composition by looking closely at the script, starting from the location of the *choros* in the open space of the *orchestra* and drawing inferences about the approach and address of actors/characters to the *choros.* Some parts of the playing space may be further defined by an additional focus in the early surviving tragedies—a mound, images, or a tomb—but the danced songs must always occur on the open ground.

In the three linked tragedies of Aeschylus's *Oresteia,* written toward the end of his life, we can observe the impact of the *skene* and the presence of three (rather than two) actors on this mode of composition and detect continuities and adjustments. As I commented, the "intimacy and directness" of the exchanges between Orestes and Electra in *Libation Bearers* mark one change, and later in that tragedy the three actors (and even a fourth, or a silent performer) are used for a swift and remarkable sequence at the door of the *skene.*

Three actors are also plainly apparent to the audience in the trial scene of *Eumenides,* but much of the *Oresteia* relies on the established mode of composition, with one or two performers closely engaged with the *choros,* coming to it and addressing it throughout the trilogy. Aeschylus plays with the impact of the *skene* on the open playing space, with characters moving to their death inside it and other characters attempting to assert their authority from it, but being constantly drawn into the open ground and into address and engagement with the successive *choroi.* My general conclusion was that, in the *Oresteia,* the three actors remain a function of composition for the *choros* . . . in the playing space.

For the period after Aeschylus and the *Oresteia,* I presented a variety of evidence that allows us to confirm composition for the open ground of the playing space in the surviving tragedies of Sophocles and Euripides. The presence of an altar, tomb, or shrine in a number of tragedies permits us to trace the disposition of actors/characters and *choros* in scenes or sequences in the scripts. In some tragedies, such as Euripides' *Helen,* these sequences with the tomb as a focus continue throughout the play. This kind of evidence allows us to make greater sense of our impression that in other tragedies (e.g., Euripides' *Suppliants,* Sophocles' *Oedipus at Colonus*) the *skene* is marginal to the action, and its resource only briefly, if significantly, allowed to affect continuous composition for actors/characters and *choros* in the playing space.

A second tangible indicator of the continuity of this kind of composition is provided by the presence of vehicles (probably carriages) in the playing space. These are used in at least two of the surviving tragedies of Aeschylus, and there are scenes or sequences in a number of later tragedies, notably in Euripides' *Trojan Women,* that give us a vivid picture of composition for the open ground and indications of the disposition of performers, actors and extras alike.

Consideration of the scripts as compositions for the voice, modulating through speaking, chanting, and singing, may also introduce implications for movement on the part of the actors. I have suggested that when actors/characters sing, they also dance, and if accepted this conclusion would affect our interpretation of movement in a number of specific scenes, as well as our sense of the art form of tragedy as a whole, including such issues as the enactment (through singing and dancing) of debility, sickness, severe injury, and old age.

Through chanting and singing, as well as speaking, actors/characters interact with the *choros* in the open playing space in many tragedies, an aspect of performance that is apparent from the earliest until the latest surviving fifth-century tragedies. It should be plain that we need to regard tragic composition as an art that aims to realize exciting opportunities for singing and dancing by actors/characters as readily as it accepts the centrality of the presence of the *choros* and *choreia* in the playing space. Tragic perversions of wedding customs and laments for death, which may be an accompaniment to the introduction of corpses into the playing space, are occasions for composed sequences of this kind, and the violent seizure of characters is another.

When combined, the indications that I traced in the review of composition for the playing space after Aeschylus would allow us to form a relatively strong impression—notably but not just in relation to movement—of much of the full extent of a number of tragedies by Sophocles and Euripides. This is something that silent and static diagrams and drawings cannot do, but they may help in clearing the ground for the creation of that impression.

The *choros* in ancient Greek tragedy and culture poses a problem of comprehension for us in the modern era, which when examined proves to be a series of interrelated problems. The broader context is essential to any more sharply defined inquiry, and I have discussed the gradual emergence of the *choros* into our view, through the narrative filter of the epic poems and in relation to early fragments and texts of songs. Much of the post-Homeric evidence relates to composition for *choroí,* and the context for composition is one of commission, whether in connection with religious festivals or secular occasions, such as the songs accompanying weddings and death within an aristocratic elite. Some kinds of celebration may have involved more traditional forms of singing and dancing groups, but a composed *choros,* as I stated, is never going to be a casual or spontaneous event.

Choreía comprises what we would call music and dance, and both of these aspects of culture in ancient Greece pose great problems for us, since records of sound and movement are inevitably lacking. In addition, music and dance are conjoined in composed Greek *choreía* through the medium of the words of the song, since the rhythm comes *from* the profile of short and long syllables and not from a stress placed *on* the syllables. This rhythmic profile of the surviving texts of *choreía,* such as we see in the choral sections of a tragic script, is known to us as meter, and attempts have been made to trace some qualities of musicality and dance through an analysis of meter. The results, however, are disappointing, with few specific meters yielding consistent characteristics and with the attendant danger of arbitrary associations being attached to them.

There is little or nothing left of musical notation from that period of antiquity and, so, nothing of melody. The modes of ancient Greek music are an intriguing subject, but our understanding of them is obscured by an ideological debate about the "proper" form of music that dates back to the time of Plato and, beyond, into the end of the fifth century BCE. It is perhaps fair to say that a review of the evidence for *mousíke* can warn us against making a number of misleading assumptions but cannot greatly substantiate our sense of the music.

The dance, or dancing as I have preferred to think of it, offers another set of problems and may be similarly prone to ideologically charged views or debates, in either the modern or the ancient period. There have been method-

204

ologically distinct attempts to work back to a convincing picture or embodiment of ancient Greek dancing. These have, variously, suggested specific, mobile associations for different meters in the texts; investigated ancient terms applied to dancing; or employed practice as research into possible affinities between what is seen on vase paintings of ancient Greek dancers and the repertoire of modern dance steps and movements.

All of the approaches face great difficulties, and it may not be possible to extract much from them that encourages confidence. We can be sure that there were *schemata* for dancing, but the precise implications of the term (poses or figures? smaller or larger units of movement? a fixed or an innovative vocabulary?) are hidden from us, as is the relationship of such *schemata* to *cheironomia* (bodily gesture?), or to what was seen as a classic "form" or "type" of tragic dancing, *emmeleia*. The images on vases must tell us something of the visual impression conveyed by ancient dancing, but static representations (even when grouped in categories) are stubbornly resistant to the formation of what we need, which is an aesthetic sense of movement.

The situation is not helped by a dominant theoretical tradition stemming from Plato that introduces the idea of mimetic dancing, one that is hard to interpret practically even in its own terms but that cannot be used to insist on a "show and tell" quality for tragic *choreia*. The existence of formal structure in composed songs—the metrically corresponding strophe and antistrophe pattern, often concluded with an epode—has also prompted speculation, with proposals made about the repetition, inversion, or directional movement of the accompanying dances. But these proposals rest on questionable interpretations of the key terms and have to rely either on tenuous associations for specific meters or on mimetic assumptions, the figuring in dance of verbal images in texts, in order to offer anything substantial to our imaginations.

There can be no doubt that the theatrical *choreia* performed at the festivals of Dionysus in Athens were compositions, and that would include the dithyramb. But there is frustratingly little text that can be securely assigned to this intriguing "circular" *choreia* at Athens, despite its constant presence in the festivals and its involvement of large numbers of citizen singers each year. In my comparative survey of the kinds of composition presented by the dithyramb, the satyr drama, comedy, and tragedy, I tried to highlight a number of characteristics that might help to distinguish the four theatrical forms of *choreia* from each other, noting the relationship with citizenship and the Dionysian in the *polis* of Athens. I ended with particular attention to qualities such as aggression and pursuit, and such as insecurity and the demand for reassurance, and to the corresponding dynamics of the relationship between leading figures and the *choros* in the broad evidence of the surviving comic and tragic scripts from the fifth century.

In writing this book as a review of different kinds of evidence on two important aspects of tragic performance, I assumed that one of the obvious advantages was that readers might feel able to draw their own conclusions from the evidence, to disagree with mine, or feel encouraged to pursue their own researches or practical explorations. There can be no sweeping resolution to the problems outlined in this book, and the evidence will not, unfortunately, always yield the kinds of insight that we would like. Nonetheless, there is a great deal that can enhance our understanding, and I have tried at all times to advance perceptions that I feel can contribute to an enlarged sense of the art form of ancient Greek tragic performance.

Yet it would be misleading to suggest that the book does not constitute an argument or lead to a more general conclusion. In both chapters, I have concentrated on the centrality of the *choros* to the performance of tragedy, insisting respectively on the presence of the *choros* as a means to grasp the mode of tragic composition and on the cultural vitality of *choreia* in all the theatrical forms that are developed at Athens. The contemporary tendency, as I write, is to look to terms such as "music theater" or "dance drama" to embrace works that do not readily conform to established categories or genres of performance. Greek tragedy was undoubtedly a performance that was both of these, and we shall get further in understanding it if we do not expect it to be familiar.

In that respect, exposure to what are conventionally called the traditional theaters of China, Japan, or India—to Peking Opera, *noh,* Kathakali or Kutiyattam—will not tell us what Greek tragedy was like but will provide a shock to our perceptions if we do not come from those cultures or are unfamiliar with the forms.[1] This kind of realignment of our aesthetic judgment and assumptions is a sound basis for an approach to ancient Greek performance that is willing to accept its difference and that does not see its value uniquely in its capacity to be assimilated to our prevalent theatrical tastes. The theatricality of Greek tragedy deserves to be appreciated on its own terms; and it will be a less predictable stimulus to our own multicultural theater if that appreciation is allied constructively to our desire to attempt its realization in the present.

---

1. It is worth noting that what we now see, in these "traditional" forms, is not necessarily or even probably what they have always been. For the evolution of Kathakali, to take one example, see Zarrilli (2000, chap. 2, 17–38).

References

Anderson, W. D. 1955. "The Importance of Damonian Theory in Plato's Thought." *Transactions and Proceedings of the American Philological Association* 86:88–102.
———. 1966. *Ethos and Education in Greek Music*. Cambridge MA: Harvard University Press.
———. 1994. *Music and Musicians in Ancient Greece*. Ithaca, NY, and London: Cornell University Press.
Arnott, P. D. 1962. *Greek Scenic Conventions*. Oxford: Oxford University Press.
———. 1989. *Public and Performance in the Greek Theatre*. London and New York: Routledge.
Arrowsmith, William, trans. 1956. *Euripides II: "The Cyclops" and "Heracles."* The Complete Greek Tragedies, vol. 4, ed. David Grene and Richmond Lattimore. Chicago: University of Chicago Press.
Ashby, C. 1991. "Where Was the Altar?" *Theatre Survey* 32:3–21.
———. 1999. *Classical Greek Theatre*. Iowa City: University of Iowa Press.
Aylen, L. 1985. *The Greek Theater*. Cranbury, NJ, and London: Associated University Presses.
Bain, D. 1981. *Masters, Servants and Orders in Greek Tragedy*. Manchester: Manchester University Press.
Bamber, L. 1982. *Comic Women, Tragic Men: A Study of Gender and Genre in Shakespeare*. Stanford, CA: Stanford University Press.
Barba, E., and N. Savarese. 1991. *A Dictionary of Theatre Anthropology*. London and New York: Published for the Centre for Performance Research by Routledge.
Barker, A. 1984. *Greek Musical Writings*. Vol. 1, *The Musician and His Art*. Cambridge: Cambridge University Press.
Barrett, W. S. 1964. *Euripides: Hippolytos*. Oxford: Oxford University Press.
Boedeker, D. D. 1974. *Aphrodite's Entry into Greek Epic*. Leiden: Brill.
Bond, G. 1981. *Euripides: Heracles*. Oxford: Oxford University Press.
Brown, A. L. 1982. "Some Problems in the *Eumenides* of Aeschylus." *Journal of Hellenic Studies* 102:26–32.
Burnett, A. P. 1985. *The Art of Bacchylides*. Cambridge MA: Harvard University Press.

Calame, C. 1997. *Choruses of Young Women in Ancient Greece: Their Morphology, Religious Role, and Social Function.* Translated by Derek Collins and Janice Orion. 2d ed. Lanham, MD, and London: Rowman & Littlefield.

Calder, W. 1959. "The Staging of the Prologue of *Oedipus Tyrannus.*" *Phoenix* 13:119–29.

Campbell, D. A. 1988. *Greek Lyric.* Vol. 2, Anacreon, Anacreontea. Cambridge MA: Harvard University Press.

———. 1991. *Greek Lyric.* Vol. 3, Stesichorus, Ibycus, Simonides, and Others. Cambridge MA: Harvard University Press.

———. 1992. *Greek Lyric.* Vol. 4, Bacchylides, Corinna, and Others. Cambridge MA: Harvard University Press.

Carey, C. 1991. "The Victory-Ode in Performance: The Case for the Chorus." *Classical Philology* 86:192–200.

Case, S.-E. 1985. "Classic Drag: The Greek Creation of Female Parts." *Theatre Journal* 37, no. 3:317–27.

Chaikin, Joseph. 1972. *The Presence of the Actor.* New York.

Chancellor, G. 1986. "Implicit Stage Directions in Ancient Greek Drama: Critical Assumptions and the Reading Public." *Arethusa* 12:133–52.

Collard, C., ed. 1975. *Supplices,* by Euripides. Vols. 1–2. Groningen: Bourma's Boekhuis.

———, trans. 1991. *Hecuba,* by Euripides. Warminster: Aris & Phillips.

Connor, W. R. 1989. "City Dionysia and Athenian Democracy." *Classica and Medievalia* 40:7–32.

Cropp, M., K. Lee, and D. Sansone, eds. 2000. *Euripides and Tragic Theatre in the Late Fifth Century.* Illinois Classical Studies 24–25. Champaign, IL: Stipes Publishing.

Csapo, E. 2004. "The Politics of the New Music." In *Music and the Muses: The Culture of "Mousike" in the Classical Athenian City,* ed. P. Murray and P. Wilson, 207–48. Oxford: Oxford University Press.

Csapo, E., and M. Miller, eds. 2003. *Poetry, Theory, Praxis: The Social Life of Myth, Word and Image in Ancient Greece.* Oxford: Oxbow.

Csapo, E., and W. J. Slater. 1994. *The Context of Ancient Drama.* Ann Arbor: University of Michigan Press.

D'Alessio, G. B. 1994. "First-Person Problems in Pindar." *Bulletin of the Institute of Classical Studies* 39:117–39.

Dale, A. M. 1967. *Euripides: Helen.* Oxford: Oxford University Press.

———. 1968. *The Lyric Metres of Greek Drama.* 2d ed. Cambridge: Cambridge University Press.

———. 1969. *Collected Papers.* Cambridge: Cambridge University Press.

Davidson, J. F. 1986. "The Circle and the Tragic Chorus." *Greece and Rome* 33, no. 1:38–46.

Diggle, J. 1974. "On the 'Heracles' and 'Ion' of Euripides." *Proceedings of the Cambridge Philological Association* 20:28–30.

Dobrov, G. W., ed. 1995. *Beyond Aristophanes: Transition and Diversity in Greek Comedy.* Atlanta: Scholars Press.

Dobrov, G. W., and E. Urios-Aparisi. 1995. "The Maculate Muse: Gender, Genre and the *Chiron* of Pherecrates." In *Beyond Aristophanes: Transition and Diversity in Greek Comedy,* ed. G. W. Dobrov, 139–74. Atlanta: Scholars Press.

Dover, K. J. 1972. *Aristophanic Comedy*. Berkeley and Los Angeles: University of California Press.

Easterling, P. E. 1987. "Women in Tragic Space." *Bulletin of the Institute of Classical Studies* 34:15–26.

———, ed. 1997. *The Cambridge Companion to Greek Tragedy*. Cambridge: Cambridge University Press.

Easterling, P. E., and E. Hall, eds. 2002. *Greek and Roman Actors: Aspects of the Ancient Profession*. Cambridge: Cambridge University Press.

Ewans, M., ed. 1995. *The Oresteia*, by Aeschylus. London: J. M. Dent; Rutland, VT: C. E. Tuttle.

———, ed. 1996. *Suppliants and Other Dramas*, by Aeschylus. London: J. M. Dent; Rutland, VT: C. E. Tuttle.

———, ed. 1999. *Four Dramas of Maturity*, by Sophocles. London: J. M. Dent; Rutland, VT: C. E. Tuttle.

———, ed. 2000. *Three Dramas of Old Age*, by Sophocles. London: J. M. Dent; Rutland, VT: C. E. Tuttle.

Fitton, J. W. 1973. "Greek Dance." *Classical Quarterly* 23, no. 2:254–74.

Foley, H. P., ed. 1981. *Reflections of Women in Antiquity*. New York: Gordon & Breach Science Publishers.

———. 2001. *Female Acts in Greek Tragedy*. Princeton, NJ: Princeton University Press.

Fraenkel, E., ed. 1950. *Agamemnon*, by Aeschylus. Vols. 1–3. Oxford: Oxford University Press.

Gardiner, C. P. 1987. *The Sophoclean Chorus*. Iowa City: University of Iowa Press.

Georgiades, T. 1973. *Greek Music, Verse and Dance*. New York: Da Capo Press.

Ginner, R. 1933. *The Revived Greek Dance*. London: Methuen & Co.

Golder, H., and S. Scully, eds. 1995. "The Chorus in Greek Tragedy and Culture, One." Special issue, *Arion* 3, no. 1.

———, eds. 1996. "The Chorus in Greek Tragedy and Culture, Two." Special issue, *Arion* 4, no. 1.

Goldhill, S. 1990. "The Great Dionysia and Civic Ideology." In *Nothing to Do with Dionysos? Athenian Drama in Its Social Context*, ed. J. J. Winkler and F. R. Zeitlin, 97–129. Princeton, NJ: Princeton University Press.

Goldhill, S., and R. Osborne, eds. 1999. *Performance Culture and Athenian Democracy*. Cambridge: Cambridge University Press.

Gould, J. 1973. "Hiketeia." *Journal of Hellenic Studies* 93:74–103.

———. 1996. "Tragedy and Collective Experience." In *Tragedy and the Tragic: Greek Theatre and Beyond*, ed. M. S. Silk, 217–43. Oxford: Oxford University Press.

———. 2001. *Myth, Ritual, Memory, and Exchange: Essays in Greek Literature and Culture*. Oxford: Oxford University Press.

Green, J. R. 1991. "On Seeing and Depicting the Theatre in Classical Athens." *Greek, Roman and Byzantine Studies* 32:15–50.

Grene, D., and R. Lattimore, eds. 1956. *The Complete Greek Tragedies*. Vol. 4, *Euripides II*. Chicago: University of Chicago Press.

Griffith, M. 1977. *The Authenticity of Prometheus Bound*. Cambridge: Cambridge University Press.

Gulick, C. B. 1950. *Athenaeus: The Deipnosophists.* Vol. 6. Cambridge, MA: Harvard University Press.

Hall, E. 1999. "Actor's Song in Tragedy." In *Performance Culture and Athenian Democracy,* ed. S. Goldhill and R. Osborne, 96–122. Cambridge: Cambridge University Press.

———. 2002. "The Singing Actors of Antiquity." In *Greek and Roman Actors,* ed. P. E. Easterling and E. Hall, 3–38. Cambridge: Cambridge University Press.

Halleran, M. R. 1985. *Stagecraft in Euripides.* London: Croom Helm.

Hamilton, R. 1987. "Cries within and the Tragic Skene." *American Journal of Philology* 108:585–99.

Hammond, N. G. L. 1972. "The Conditions of Dramatic Production to the Death of Aeschylus." *Greek, Roman and Byzantine Studies* 13, no. 4:387–450.

———. 1988. "More on Conditions of Production to the Death of Aeschylus." *Greek, Roman and Byzantine Studies* 29, no. 1:5–33.

Harvey, A. E. 1955. "The Classification of Greek Lyric Poetry." *Classical Quarterly* 5:157–75.

Harvey, D., and J. Wilkins, eds. 2000. *The Rivals of Aristophanes.* London: Duckworth and the Classical Press of Wales.

Haskell, A. 1938. *Ballet.* Harmondsworth: Penguin.

Heinrichs, A. 1995. "'Why Should I Dance?' Choral Self-referentiality in Greek Tragedy." *Arion* 3, no. 1:56–111.

Herington, C. J. 1963. "The Influence of Old Comedy on Aeschylus' Later Trilogies." *Transactions and Proceedings of the American Philological Society* 94:113–23.

Herington, J. 1985. *Poetry into Drama: Early Tragedy and the Greek Poetic Tradition.* Berkeley and Los Angeles: University of California Press.

Hourmouziades, N. C. 1965. *Production and Imagination in Euripides.* Athens: Greek Society for Humanistic Studies.

Hubbard, T. K. 1991. *The Mask of Comedy: Aristophanes and the Intertextual Parabasis.* Ithaca, NY: Cornell University Press.

Hutchinson, G. O., ed. 1985. *Aeschylus: Septem contra Thebas.* Oxford: Oxford University Press.

Huxley, G. L. 1969. *Greek Epic Poetry from Eumelos to Panyassis.* London: Faber.

Jaeger, W. 1939. *Paideia: The Ideals of Greek Culture.* Oxford: Oxford University Press.

Janko, R. 1982. *Homer, Hesiod and the Hymns.* Cambridge: Cambridge University Press.

Jardine, L. 1989. *Still Harping on Daughters: Women and Drama in the Age of Shakespeare.* 2d ed. New York: Columbia University Press.

Jebb, R. C., ed. and trans. 1928. *Sophocles: The Plays and Fragments.* Pt. 2, *The Oedipus Coloneus.* Cambridge: Cambridge University Press.

Kaimio, M. 1988. *Physical Contact in Greek Tragedy.* Helsinki: Suomaliainen Tiedeakatemia.

Käppel, L. 1992. *Paian: Studien zur Geschichte einer Gattung.* Berlin: Walter de Gruyter.

Kitto, H. D. F. 1955. "The Dance in Greek Tragedy." *Journal of Hellenic Studies* 75:36–41.

Kranz, W. 1933. *Stasimon.* Berlin: Weidmann.

Landels, J. G. 1999. *Music in Ancient Greece and Rome.* London and New York: Routledge.

Lattimore, R. 1960. *Greek Lyrics.* 2d ed. Chicago: University of Chicago Press.

Lawler, L. B. 1939. "The Dance of the Owl and Its Significance in the History of

Greek Religion and the Drama." *Transactions and Proceedings of the American Philological Association* 70:482–502.

———. 1954. "Phora, Schema, Deixis in the Greek Dance." *Transactions and Proceedings of the American Philological Association* 85:148–58.

———. 1964a. *The Dance in Ancient Greece.* London: A. & C. Black.

———. 1964b. *The Dance of the Ancient Greek Theatre.* Iowa City: University of Iowa Press.

Lee, K., ed. 1976. *Troades,* by Euripides. Basingstoke: Macmillan.

Lefkowitz, M. R. 1991. *First-Person Fictions: Pindar's Poetic "I."* Oxford: Oxford University Press.

———. 1995. "The First Person in Pindar Reconsidered—Again." *Bulletin of the Institute of Classical Studies* 40:139–50.

Ley, G. K. H. 1991a. "Scenic Notes on Euripides' *Helen.*" *Eranos* 89:25–34.

———. 1991b. *A Short Introduction to the Ancient Greek Theater.* Chicago: University of Chicago Press.

———. 1993. "Monody, Choral Song and Athenian Festival Performance." *Maia* 45, no. 2:105–24.

———. 1994. "Performance Studies and Greek Tragedy." *Eranos* 92:29–45.

———. 1999. *From Mimesis to Interculturalism: Readings of Theatrical Theory Before and After 'Modernism.'* Exeter: University of Exeter Press.

———. 2000. "Aristotle's *Poetics,* Bharatamuni's *Natyasastra,* and Zeami's *Treatises:* Theory as Discourse." *Asian Theatre Journal* 17, no. 2:191–214.

Lonsdale, S. H. 1994. *Dance and Ritual Play in Greek Religion.* Baltimore, MD: Johns Hopkins University Press.

Maehler, H., ed. 2004. *Bacchylides: A Selection.* Cambridge: Cambridge University Press.

Marchant, E. C., and O. C. Todd, trans. 1923. *Xenophon in Seven Volumes.* Vol. 4, *Memorabilia, Oeconomicus, Symposium, Apology.* Cambridge MA: Harvard University Press.

Mastronarde, D. J. 1979. *Contact and Discontinuity: Some Conventions of Speech and Action on the Tragic Stage.* Berkeley and Los Angeles: University of California Press.

———. 1990. "Actors on High: The Skene Roof, the Crane, and the Gods in Attic Drama." *Classical Antiquity* 9:247–94.

Moretti, J.-C. "The Theater of the Sanctuary of Dionysus Eleuthereus in Late Fifth-Century Athens." In *Euripides and Tragic Theatre in the Late Fifth Century,* ed. M. Cropp, K. Lee, and D. Sansone, 377–98. Illinois Classical Studies 24–25. Champaign, IL: Stipes Publishing.

Mullen, W. 1982. *Choreia: Pindar and Dance.* Princeton NJ: Princeton University Press.

Murray, P., and P. Wilson, eds. 2004. *Music and the Muses: The Culture of "Mousike" in the Classical Athenian City.* Oxford: Oxford University Press.

Naerebout, F. G. 1997. *Attractive Performances: Ancient Greek Dance: Three Preliminary Studies.* Amsterdam: J. C. Gieben.

Osborne, R. 1993. "Competitive Festivals and the Polis: A Context for Dramatic Festivals at Athens." In *Tragedy, Comedy and the Polis,* ed. A. H. Sommerstein, S. Halliwell, J. Henderson, and B. Zimmermann, 21–38. Bari: Levante editori.

Osborne, R., and S. Hornblower, eds. 1994. *Ritual, Finance, Politics.* Oxford: Oxford University Press.

Page, D. 1934. *Actors' Interpolations in Greek Tragedy.* Oxford: Oxford University Press.

211

Parke, H. W. 1977. *Festivals of the Athenians.* London: Thames & Hudson.

Pickard-Cambridge, A. W. 1946. *The Theatre of Dionysus at Athens.* Oxford: Oxford University Press.

———. 1962. *Dithyramb, Tragedy, and Comedy.* 2d ed. Revised by T. B. L. Webster. Oxford: Oxford University Press.

———. 1988. *The Dramatic Festivals of Athens.* 2d ed. Revised by J. Gould and D. M. Lewis. Oxford: Oxford University Press.

Podlecki, A. J., ed. 1989. *Eumenides* by Aeschylus. Warminster: Aris & Phillips.

Poe, C. P. 1989. "The Altar in the Fifth-Century Theater." *Classical Antiquity* 8:116–39.

Privitera, G. A. "Il Ditirmabo come Spettacolo Musicale: Il Ruolo di Archiloco e Arione." In *La Musica in Grecia,* ed. B. Gentili and R. Pretagonisti, 123–31. Rome: Editori Laterza.

Prudhommeau, G. 1965. *La danse grecque antique.* Paris: Éditions du Centre national de la recherche scientifique.

Race, W. H., ed. 1997. *Pindar.* Vol. 2, *Nemean Odes, Isthmian Odes, Fragments.* Cambridge MA: Harvard University Press.

Rehm, R. 1988. "The Staging of Suppliant Plays." *Greek, Roman and Byzantine Studies* 29, no. 3:263–307.

———. 1992. *Greek Tragic Theatre.* London and New York: Routledge.

———. 1994. *Marriage to Death: The Conflation of Wedding and Funeral Rituals in Greek Tragedy.* Princeton, NJ: Princeton University Press.

———. 1996. "Performing the Chorus: Choral Action, Interaction, and Absence in Euripides." In "The Chorus in Greek Tragedy and Culture, Two," ed. H. Golder and S. Scully, 45–60. Special issue, *Arion* 4, no. 1.

———. 2002. *The Play of Space: Spatial Transformation in Greek Tragedy.* Princeton, NJ: Princeton University Press.

Rimer, J. T., and Y. Masakazu. 1984. *On the Art of the Noh Drama: The Major Treatises of Zeami.* Princeton, NJ: Princeton University Press.

Rosen, R. M. 1988. *Old Comedy and the Iambographic Tradition.* Atlanta: Scholars Press.

Rosenmeyer, T. G. 1982. *The Art of Aeschylus.* Berkeley and Los Angeles: University of California Press.

Rutherford, I. 1995. "Apollo in Ivy: The Tragic Paean." In "The Chorus in Greek Tragedy and Culture, One," ed. H. Golder and S. Scully, 112–35. Special issue, *Arion* 3, no. 1.

———. 2001. *Pindar's Paeans: A Reading of the Fragments with a Survey of the Genre.* Oxford: Oxford University Press.

———. 2004. "Song-Dance and State Pilgrimage at Athens." In *Music and the Muses: The Culture of "Mousike" in the Classical Athenian City,* ed. P. Murray and P. Wilson, 67–90. Oxford: Oxford University Press.

Scodel, R. 1980. *The Trojan Trilogy of Euripides.* Göttingen: Vandenhoeck & Ruprecht.

———, ed. 1993. *Theater and Society in the Classical World.* Ann Arbor: University of Michigan Press.

Scott, W. C. 1984. *Musical Design in Aeschylean Theater.* Hanover, NH: Published for Dartmouth College by University Press of New England.

———. 1996. *Musical Design in Sophoclean Theater.* Hanover, NH: Published for Dartmouth College by University Press of New England.

Scullion, S. 1994. *Three Studies in Athenian Dramaturgy.* Stuttgart and Leipzig: G. B. Teubner.

Seaford, R. 1977–78. "The 'Hyporcheme' of Pratinas." *Maia* 29:81–94.

———, ed. 1984. *Cyclops* by Euripides. Oxford: Oxford University Press.

Seale, D. 1982. *Vision and Stagecraft in Sophocles.* London: Croom Helm.

Seidensticker, B. 2003. "The Chorus in Greek Satyrplay." In *Poetry, Theory, Praxis: The Social Life of Myth, Word and Image in Ancient Greece,* edited by E. Csapo and M. Miller, 100–121. Oxford: Oxbow.

Shenfield, L. W. 2001. "Chariots in Early Greek Culture." Ph.D. thesis, University of Exeter.

Sifakis, G. M. 1971. *Parabasis and Animal Choruses.* London: Athlone Press.

Silk, M. S., ed. 1996. *Tragedy and the Tragic: Greek Theatre and Beyond.* Oxford: Oxford University Press.

Smethurst, M. J. 1989. *The Artistry of Aeschylus and Zeami: A Comparative Study of Greek Tragedy and Nô.* Princeton, NJ: Princeton University Press.

Sommerstein, A. H., ed. 1989. *Eumenides* by Aeschylus. Cambridge: Cambridge University Press.

———. 1996. *Aeschylean Tragedy.* Bari: Levante editori.

Sommerstein, A. H., S. Halliwell, J. Henderson, and B. Zimmermann, eds. 1993. *Tragedy, Comedy and the Polis.* Bari: Levante editori.

Stehle, E. 1997. *Performance and Gender in Ancient Greece: Non-dramatic Poetry in Its Setting.* Princeton, NJ: Princeton University Press.

Sutton, D. F. 1980. *The Greek Satyr Play.* Meisenheim: Hain.

Taplin, O. 1977a. "Did Greek Dramatists Write Stage Instructions?" *Proceedings of the Cambridge Philological Society* 203:121–32.

———. 1977b. *The Stagecraft of Aeschylus.* Oxford: Oxford University Press.

———. 1978. *Greek Tragedy in Action.* London: Methuen.

———. 1986. "Fifth-Century Tragedy and Comedy: A *Synkrisis.*" *Journal of Hellenic Studies* 106:163–74.

Thomas, R. 1992. *Literacy and Orality in Ancient Greece.* Cambridge: Cambridge University Press.

Tredennick, H., trans. 1970. *Memoirs of Socrates and Symposium* by Xenophon. Harmondsworth: Penguin Books.

Van Gennep, A. 1960. *The Rites of Passage.* Chicago: University of Chicago Press.

van der Weiden, M. J. H. 1991. *The Dithyrambs of Pindar.* Amsterdam: J. C. Gieben.

Wallace, R. W. 2004. "Damon of Oa: A Music Theorist Ostracized?" In *Music and the Muses: The Culture of "Mousike" in the Classical Athenian City,* ed. P. Murray and P. Wilson, 249–67. Oxford: Oxford University Press.

Webster, T. B. L. 1967. *The Tragedies of Euripides.* London: Methuen.

———. 1970. *The Greek Chorus.* London: Methuen.

Weir Smyth, H., and H. Lloyd-Jones, eds. 1957. *Aeschylus.* Vol. 2, *Agamemnon, Libation-Bearers, Eumenides, Fragments.* Cambridge, MA: Harvard University Press.

West, M. L. 1981. "The Singing of Homer and the Modes of Early Greek Music." *Journal of Hellenic Studies* 101:113–29.

———. 1982. *Greek Metre.* Oxford: Oxford University Press.

———. 1989. "The Early Chronology of Greek Tragedy." *Classical Quarterly* 39:251–4.

———. 1992. *Ancient Greek Music.* Oxford: Oxford University Press.

———. 1993. *Greek Lyric Poetry.* Oxford: Oxford University Press.

Wiles, D. 1997. *Tragedy in Athens.* Cambridge: Cambridge University Press.

———. 2000. *Greek Theatre Performance.* Cambridge: Cambridge University Press.

Wilkins, J. 1993. *Euripides: Heraclidae.* Oxford: Oxford University Press.

Wilson, P. 1999. "The *aulos* in Athens." In *Performance Culture and Athenian Democracy,* ed. S. Goldhill and R. Osborne, 58–95. Cambridge: Cambridge University Press.

———. 2000. *The Athenian Institution of the Khoregia: The Chorus, the City and the Stage.* Cambridge: Cambridge University Press.

———. 2002. "The Musicians among the Actors." in *Greek and Roman Actors: Aspects of the Ancient Profession,* ed. P. E. Easterling and E. Hall, 39–68. Cambridge: Cambridge University Press.

———. 2004. "Athenian Strings." In *Music and the Muses: The Culture of "Mousike" in the Classical Athenian City,* ed. P. Murray and P. Wilson, 269–306. Oxford: Oxford University Press.

Winkler, J. J. 1990. "The Ephebes' Song: Tragodia and the Polis." In *Nothing to Do with Dionysos? Athenian Drama in Its Social Context,* ed. J. J. Winkler and F. R. Zeitlin, 20–62. Princeton, NJ: Princeton University Press.

Winkler, J. J., and F. R. Zeitlin, eds. 1990. *Nothing to Do with Dionysos? Athenian Drama in Its Social Context.* Princeton NJ: Princeton University Press.

Wohl, V. 2004. "Dirty Dancing: Xenophon's *Symposium.*" in *Music and the Muses: The Culture of "Mousike" in the Classical Athenian City,* ed. P. Murray and P. Wilson, 337–63. Oxford: Oxford University Press.

Yavis, C. G. 1949. *Greek Altars.* Saint Louis: Saint Louis University Press.

Zarrilli, P. 2000. *Kathakali Dance-Drama: Where Gods and Demons Come to Play.* London and New York: Routledge.

Zeitlin, F. R. 1990. "Playing the Other: Theater, Theatricality, and the Feminine in Greek Drama." In *Nothing To Do With Dionysos? Athenian Drama in Its Social Context,* ed. J. J. Winkler and F. R. Zeitlin, 63–96.

Zimmermann, B. 1992. *Dithyrambos: Geschichte einer Gattung.* Göttingen: Vandenhoeck & Ruprecht.

Index

Note: Italicized page numbers indicate figures.

accents, 137

Acharnians (Aristophanes), 112, 187, 189

actors: addition of second, 5, 6, 7; addition of third, 5, 6, 7, 28; audience knowledge of introduction of third, 28; chanting, singing, and dancing in playing space, 91–111; composer as, 5, 7, 87; dancing by, 87–91; emergence of, 176–77; modern emphasis on, 6, 6n15; *Oresteia* requiring three, 5, 7, 24, 28, 202–3

Adrastos, 175–76

Aeolian mode, 144–45

Aeschylus: chronology of surviving plays, 112; Dionysian tragedies of, 196n; early tragic performance and surviving tragedies of, 4–9, 202–3; as performer in his own compositions, 87; second actor introduced by, 5; two modes of composition in, 7–8; vehicles in playing space of, 69–70. See also *Oresteia; Persians; Seven against Thebes; Suppliants*

Agamemnon (Aeschylus): Aegisthus, 30, 32, 34; Agamemnon, 30–32, 33, 70, 71, 72, 74, 77; arrival in vehicle in, 11, 30, 70–71, 76–77; Cassandra, 28, 30, 32, 70, 77, 80, 92; *choros,* 25, 28, 29, 30–31, 32–33, 77, 92, 163, 166, 196; close of, 32–33; Clytemnestra, 28, 29, 30, 31–32, 33, 40, 92; composition for playing space in, 28–33; confrontation between

choroi and leading figures in, 196; continuity with earlier plays, 25; corpses displayed in, 32, 39, 41; dating of, 4, 112; *ekkuklema* in, 39–41; *Electra* of Euripides alluding to, 77, 78; Herald, 28, 29; meter in, 140; murder of Agamemnon, 32, 33; *orchestra* in, 32–33; and Plato's ethical theory of *choreia,* 166; playing space defined by speech from actors, 25; pulling Agamemnon's boots off, 71, 72, 74; singing and chanting in, 92; *skene* in, 7, 28–30, 32–33; third actor in, 28; Watchman, 28

Agathon, 135, 146, 168–69

aggression: in comic *choroi,* 189–90, 194; in tragic *choroi,* 194–95

agitation in tragic *choroi,* 196–99

agon, 189–90

agora, 51n90

Ajax (Sophocles): *choros,* 193; dating of, 112; *ekkuklema* in, 39, 101n; military action in, 193

Alcestis (Euripides), 89, 163, 112, 113n

Alcman, 124, 125, 126–27, 128, 131, 155, 178, 200

Alexandros (Euripides), 198n233

alien status, identification with, 191

altars: to Olympian gods in *Suppliants* of Aeschylus, 18–19, 20; placed outside temples, 47; in playing space after Aeschylus, xvii, 46–69, 203

216

225